LIFE IN THE MEDIEVAL CLOISTER

Life in the Medieval Cloister

Julie Kerr

continuum

Continuum UK, The Tower Building, 11 York Road, London SE1 7NX
Continuum US, 80 Maiden Lane, Suite 704, New York, NY 10038

www.continuumbooks.com

Copyright © Julie Kerr 2009

First published 2009

British Library Cataloguing-in-Publication Data
A catalogue record for this book is available from the British Library.

ISBN 978 1 84725 161 9

Typeset by Pindar NZ, Auckland, New Zealand
Printed and bound by MPG Books Ltd, Cornwall, Great Britain

Contents

Illustrations

For Simone

Acknowledgements

I am indebted to a number of people for their help and support in the preparation of this book. In 2001 I had the good fortune to join the Cistercians in Yorkshire Project at the University of Sheffield, directed by Professor Sarah Foot. This was an opportunity to work with experts from a wide range of disciplines, to develop my understanding of the Cistercian Order and, under Sarah's guidance, to shake off the rather turgid style of a doctoral student and write more freely for a diverse readership. I am grateful to my parents, Betty and Bob, who have taken an avid interest in this as in all my monastic enterprises, and to my nephew and niece, Jamie and Katie, who offered their thoughts on the illustrations with great enthusiasm. My husband, Haki Antonsson, a fellow medievalist, has been a patient listener and a willing reader who has supported and advised me throughout the venture. My greatest thanks are to Dr Simone C. Macdougall who introduced me to the world of the medieval cloister as an undergraduate of the University of St Andrews and whose passion and knowledge has since nurtured my love for the subject. Simone was instrumental in the conception, planning and writing of this book, offering guidance, inspiration and a fund of quirky anecdotes. Simone's comments on the manuscript and suggestions for improving the text have been invaluable; without her this book would certainly never have been written. Finally, I would like to thank Michael Greenwood and Eva Osborne of Continuum for their advice and enduring patience.

Abbreviations

CS Camden Society

ns new series

PL *Patrologia Cursus Completus, Series Latina*, ed. J. P. Migne *et al.*, 221 vols (Paris, 1844–64)

RS Rolls Series

SS Surtees Society

Preface

Leave your body at the door; here in the kingdom of souls the flesh has nothing more to do with it.[1]

This study aims to offer an insight into the daily life of the medieval monk; to explore what it really meant for the men and women who entered the monastery to take vows of poverty, obedience and chastity and subject themselves to the silence and austerities of the cloister. How did they cope with the transition to this highly regimented way of life that required them to sever links with the outside world and exercise humility and self-abnegation? How difficult was it to adjust to the confinement and lack of privacy, and was there scope for them to forge personal friendships and ties within the cloister? These and other questions are explored to understand more clearly the medieval monk's experience of claustral life.

Previous studies of monasticism have examined the monks' personal writings and also legislative works to consider the organizational structure of the various religious orders, their ideals and key individuals within the monastic movement. This diverse body of sources includes letter collections, chronicles, biographies, books of customs (customaries) that record liturgical and administrative arrangements in the monastery and visitation reports that were intended to regularize monastic observance. Here, by contrast, these same sources are used to evoke the reality of everyday life in the monastery, to explore the trials and tribulations experienced by the brethren, the transgressions they committed, the physical and mental impact of claustral life as well as relationships both within and outside the monastery. The analysis is Europe-wide but with a special interest in the British Isles and a particular focus on the late eleventh to the sixteenth centuries.

An overview of monasticism, charting its origins, evolution and defining features offers an introduction to the key monastic Orders, namely the Benedictines, Cluniacs, Cistercians and Carthusians, with some attention accorded to female religious, for while the nuns' way of life might differ from that of their male counterparts they were nevertheless an integral part of the monastic movement. Some reference is made to the customs of the Regular Canons for although they were not strictly speaking monks – they followed the *Rule of St Augustine* rather than the *Rule of St Benedict*, modelled their life on the Apostles and did not take the three monastic vows of poverty, chastity and obedience – their daily regime was similar to that of the monks and significantly, their customaries may have influenced those compiled by the Benedictines.[2] The Military Orders (Knights Templar and Knights Hospitaller) that developed as part of the Crusading movement and the Mendicant Orders that emerged in the thirteenth century fall outside the scope of this study.

This survey of medieval monasticism is continued with a brief outline of the monastic precinct, the people who made up the community or were in some way associated with the monastery, and the daily routine in the cloister, thereby establishing the physical context, personnel and daily rhythm of monastic existence. Subsequent chapters reveal that the monk's life was demanding if rewarding. Most found the dietary restrictions, the cold and lack of sleep particularly challenging. One monk's craving for wine was so great it caused him to hallucinate and see wine cups in the choir; another gnawed wood thinking it was meat. Concessions might be granted to ease the hardships and in some northern countries the monks were given special dispensation to wear caps in church to combat the cold; others were excused from processing barefoot. The obligation to rise each night to celebrate Vigils in the church was perhaps the most gruelling aspect of claustral life, especially for newcomers, but some found that chewing on a peppercorn during the Office prevented them from nodding off. The austerities of the cloister could have a considerable impact on the monk's physical and mental well-being. Fasting and abstinence meant that stomach problems were not uncommon while back strain might be caused by ringing heavy bells. Antipathy and depression could strike those who missed their family, friends and the delights of the world, prompting them to consider leaving the monastery or, in extreme cases, to contemplate suicide. It was thus important to keep the monks in good health and high spirits; while the routine bloodletting sessions were believed to prevent sickness, fresh air, exercise and a break from the confinement of the cloister were often recommended to dispel gloominess and torpor.

It was vital that the cloister was preserved as a place of contemplation and that silence was observed here so that the monks could read, meditate and advance on the path to Truth and Understanding. Accordingly, restrictions were imposed on speech, and essential communication was made by signing. Newcomers had therefore to learn the community's system of sign language but were warned that this was only to be used when necessary. The silence of the cloister was, however, relative. Bells sounded throughout the day to summon the monks to the church or refectory, there was often the noise of workmen carrying out construction or repairs, and the sound of animals in the outer court of the precinct or even in the claustral area. The monks of Bury St Edmunds (Suffolk) raised a billy goat that would cavort around the cloister and wander into the church; elsewhere there were lapdogs, monkeys and even sheep.

Daily life in the monastery was strictly regulated but on occasion this routine was interrupted by the arrival of a visiting dignitary, by storms or even intruders. The monks of Meaux Abbey were blown out of their choir stalls when an earthquake hit Yorkshire in 1349, while the Palm Sunday procession at Øm Abbey, Denmark, was brought to an abrupt standstill in the late twelfth century when local women stripped down to their underwear before the monks. The night could be equally eventful and even fearful. The communal sleeping arrangements meant that the monks might be disturbed by the snores or cries of their companions. Their slumbers might also be disrupted by the appearance of a saint come to chasten or to cure or, conversely, by the devil seeking to lead the monks into temptation. He might take on any number of guises to succeed in this malevolence, appearing as a black crow, a raving hound or even an alluring maiden. In the dark and quiet of the night the monk was vulnerable to his own worries and anxieties. Consequently, insomnia was not uncommon in the medieval monastery and was not taken lightly – various remedies were prescribed to combat sleeplessness.

The monastic life was founded on obedience – to God, to the *Rule of St Benedict* and to the superior of the house. By living as a community rather than as solitaries it was hoped that the monks could support each other to resist temptation and exercise self-control. Measures were also taken to enforce obedience and misdemeanours were punished. The nature of crimes varied considerably. Minor transgressions included lateness and talking; serious offences were murder, arson and breach of chastity. One twelfth-century nun whose amorous behaviour resulted in her pregnancy was beaten up and imprisoned by her fellow sisters, who then forced her to castrate her lover, whose severed parts were duly thrust into her mouth. Punishment was an effective deterrent but it was also essential if the miscreant was to be absolved of his or her sins and progress, unfettered, on the path to salvation.

The monastic life was twofold – as a member of the community each monk was expected to join his fellow brethren in corporate worship and activities; moreover, the monks ate and slept in common. Yet the monastic life was a solitary one with time for private devotion and prayer. This duality meant that camaraderie and strong friendships were often forged among members of the community, that tensions and hostilities might develop and that the monk might suffer from a lack of privacy or, conversely, from loneliness. A final section considers these two aspects of the monastic life, the nature of relationships within the cloister and the impact of death. What happened when friendships soured or there were divisions within the community and what caused them; how great was the desire for privacy and what effect did the death of a member have on general morale? While some took great comfort from the presence of their companions and might, for example, fear sleeping alone, others craved solitude lest their appearance or behaviour startled or revolted their fellow brethren. Deformity drove one monk to leave his monastery and withdraw to a nearby island, for he believed that others would find his demeanour repulsive. A nun who was prone to fits of ecstasy sought to meditate in private so that she could freely succumb to her emotions without causing her companions alarm.

While the monastic life was challenging and for some unduly hard, it clearly brought great joy and true contentment to many, who found serenity and fulfilment in a life dedicated to God and the salvation of the soul.

Whoever sits in solitude and is at peace is rescued from three wars, that is wars of hearing, speech and sight; he shall have only one thing to fight against – the heart.[1]

Introduction

THE ORIGINS OF MONASTICISM[2]

*It is well for those who wish to enter upon the warfare of life in the cloister
in which it is well known not only the habit and customs of a man's past life
but nature herself must change to know both by practice and by force of habit
certain ways of behaviour which form as it were an introduction and preface
to the Rule of our holy Father Benedict.*[3]

THE INFLUENCE OF THE EAST

The origins of monasticism lie in Egypt, Palestine and Syria with St Anthony
(d. 356) and the Desert Fathers, whose austere way of life provided the impulse
and model for later developments. These solitaries emulated Christ's time in the
wilderness. They lived alone and spent their days in prayer, but their cells were
within walking distance of each other and the men came together occasionally
for communal worship and support. The beginnings of monasticism as we think
of it, that is groups of men living together under a rule and subject to a superior,
stems from Pachomius in the fourth century. In the fifth century the Greek term
monos – alone – which had been used to describe the solitaries and their hermit
or eremitic way of life was instead applied to the coenobites, namely men living
in communities who engaged in corporate devotion. From this time there was
thus a distinction between two ways of life – the eremitic and the coenobitic; a
third group, anchorites, lived alone but unlike hermits remained rooted to the
one place.

It was essentially through the writings of St Jerome (d. c. 420), St Basil (d. 379)
and St John Cassian (d. c. 435) that Eastern monasticism was made known to the
Latin West and influenced the development of Christian monasticism. Cassian,
who visited and lived among the Desert Fathers, wrote about their life and

compiled his own prescriptions based on his observances. These saw fruition in the monastery of St Victor, Marseilles, that he founded in c. 415. Western monasticism was also influenced profoundly by the vast corpus of writings compiled by St Augustine of Hippo (d. c. 430). This included theological works and three rules, one of which was specifically for women. Augustine stressed the importance of charity, obedience and individual poverty, and set down a daily schedule for communal devotion.

THE RULE OF ST BENEDICT

> *Whoever you are hastening to the Heavenly country, fulfil this little rule*
> *for beginners with Christ's help; at length you shall arrive, under God's*
> *protection at the lofty summits of doctrine and virtue.*[4]

In c. 530 Benedict of Nursia compiled a rule for the monks of his own abbey of Monte Cassino (S. Italy) and others that would provide stability for a small group living under a superior and united in brotherly love. The monks were to take three vows – obedience, poverty and chastity – to exercise humility and observe stability both to the monastery and the way of life. Benedict provided an outline for the monk's daily regime which essentially comprised three elements – liturgical observance (*Opus Dei*), spiritual reading (*Lectio Divina*) and manual labour. He stressed the importance of sleeping and eating in common and of sharing the various chores to suppress rivalries and preserve harmony within the monastery. Benedict also gave advice on the monks' diet and clothing, their reading material and sleeping arrangements. Benedict modestly described this as 'a little rule for beginners' and evidently considered it a framework for others to modify in accordance with their particular needs. He could hardly have anticipated that his rule would become the bedrock of Western monasticism.

It was largely thanks to Benedict of Aniane (d. 821) that the *Rule of St Benedict* became and remains the rule par excellence in the West and St Benedict of Nursia was regarded as the Father of Monasticism. Benedict of Aniane led a Benedictine revival in the late eighth and early ninth century and received royal backing from Charlemagne (d. 814) and his son, Louis the Pious (d. 840). Benedict founded a monastery at Aniane in 779 which became a centre of reform in France. He played a prominent role in the Synod of Aachen (816) where clerical and monastic reform was addressed and where he hoped to make it obligatory for all monastic Orders to follow the *Rule of St Benedict*. A second synod was held the following

St Benedict delivering his Rule, British Library, Additional 16979, f. 21v.

year to modify some of the regulations of 816 but Aachen had successfully launched the *Rule of St Benedict* as the cornerstone of Western monasticism – some 300 years after it had been compiled. Not least, Aachen made the *Rule* and obedience to it the defining characteristic of the monk. This was no longer a term used to describe any member of a community of religious men but denoted followers of the *Rule of St Benedict*; accordingly the monastic life was now the life of the *Rule*. Benedict of Aniane's monasticism was a reinterpretation of the *Rule*, and while he considered it important that the monks should help with the various tasks in the monastery, he regarded agricultural work and heavy labour as inappropriate. Further, he promoted the primacy of prayer – the monks were to pray for the sins of the world – and developed an elaborate and time-consuming liturgy. Benedict of Aniane's monasticism was highly organized and conducted within opulent surroundings that were intended to honour God and inspire the monk to greater devotion.

It was not until the tenth century that the impact of the *Rule of St Benedict* was felt on England's shores. This was a consequence of the reform movement instigated by Dunstan, Abbot of Glastonbury and later Archbishop of Canterbury (d. 988), and continued by Bishop Oswald of Worcester (d. 992) and Abbot Aethelwold of Abingdon, who became Bishop of Winchester (d. 984). This triumvirate brought Continental practice and reform to England, where they worked in tandem with King Edgar (d. 975) and his queen to found and restore monasteries and nunneries throughout the kingdom. This culminated in the promulgation of the *Regularis Concordia* at Winchester in c. 970, a legislative document that was based on the *Rule of St Benedict* and the revisions of Benedict of Aniane and was intended to unify monastic practice in England. Reform centred on the south of England where the king had authority; monastic life in the north of England had been devastated by the Danish raiders but the religious landscape there and also in Scotland and Wales was later transformed, following the Norman Conquest of 1066.

WAVES OF REFORM

Periods of apathy and decline in the monastic life were interspersed with waves of renewal and reinvigoration, notably the tenth-century reform movement that was spearheaded by the Burgundian abbey of Cluny and the regeneration of monastic life in the eleventh century. The latter led to the emergence of new religious Orders, which ended the Benedictine monopoly of monastic life. However, the proliferation of new Orders was so great that at the Fourth Lateran Council of 1215, Pope Innocent III ruled against the creation of any more. From then on all new communities had to adopt an existing rule, whether Benedictine, Cistercian, Carthusian or Canonical. These revivals had a profound impact on the nature and subsequent development of monasticism in the West and effectively reshaped the monastic landscape of Europe.

The Burgundian abbey of Cluny, founded in 909 by William of Aquitaine, promoted the monasticism espoused by Benedict of Aniane and dominated monastic life in the tenth and eleventh centuries. The abbey came to represent the restored Benedictine life and established a large and influential network of houses from those it had reformed. All of these dependencies were subject to Cluny and were priories; Cluny alone was accorded the status of abbey. Cluny and her dependencies were effectively powerhouses of prayer, and the monks' day revolved around an elaborate liturgy in magnificent buildings. In the late eleventh century a new spirit pervaded society, causing men and women to question how best to lead the monastic life, which was considered the most perfect way to the Christian life. There was a desire to return to a simpler form of monasticism with the emphasis on personal devotion, in accordance with the *Rule of St Benedict*, and on small communities – twelve monks and an abbot. This energy gave rise to new modes of religious life initiated by austere hermit groups such as the Italian Camaldolese, founded c. 1024 in Arezzo. This was the first eremitical Order in the West and the initiative of an ex-Cluniac, Romuald (d. 1027). The Tironensians, founded in northern France by Bernard of Tiron (d. 1117), was the first of these new groups to expand internationally. The Tironensian monks were brought to Scotland by King David (d. 1153), who visited Tiron in 1116 and was so impressed with what he witnessed that he returned to his kingdom with a group of these monks, whom he settled at Selkirk in the Scottish Borders. In 1128 the monks relocated to Kelso and some fifty years later a second community was founded at Arbroath by William the Lion (d. 1214).

A group that successfully combined coenobitic with eremitic living and established an Order that achieved international prominence and renown was the Carthusians. This was the inspiration of Bruno of Cologne, who in 1084 settled with a small band of followers in the Chartreuse mountains, north of Grenoble, seeking austerity, simplicity and solitude. While the monks lived as a community and came together for some services and meals, most of their time was spent alone in their private cells, where they could find unity with God. The cell was regarded as the essence of Carthusian life and as essential to the monk's being; hence, a Carthusian out of his cell was compared to a fish out of water or a sheep out of his pen. The Carthusians arrived in England in around 1178 and settled at Witham in Somerset. The house was founded by Henry II (1154–89) in part penance for his failure to go on a pilgrimage to the Holy Land. After an inauspicious start the community flourished under the guidance of its first prior, St Hugh of Avalon, later bishop of Lincoln (d. 1200). The Carthusians were renowned for their uncompromising attitude to monastic life; silence was strictly observed, meat was prohibited and the way of life was demanding – hence nobody under the age of twenty was permitted to join and numbers were restricted. Despite the hardships of Carthusian life the Order attracted a diversity of recruits and sustained its appeal throughout the Middle Ages. Indeed, those wishing to join might have to wait some time for a vacant cell before they could embark on their Carthusian journey. In the 1520s the Yorkshire priory of Mount Grace had a waiting list of four for one cell.[5]

There was one Order that stood out from all the others and effectively became synonymous with reform. This was the Cistercians, or the White Monks as they were also known since they wore habits of undyed wool. The impulse for Cistercian life came from Abbot Robert of Molesme, who in 1098 left his Benedictine monastery seeking solitude and seclusion in the marshy forest of Cîteaux, south of Dijon. Robert was joined by several companions and while he himself was recalled to Molesme to resume his abbatial duties, the group remained and expanded. They sought above all to return to the simplicity of the *Rule of St Benedict* and restore what they considered was the true form of monasticism. The third abbot, Stephen Harding (d. 1134), was an Englishman and promulgated the 'Charter of Charity' (*Carta Caritatis*). This constituted the monks as a fully fledged Order and made them the first to have a written constitution. This pioneering document marked the Cistercians out and became a model for others. The 'Charter of Charity' sets out the federal arrangement of the abbeys, which were joined in a familial relationship and united through bonds of charity and uniformity of practice. All houses of the Order were to observe the same customs and were visited annually to make sure that standards were maintained. Moreover, the abbots were required to attend an annual assembly at the mother-house of Cîteaux to discuss new legislation and deal with disciplinary matters. The Cistercians sought simplicity in every aspect of their life, from their food and clothing to the nature of the liturgy and the design of their buildings. They were also concerned that manual labour should be an integral part of the day, as prescribed in the *Rule of St Benedict*. The monks were helped by lay brothers (*conversi*), who took vows and were professed members of the community but spent most of their time labouring rather than praying, leaving the monks free to fulfil their liturgical duties. The lay brothers effectively formed a separate community, having their own quarters and occupying a separate part of the church – their stalls were in the nave while the monks' choir was in the east. The Cistercians were not the first to introduce lay brothers but were the first to make these men an integral part of their community. In doing so they opened the monastic life to the illiterate, who had hitherto been excluded, and, not least, succeeded in making their abbeys self-sufficient units.

The Cistercians' success can be attributed to the efficiency of their administrative organization but also, and crucially, to the drive and energy of St Bernard of Clairvaux (d. 1153). Bernard joined the Order in c. 1112 and was largely responsible for making the Cistercians a truly international Order that had houses the length and breadth of Western Christendom by the mid-twelfth century. Bernard himself became an internationally renowned figure who was a friend and advisor to rulers and popes, a prolific writer and a charismatic speaker. Bernard preached the Second Crusade (1147–9) throughout Europe, and his eloquence incited many to take the Cross. Thanks to Bernard's zeal and prominence Cistercian life flourished in the first half of the twelfth century and the Order dominated monastic reform. Bernard was directly responsible for the expansion of the Order throughout the British Isles. This was achieved through the foundation of Rievaulx Abbey in North Yorkshire as a daughter-house of Clairvaux (Langres); this meant that Bernard sent monks from his own abbey of Clairvaux to colonize the new community. Bernard intended Rievaulx to be an outpost from which the White Monks could infiltrate the country and spread across the British Isles; houses were duly founded in Scotland, Ireland and Wales. The extent and speed of Cistercian expansion in Europe was quite remarkable, prompting Orderic Vitalis (d. c. 1142), a monk of St Evroul (Normandy), to remark that the swarm of these monks with their white cowls spread over the whole earth.[6] Not least, the Cistercians' pioneering legislation and tight administrative structure had a profound impact on contemporary practice and future developments.

WOMEN RELIGIOUS

The nuns who professed the religion of the Cistercian Order multiplied like the stars of heaven and vastly increased – convents were founded and built, virgins, widows and married women who had gained their husbands' consent rushed to fill the cloisters.[7]

There were few formal established houses for women prior to the mid-tenth century and those that existed were mostly hierarchical institutions, founded and presided over by royalty and noblewomen and intended for those of standing – the nobility sent their daughters to be educated in the nunneries, widows retired there and some withdrew to the convent to escape an enforced marriage.[8] Matilda of Scotland (d. 1118), the future wife of Henry I, was sent as a girl to Romsey Abbey (Hampshire), where her Aunt Christine was the abbess; the following century King Stephen's (1135–54) daughter, Mary of Blois, presided over Romsey. There was, however, more informal provision for women religious. Groups of these females might live adjacent to a male house, follow their customs and receive spiritual direction from the priests of the monastery since women relied upon men for spiritual guidance and to minister the sacraments. Thus, the Ladies of St Peter stood beside the male house of St Peter's, Salzburg. The community of female recluses at Sopwell was about half a mile from St Albans (Hertfordshire), whose abbot, Geoffrey de Gorham (1119–46), supported the group and helped regulate their way of life. Abbot Geoffrey similarly supported Christina of Markyate (d. c. 1160) and her female companions and helped convert Markyate into a priory. Monasteries might establish a female community specifically to provide for the relatives of the men who had joined their cloisters. In 1056 Cluny founded Marcigny in Burgundy for the wives and mothers of those who had taken the habit at Cluny, but stipulated that the women should be at least twenty years of age and limited numbers to nineteen. These nuns observed a similar liturgical cycle to the men but were ministered to by priests from Cluny and, like all female religious, were subject to more severe restrictions regarding their claustration.

A number of Benedictine nunneries were founded for women during the eleventh and twelfth centuries. While the Cistercians supported female religious throughout the twelfth century they were rather wary of embracing them as part of the Order, but bowed to pressure in the thirteenth century when various nunneries were incorporated within the Cistercian family. Others called themselves Cistercian and followed the customs of the Order yet were not officially recognized by the Cistercian General Chapter. The same period gave rise to Orders specifically for women, such as the double foundation of Fontevrault in Anjou that was established in c. 1101 by a preacher, Robert of Arbrissel, and the Order of Sempringham, or Gilbertines as they were also known after their founder, St Gilbert of Sempringham (d. 1189). While all female communities were dependent on males to minister to their spiritual needs and help with heavy labour, these double houses formally incorporated the male element within their organizational framework. The men lived within the precinct but strict measures were taken to segregate the two, for there was always a fear or suspicion of sexual scandal. Fontevrault was originally intended for women from all walks of life – the educated sang in the choir while the illiterate served. However, the community soon became more exclusive, attracting royal and noble recruits. One renowned resident was Eleanor of Aquitaine, who died here in 1204; she and her husband Henry II (d. 1189) were buried at Fontevrault and their tombs can still be seen. The Order of Sempringham was the only English Order that was established and had its roots in Lincolnshire, where indeed most of the houses were founded; the Gilbertines never spread to the Continent. The Order effectively comprised four communities – the nuns, who followed the *Rule of St Benedict*, the canons who ministered to them and observed the *Rule of St Augustine*, lay sisters who were mostly engaged in domestic chores, and lay brothers who undertook heavy labour. While the males and females occupied separate parts of the precinct they shared the church, but this was divided to keep the two apart. The Gilbertines were greatly influenced by the Cistercians and Gilbert in fact attended the Cistercian General Chapter of 1147 hoping that they might incorporate his own congregation within their family. The Cistercians refused for they were reluctant at this time to embrace female communities within the Order, but offered Gilbert their support.

THE ETHOS OF THE MONASTIC LIFE

So whether you eat, drink or do anything else do everything in the name of the Lord, devoutly, reverently and religiously.[9]

Western monasticism was characterized by life in a community where time was spent in corporate devotion, private prayer and work. The monk's life was a spiritual journey directed towards salvation, which was to be attained through prayer, meditation and adherence to the *Rule of St Benedict* and the monastic way of life. The monk was required to exercise humility, observe stability and take the three vows of poverty, chastity and obedience. Poverty was individual rather than corporate and the community might collectively have ownership. Indeed, it was often expected that recruits would make a donation to the monastery upon their entry and perhaps sign over all their material possessions to the community. Obedience was the cornerstone of monastic observance and required adherence to the *Rule of St Benedict* and subjection to the superior of the house, who stood in place of God as father (*abba*) of the community and was to be obeyed in all matters unless this ran counter to the *Rule*. It was only through obedience, the abnegation of self-will, that the monk could be truly free.

What precisely it meant to lead the monastic life and how best this could be achieved changed over time and was affected by social and economic developments. For example, a higher standard of living in the later Middle Ages made many in the cloister less tolerant of the austere diet and living conditions their predecessors had endured and a growing demand for privacy resulted in monasteries creating private cells and cubicles for the monks. Another important development that had a profound impact on the structure of monastic life and altered the very meaning of stability was the development of the universities. From the mid-thirteenth century it became common for the religious Orders to establish their own colleges in the university towns so that their monks could live and study in appropriate surroundings. The Cistercians stood at the vanguard of this movement with the foundation of St Bernard's in Paris in c. 1246; the Benedictines and Cluniacs followed suit, establishing colleges at Oxford, Montpellier, Bologna, Salamanca and other university towns. Study was now promoted as an integral part of monastic life and a university education effectively became a requirement for promotion to office. It was also considered a legitimate reason to leave the cloister and effectively break the vow of stability. In fact, the monasteries were encouraged and in some cases instructed to send representatives from their communities to study at the universities. In 1292 Cistercian abbots were ordered to send one monk for every twenty in the community to the local *studium*. In the sixteenth century Andrew Forman, Archbishop of St Andrews (1512–21), instructed each of the nine greater monasteries in his diocese to send two monks to reside and study continuously at the University of St Andrews (Fife) while the four lesser houses were to send one. Forman hoped that the university education would equip the monks better to oppose heresies and that their presence would in turn enhance university life by bringing to it the spirit of the cloister.[10]

Despite these modifications the fundamental spirit of monasticism was unaltered – the monks' goal remained the same even if how precisely this was to be achieved changed. Accordingly, those who entered the cloister embarked on a life dedicated to the pursuit of salvation and founded on poverty, chastity and obedience. Importantly, the communal life of the cloister was regarded as a training ground, the first steps on the road to perfection. This image is vividly evoked by the monastic reformer, Peter Damian (d. 1072), who considered the monastery simply as a resting place and preparation for a solitary existence in the desert.[11]

THE APPEAL OF THE MONASTIC LIFE

Flee from the midst of depravity and perversity, from danger to security, from work to quietude, from shadow to light, from the corruption of the flesh to delight in the spirit.[12]

In his 'Dialogue on Miracles', Caesarius of Heisterbach (d. c. 1240) discussed the various reasons that prompted men to take the habit and enter the cloister. Whereas some were called directly by God, others joined on a whim, but the majority were recruited through the ministry of the brethren, whether by their exhortation, prayer or example. A few, however, fled to the monastery on account of sickness, poverty, shame or even fear of death; in other words to escape problems of an earthly nature. Caesarius also commented on what might deter men from joining the community, such as the fear of silence and even of the vermin and lice that commonly infested the brethren's robes.[13]

Caesarius' account is a testimony to the variety of factors that might compel men and women to take the habit and embark on claustral life. For some the monastery provided a refuge from worldly concerns and might offer security with a reliable source of food and drink, accommodation and a structured daily routine. The spiritual impetus was, however, strong and the monastic life was regarded as a way to safeguard one's salvation. The austerities and hardships that the monk endured in this world would be generously rewarded with eternal life. Bernard of Clairvaux (d. 1153) considered his monastery Jerusalem and maintained that everyone who entered would have a direct and more certain passage heavenwards.[14] Bernard, like others who had taken the habit, actively sought to win recruits and extend the cloister. This was achieved through writing letters urging the recipients to share their great joy and the guarantee of salvation. As St Anselm (d. 1109), who was one of the most prodigious and persuasive letter writers, explained,

Anyone who imagines that foregoing the pleasures of the world and persevering in the exercises of virtue is extremely hard, even impossible, has never experienced how praiseworthy and delightful it is not to submit to but to command one's vices through love and the hope of the heavenly kingdom.[15]

Preaching was another way to win recruits. Bernard of Clairvaux was regarded as such a charismatic and compelling preacher that mothers allegedly hid their sons from him and wives their husbands, lest these men were drawn to take the Cistercian habit. During Bernard's life, numbers at Clairvaux (Langres) and in the Cistercian Order soared. At the time of Bernard's death there were apparently some 900 applications in the Clairvaux archives.[16] Adam of Eynsham, who wrote a biography of St Hugh of Lincoln (d. 1200), claimed that monks and canons of other Orders transferred to Witham (Somerset) so that they might live under Prior Hugh, 'prudently deciding that the monotony of the material food would be amply compensated for by the scrumptiousness of the spiritual fare'.[17] Some recruits were incited to take the habit after a personal visit to the monastery. A well-known example is St Aelred's visit to the Yorkshire abbey of Rievaulx in 1134, when he was steward to the king of Scotland. Aelred was so impressed with what he saw that he decided to stay; he was later promoted to the abbacy of the house and became one of the leading figures in the Order. Andrew, the archdeacon of Verdun, had a similar conversion when he visited the monks of Clairvaux to request prayers. Andrew entered their chapter house and was so moved at the sight of their angelic devotion that he abandoned everything and remained at the abbey.[18]

While some recruits acted on impulse and took the habit having had no prior intention of doing so, for others this was a fulfilment of their destiny. Abbot Samson's (d. 1211) decision to enter the monastery of Bury St Edmunds was evidently made following a dream he had as a nine-year-old boy. Samson dreamt he was in front of the cemetery gate of a monastery when the devil tried to seize him. Fortunately he was rescued by St Edmund, who took the boy in his arms, prompting Samson to cry out in his sleep, 'St Edmund, help me.' His mother was astonished by the vehemence of Samson's cry but also as he had called out the name of Edmund, since he had never before heard of the saint. She subsequently brought Samson to Edmund's shrine at Bury, where he realized that this was the monastery in his dream and concluded that the saint wished him to become a monk of the house. Some years later Samson entered the monastery at Bury, where he was professed as a monk in 1166 and succeeded to the abbacy in 1182.[19]

The promise of eternal life and joyous rewards in heaven gave the monastic life considerable appeal and incited many to consider taking the habit. Moreover, as St Anselm warned, it was easier for men to live a holy life in the cloister among their brethren than alone in the world and faced with temptation.[20] The monastic life was not, however, to be embarked upon lightly. It demanded total commitment and a change of attitude as well as clothing. As Caesarius of Heisterbach colourfully remarked, it was unnatural to carry a wolf's heart beneath sheep's clothing, yet this was not uncommon.[21]

Just as the oyster is safe within its shell yet is prey to the crabs and other enemies when it comes out, so the monk is safe within the convent walls, but outside is exposed to the snares of evil.[1]

1

The Precinct, the People, the Daily Regime

THE MONASTERY PRECINCT

The medieval monastery was a hive of industry as well as a place of solitude. Monks traditionally sought to live apart from the world and some chose secluded landscapes. The Cistercians were concerned that their sites should be 'far from the haunts of men' and mostly settled in rural locations. But these were not usually remote. For example, the Scottish abbey of Melrose was situated along the Roman road connecting England to Tweedale and the Lothians. Melrose was thus a popular stopping-off point for those travelling between England and Scotland and a choice meeting place for royal and ecclesiastical dignitaries. The abbeys of Margam, Basingwerk, Whitland and Neath were located on the Welsh coast and accordingly inundated with visitors travelling to and from Ireland. A number of religious houses were founded in towns and cities. The urban location afforded protection and resources but there was inevitably a risk of noise and disruption. This was the cause of dissension amongst the monks of Marienkroon in the fifteenth century. Their monastery was in the town of Heusden (Netherlands) and while some of the brethren wished to remain there, others sought to move, complaining that they were disturbed by the townsfolk chattering and women entering the church. In some cases the town grew up around the monastery which, like the Benedictine abbey of St Albans (Hertfordshire), subsequently found itself at the hub of urban life and hosted fairs and markets in its outer court. Monasteries often forged strong links with the local community but rivalries and antagonisms might instead develop and result in violence. In 1327 hostilities between the abbey and townsfolk of Bury St Edmunds culminated in the locals launching a three-day riot at the monastery, which caused extensive damage.

THE LAYOUT OF THE PRECINCT

*Monks are like fish that swim in ponds; some are very fat since they serve God
in the cloister. For monasteries can rightly be compared to ponds where the
fish are all held captive.*[2]

The medieval monastery was much more than simply a church and cloister.
Today, however, it is often difficult to appreciate just how extensive these
precincts were and their impact on the locality. Standing remains, excavations
and topographical surveys have done much to reveal the size and layout of the
monastic precinct, but there are often problems in identifying what the particular buildings were used for and how their function may have changed over the
years in accordance with the community's needs. The task of understanding the
monks' use of space is helped greatly by the survival of two medieval plans. The
first is the plan of St Gall (Switzerland), compiled c. 819–26 at the Benedictine
monastery of Reichenau. This represents an idealized plan of the monastery for
it was never actually executed. It is nonetheless an outstanding source which
depicts and crucially labels some forty buildings, as well as walls, gardens and
fences.[3] In contrast, the Waterworks Plan of c. 1165 shows the layout of the
cathedral priory of Christ Church, Canterbury, as it was in the twelfth century –
and beyond, for despite repairs and renovations the basic arrangement remained
almost the same until the reconstitution of the priory in the sixteenth century.
It is the only known plan of a real western monastery prior to the sixteenth
century. This unique plan was drawn up by Prior Wibert (1155–67) of Christ
Church and was seemingly intended as a guide for repairs and building work
within the precinct. It is subsequently highly technical. The buildings are not,
however, always shown in proportion but are labelled and therefore offer a
valuable and exceptional insight into the layout of the medieval monastery and
the use of space therein.[4]

The precise arrangement of the precinct varied depending on the size and
needs of the individual community as well as the Order, but could be extensive
and cover many acres with stables and smithies as well as gardens, orchards and
also vineyards if the climate supported viticulture. Some houses had fish stews
to provide the community with a supply of fresh water fish, others had hives
for honey; there was even a swannery at Norwich Cathedral Priory.[5] Cistercian
precincts were generally larger than others since the White Monks sought to
establish self-sufficient communities with everything they required within

the confines of the monastery. Whereas the Cistercian abbey of Rievaulx in Yorkshire covered about ninety acres, the Benedictine monastery at Abingdon was about eighteen acres.

THE CHURCH AND CLOISTER

The church and cloister stood at the heart of the precinct and were at the core of monastic life. All of the buildings that were needed for daily living could be accessed from the cloister so that the monks had no need to leave this area, and indeed they required permission to do so. The monks' day revolved around the cycle of liturgical offices celebrated in the church and the times set aside for spiritual reading in the cloister. The cloister was symbolic of the Heavenly Paradise and was a place for contemplation. It was sheltered from the noise of the outer court and access to visitors was restricted, lest they disrupted monastic observance. Accordingly, the cloister door was monitored during the day and locked at night after the Office of Compline. The cloister was not simply a place for contemplation but was for communal living. The monks washed and were shaved here, and even hung the washing out to dry. Most cloisters faced southwards, to make the optimum use of heat and light from the sun, but at some sites the nature of the landscape necessitated a north-facing cloister for drainage and construction purposes.

THE CLAUSTRAL RANGES

The chapter house, library, parlour and dormitory were usually situated in the east cloister range. The chapter house was an important place in the monastery because every day the community met here to discuss any business and deal with disciplinary matters. Each meeting began with a chapter of the *Rule of St Benedict*, which was read aloud, and it was this which gave the building its name. Chapter meetings were private and no outsiders were permitted to attend or even enter the cloister when the meeting was in progress. But the chapter house as such was not out of bounds and visitors might listen to a sermon here, present a gift to the community or visit any shrines or relics. The library or book cupboard was generally beside the chapter house. Every year at Lent the monk received a book from the library which he was to read and meditate over in the daily period accorded to *Lectio Divina* (Divine Reading). While the monks were to preserve silence in the cloister, essential matters could be discussed in a small chamber known as the parlour. In Cistercian houses the monks gathered in the parlour every day to receive their work tools from the prior, for manual labour was an important part of their daily regime. The monks' dormitory occupied the upper level of the eastern range and was accessed externally from the cloister by a set of steps and internally by the nightstairs that provided sheltered access to the choir for the night Office of Vigils. The monks were permitted to go to the dormitory whenever they wished – presumably as their toilet blocks (*reredorters*) were often located at the far end of the dormitory – but were not allowed to communicate with each other in any way. Outsiders were forbidden from entering the dormitory unless they had received special permission and perhaps wished to tour the buildings. Women, however, were strictly prohibited to prevent scandal arising. The dormitory was a large, long room and the monks slept here in common although novices were sometimes allocated separate quarters and abbots often had their own private lodgings. The dormitory was generally unheated and simply furnished, with each brother having his own bed and perhaps a hook and shelf for his clothes. The floor would have been strewn with rushes that were changed once or twice a year.

The south side of the cloister commonly housed the refectory and kitchen, as well as the warming house which was, in theory, the only heated building within the cloister. The monks dined together in the refectory once a day in winter but twice in summer when a light supper was served to sustain them through the longer day. A *lavatorium* or wash basin stood outside the refectory, for the monks were obliged to wash their hands before entering, a practical and symbolic gesture of cleansing. Some refectories were large and impressive. At the Cistercian abbey of Rievaulx, the refectory stood about fifteen metres high and was evidently a splendid building, for traces of paint reveal that it was lime-washed pink with mock masonry lines drawn in red. The floor here, as elsewhere, was tiled. The tables in the refectory were arranged around the sides of the room with the high table at the far end, often on a raised dais. Here the abbot or prior sat with any distinguished visitors he was entertaining. The monks sat with their backs to the walls, looking inwards, so that the servers could stand in the centre and place the dishes on the tables. Meals were eaten in silence and while the monks ate they listened to an edifying passage from the Gospels or the Lives of the Saints, thereby nourishing their minds while feasting their bodies. Any necessary communication was conveyed using sign language – for example, to sign for bread the monk made a circle with his thumb and first two fingers, since bread was usually round. Few places in the monastery were heated but from 1 November until Good Friday a fire was kept burning in the warming house, or calefactory as it was also known. The monks were allowed to gather around the fire here to warm themselves and the calefactory would have been a particularly popular spot when the weather was bad, but conversation was prohibited lest they were tempted to gossip. The warmth of the calefactory made it an ideal place for various activities such as preparing ink and greasing boots with pig fat since the fire helped to soften the grease. Scribes might bring their work here when it was cold or wet and in some monasteries bloodletting was carried out in the warming house. Elsewhere this took place in the infirmary complex. This was often situated to the east of the cloister where the sick were connected to but removed from the rest of the community. Some monasteries had a special seyney house for bloodletting.

The western range connected the cloister with the court and linked the monks' home with the outside world. It subsequently had a more secular function. The cellarer had his office here with storage space for the monastery's supplies and there was commonly an outer parlour where visitors met with members of the community and merchants and traders discussed their business. In Cistercian abbeys the western range was assigned to the lay brethren, who had their own refectory and dormitory, but in Benedictine houses it was more usual for the abbot to have private chambers here and perhaps offer accommodation to important visitors. Additional guest accommodation was situated beyond the western range, to minimize disruption to monastic observance. The guest quarters might be comprised of various apartments so that visitors could be lodged appropriately, in accordance with their standing. For example, the guest complex at the Yorkshire abbey of Fountains included an aisled hall for lower-ranking guests and two guesthouses for notable visitors. At Mortemer Abbey in Rouen two stone houses provided separate accommodation for merchants, the poor, the religious and the rich. Of course the use of space was flexible. Additional chambers within the precinct might be made available to visitors if needed and whenever the guesthouse was vacant the monks might use it for their own meetings. In the thirteenth century, the monks of Bury St Edmunds gathered in the abbey guesthouse to resolve a dispute over Hugh of Northwold's election to the abbacy.[6] It was important that the guest chambers were kept clean and tidy if visitors were to be duly impressed and perhaps be compelled to make a generous donation to the community. At the Augustinian priory of Barnwell

(Cambridgeshire) the hosteller was to ensure that there were no spiders' webs in the guest chambers, the bedding was not torn and all the food containers had been well scrubbed. He was to check that rushes were strewn on the ground and there was plenty of hay in the toilet block – the medieval equivalent of toilet paper. There was always a danger that light-fingered guests would gain access to the precinct and after each guest departed from Barnwell the hosteller's servant was to check the inventory to make sure that nothing had gone astray.[7]

THE CLEANLINESS OF THE CLOISTER

It was important that the entire precinct was well maintained to honour God and guard against slander, but also for safety reasons, since falling masonry could be hazardous. At the Burgundian abbey of Cluny the kitchen was swept every Saturday, while at Canterbury the monks' dormitory was swept once a year. At Abingdon (Berkshire) the dormitory was swept on the Assumption of Mary (15 August) and the Nativity of Mary (8 August). These were two of the most important feasts in Abingdon's calendar, when a number of visitors would have descended on the house for the celebrations and might expect to have a tour of the buildings. It would therefore have been especially important that everywhere was clean and tidy on these occasions.[8] It was not just the sight but the smell of the buildings that was of concern and measures were taken to guard against malodours. At Barnwell the refectorer threw mint and fennel in the air to make a pleasant odour in the refectory and presumably to mask cooking smells.[9]

It was imperative to keep the cloister neat and tidy since it was symbolic of the Heavenly Paradise and a place for contemplation. In a number of houses the cloister was planted with trees and flowers. The twelfth-century monks of Norwich Cathedral Priory had a rose bush in their cloister, symbolic of the Virgin Mary, while there was a juniper bush in the cloister of St Lomer, on the north bank of the Loire. Those who neglected their cloisters were liable to be reprimanded. When Abbot Herman of Stratford conducted a visitation of Hailes Abbey (Gloucestershire) in 1394 he criticized the monks, whose cloister was full of weeds and nettles, and was a disgrace rather than a thing of beauty.[10]

Not infrequently the monastic buildings were used for a different purpose than intended. For example, the brethren might be required to temporarily relocate to another building while necessary repairs were undertaken. The collapse of the great tower at Abingdon (Berkshire) in the late eleventh century left the church in a hazardous state and the monks celebrated the Divine Office in the chapter house and cloister until the building had been made safe. The extent of building work that was carried out at these houses and the impact this would have had on monastic observance is considered further in Chapter 4.

THE PEOPLE

A variety of people were associated with the monastery in addition to the monastic community. There were servants and perhaps lay brethren to help with the daily running of the house and their dealings with the outside world, visitors were received and charity was administered to the worthy poor of the locality. In the later Middle Ages it became more common for outsiders to work and reside within the grounds of the monastery; professionals might rent offices or lodgings in the outer court and lay folk might retire here, offering a grant of land or property in return for their daily upkeep. This section looks briefly at the various people within the monastic community and the offices they occupied, and thereafter considers the wider nexus of individuals who were in some way affiliated to the monastery.

THE MONASTIC COMMUNITY

The supreme obligation of monks is to keep silence and close their eyes to the aberrations of their superiors.[11]

The monastic community was made up chiefly of choir monks or nuns whose day revolved around the cycle of liturgical duties. The exact number of brethren varied from house to house and over time depending on the size and resources of the monastery, the popularity of a particular abbot and the general enthusiasm for monastic life. Aelred of Rievaulx's (1147–67) lofty reputation attracted a number of recruits to the Yorkshire abbey, doubling the size of the community. During Aelred's abbacy there were some 140 monks and 500 lay brothers but at the dissolution of the house in 1538 numbers had fallen to twenty-three. This was not uncommon. Abingdon's community increased to about eighty under Abbot Faritius (1100–17) but fell to twenty-five by the Dissolution. The size of the community might be affected by social and economic factors such as the various plagues that swept through Europe in the fourteenth century. This had a devastating impact on some houses. In the early fourteenth century thirteen monks of Crowland Abbey (Lincolnshire) died of the plague within fifteen days.[12]

THE PERSONNEL

> 'You are a fool and you speak foolishly. You should know what Solomon
> says, "Thou hast many daughters. Show not thy face cheerful before them".'
> (Eccl. 7.26)

The abbot stood at the head of the community and was a father figure who was responsible for maintaining discipline and offering consolation and advice. He was therefore to combine the lion with the lamb, to instil fear and command obedience yet comfort and console his flock. This could be an onerous and sometimes lonely role. The abbot was helped by the prior, who acted as his deputy when the abbot was occupied with external affairs. This became more common from the twelfth century when the abbot was often away from the house and it was generally the prior who was the visible voice of authority within the cloister. In cathedral priories, such as Christ Church, Canterbury, Ely and Durham, the archbishop or bishop was the nominal head of the community and stood in place of the abbot but the prior of the house effectively presided as the superior. Similarly, the heads of Cluniac monasteries were priors since all but the mother-house of Cluny were priories and subject to the abbot of Cluny.

The administration of the monastery was a complex affair and became increasingly so throughout the Middle Ages. To ensure the efficient organization of both internal and external affairs a number of monks were appointed to hold offices or 'obediences' and were known as obedientiaries. They included the cellarer, who was in charge of the community's supplies; the sacrist, who was responsible for the upkeep of the church and vestments as well as for timekeeping; the infirmarer, who cared for the sick; and the precentor, who directed the church services; the almoner exercised charity on the community's behalf and tended the deserving poor of the neighbourhood. The precise titles, duties and relative importance of the obedientiaries varied from house to house and over time depending on the needs and customs of the particular monastery. For example, while the sacrist and cellarer were the leading obedientiaries at Bury St Edmunds, the sacrist and almoner were the most influential at Peterborough. In Benedictine houses the almoner was a top-ranking official yet there was no such official in Cistercian abbeys, where the porter was responsible for distributing alms and extending charity. The obedientiaries were accorded status and shown deference on account of their office but the work involved could be stressful. Matthew of Rievaulx, who was precentor of the Yorkshire abbey in the late twelfth and early thirteenth century, attributed his ill health and insomnia to the strains of his duties and claimed he would never have accepted office had he known what was involved.[13]

THE MONKS

Most members of the monastic community were choir monks who had completed a probationary period and made their profession. Some might then take holy orders, becoming first an acolyte, then a subdeacon, deacon and eventually a priest. This became more common in the later Middle Ages. At the time of the dissolution of Kirkstall Abbey (Leeds), twenty-nine of the thirty-one monks had been ordained to the priesthood. Within the community the monks were often known by their town, village or country; for example, Hugh of Durham, Roger of Tickhill and Gervase of St Bertin. But the monks were sometimes numbered to distinguish those who shared the same name – Jocelin 1, Jocelin 2, Jocelin 3.[14] Members of the monastic community would have come from the locality but also from further afield. Indeed, the monasteries were truly international institutions and might include brothers from across Europe. Following the Norman Conquest of 1066 the brethren at Christ Church Cathedral Priory came from England, Normandy and Italy while the sub-prior of Durham Cathedral Priory was Germanic; a number of English and French monks were sent to the Cistercian abbeys in Scandinavia. This internationalism might lead to problems conversing, and create tensions and rivalries. Not least, monks who found themselves in an alien culture might struggle with the diet and customs, as well as the climate. An English monk, Philip, who was sent to preside over the Norwegian abbey of Hovedøya, resigned after seven years on account of the 'intemperate climate'. He returned to his home community at Kirkstead (Lincolnshire) and resumed his previous office as prior. Hugh of Melrose, who was in 1234 elected to the abbacy of Deer in Aberdeenshire, returned to his former house after only one year, complaining of his infirmity and 'the coldness of that place'. A fifteenth-century monk of the London Charterhouse who was a native of

Lombardy evidently had difficulty adapting to the English diet. His prior was so concerned for the monk's welfare that he acquired permission for him to return to his homeland.[15]

The monastery was a hierarchical institution, and the brethren were organized according to seniority. This was based on when they had made their profession rather than their actual age. Thus, if Robert of York was forty-two and had become a monk at twenty-three he was senior to a fifty-year-old monk who had taken the habit at forty. Whenever a member of the community died the ordering was affected, but promotion to an office – or resignation from a post – also had an impact since office-holders (obedientiaries) automatically assumed a higher place. This system of ranking determined the monks' place in choir, at the daily chapter meeting and in the refectory, but also the order in which they received their books at Lent and the positions they occupied in processions.

THE NOVICES

Recruitment was essential to the survival of any community and the group of novices formed an important component within the monastery. These newcomers sought to embark upon the religious life, which was difficult, if rewarding, and was to be carefully considered. Anyone wishing to become a monk had to first undergo a probationary period known as the novitiate, to prove his suitability for the cloister. During this time novices were supervised by the novice master, whose task was to make them 'worthy vessels of God'.[16] In theory this probationary period lasted for a year but in some houses it was simply a few months or even weeks. The novitiate was as much a time for the applicant to consider carefully his decision to become a monk as an opportunity for the community to assess his aptitude. Not everyone who began the novitiate became a fully professed monk. Some left, finding the way of life too demanding, while others lacked the necessary skills required of a choir monk. In Gilbertine houses any novice who was not proficient enough at reading might instead become a lay sister or perhaps even a lay nun, which meant she slept and ate with the rest of the nuns but engaged in manual work when the others read.[17] One Cistercian novice who threatened to leave the abbey before his novitiate was over soon changed his mind when his abbot joked that he would cut off his feet with an axe to prevent him from going.[18]

Novices were not regarded as full members of the monastic community

14th c depiction of boy received into the monastery, British Library, Royal 10D. VIII, f. 82v.

and did not participate fully in the round of monastic offices. They generally had their own quarters and received instruction on the liturgy and singing; they were taught the customs of the house and order and all importantly learnt the system of signing used by the community to preserve silence in the cloister. Henry of Kirkstead, novice-master at Bury St Edmunds (Suffolk) in the fourteenth century, compiled a sign language list specifically to instruct the novices since 'dull wits, sluggish carelessness and futile activity allow novices to become acquainted with very few signs' and particularly as 'novices acquire years sooner than understanding'.[19] The novitiate could be a difficult period for these newcomers, who were often troubled with fears, doubts and temptations. The novice-master offered encouragement and support during such times and a close relationship might develop between the two which would endure through-out their claustral life. Jocelin of Brakelond (fl. 1173–c. 1215), a monk of Bury St Edmunds, remained loyal to his former novice-master, Samson, whose policies as abbot provoked criticism and hostility from within the community. Jocelin wrote what was effectively a biography of Samson.[20] When Aelred was novice-master of Rievaulx (Yorkshire) in the twelfth century, his encouragement and compassion persuaded a novice clerk who had fled from the cloister to return. The two remained close and the former clerk eventually died in Aelred's arms in the infirmary at Rievaulx.[21]

In some houses the novices slept in the common dormitory with the rest of the brethren, but elsewhere they were assigned a separate area. The novices' quarters at Fountains Abbey (Yorkshire) were situated beneath the monks' toilet block, off the southern range of the cloister, but the exact location and the nature of this accommodation would have varied from house to house depending on their own customs and facilities. At the Burgundian abbey of Cluny, novices were kept apart from the other monks and were forbidden to enter the common dormitory until after they had been blessed; they also dined at a separate table in the refectory.[22] It was customary for novices to be separated from the monks in church and they generally occupied the area known as the retrochoir, which was immediately behind the monks' choir. Here they might be joined by sick and infirm monks who followed a less rigorous regime and were not expected to participate in the full liturgical day. The transition to monastic life could be extremely difficult. Novices followed a less punishing schedule to help them adjust to the demands of the cloister. They were often served better food than the rest of the brethren and their quarters were heated. They might also receive preferential treatment when ill and convalescing. A sixteenth-century novice of Westminster Abbey who was recovering from illness was provided with a fire and a pair of fur-lined boots with double soles that cost twice as much as those given to a healthy monk.[23]

Those who managed to stay the course and complete their novitiate were professed as monks and made full members of the community. Their reception into the monastic brotherhood took place in the chapter house, in the presence of the entire community. Here, the novice made a will and was given the tonsure by the sacrist. This symbolic shaving of the head was a visible sign of his new monastic status but might, on occasion, prompt last-minute nerves. Caesarius of Heisterbach (d. c. 1240) recounts how one novice panicked when the razor was sharpened for his tonsure and would not let the implement near him until the prior had calmed him down.[24] The ceremony moved from the chapter house to the church, where the newcomer celebrated Mass and took the monastic vows of poverty, chastity and obedience. He was given the cowl, which was the hooded cloak worn only by monks, and received the Kiss of Peace from each member of the community. In Cluniac houses the new monk spent three days alone in silence and solitude, akin to Christ's three-day entombment preceding his resurrection. During this time his head and body were robed. At the Benedictine abbey of Eynsham (Oxfordshire) the newly professed monk followed a solitary existence during this three-day period and was a rather shadowy presence within the community. He took last place in the church, cloister and chapter house, remained in the church when the others were in the cloister and stayed behind after Matins to meditate or sing the psalmody. He was also required to sleep with his hood up and sing in a low voice. At the end of these three days the monk received the Kiss of Peace at Mass and communicated. The abbot then uncovered his head in a symbolic gesture making him a full member of the community.[25]

OBLATES

> *Weeping, he gave me, a weeping child, into the care of the monk Reginald, and sent me away into exile for love and never saw me again. And I, a mere boy did not presume to oppose my father's wishes, but I obeyed him willingly in all things, for he promised me in Thy name that if I became a monk I should taste the joys of Paradise with the Innocents after my death.*[26]

Orderic Vitalis (d. c. 1142), a monk of St Evroul in Normandy, was gifted to the abbey as a child oblate by his father, Odeler, when he was ten years old. The boy was assured that this would enable him to serve God more fully and ultimately attain Paradise. The reward was therefore worth the sacrifice. Orderic did not simply leave behind his family and friends but his country and language for he was born near Shrewsbury, in Shropshire, and had therefore to cross the Channel to Normandy when he entered the monastery of St Evroul. Orderic recounts the heart-wrenching departure as both father and son wept bitterly, and recalls his arrival in an unfamiliar country where, like Joseph in Egypt, he knew no one and was unable to understand the foreign language. Yet, with God's Grace and the kindness of the brethren Orderic soon settled in the monastery, which became his home for fifty-six years.[27]

The practice of offering a child to the monastery and the service of God was widespread at this time and was known as the oblate system. A number of parents gifted a child to the monastery, often a younger son who would not inherit his father's lands or as an act of gratitude to God for the safe delivery of their offspring. These oblates received an education in the monastery and when they were seventeen years of age took the monastic vows and were professed as full members of the community. While the practice flourished in the eleventh century it was gradually phased out in the twelfth and explicitly prohibited at the Fourth Lateran Council of 1215. There were several reasons for this. The presence of these spirited young boys could severely disrupt claustral life and some, who had little interest in a monastic vocation, were troublesome and wayward. But above all it was crucial that the decision to enter the monastery was made by the postulant himself and was carefully considered. Thus the Cistercians stipulated that all recruits must be at least sixteen when they entered the monastery to embark on a one-year novitiate; in Carthusian houses aspirants had to be twenty-one years of age.

THE WORKING COMMUNITY

> *Having spurned this world's riches, behold! The new soldiers of Christ, poor*
> *with the poor Christ, began discussing by what planning, by what device, by*
> *what management they would be able to support themselves in this life, as well*
> *as their guests who came, both rich and poor, whom the Rule commands to*
> *welcome as Christ. It was then that they enacted a definition to receive, with*
> *their bishop's permission, bearded lay brothers, and to treat them as themselves*
> *in life and death – except that they might not become monks – and also hired*
> *hands; for without the assistance of these they did not understand how they*
> *could fully observe the precepts of the Rule day and night.*[28]

The monastery engaged an array of helpers to assist with the daily running of the house, relying upon a network of servants, casual workers and lay brothers. Cistercian abbeys, for example, had a community of lay brothers (*conversi*) as well as a community of monks. These lay brethren were members of the Order who took vows of obedience and were required to observe various liturgical Offices but, unlike the monks, their day was centred upon manual labour. They undertook agricultural and industrial work within the precinct as well as on the abbey's granges, farming the land, rearing livestock and helping with building and repair work. As such the lay brethren were integral to the self-sufficiency of each community and were the bedrock of the Cistercian economy. The lay brothers were physically distinguished from the monks by their appearance, for they wore work clothes rather than habits and did not receive the tonsure but remained unshaven. They were literally set apart from the monks within the precinct, having their own choir in the west end of the church and their living quarters in the western range. Other Orders similarly made use of a lay brotherhood or sorority. The Gilbertine Order, or the Order of Sempringham as it was also known, engaged a community of lay sisters to support the nuns and a group of lay brothers to help the canons and undertake heavy labour. The

Carthusian monks were assisted by a community of lay brethren who had their own quarters in the lower court, which was often about a mile from the monks' cloister. The lay brothers were responsible for exercising hospitality as well as charity, in addition to helping with manual work.

Servants and workers were engaged by monasteries to support and sustain the monastic community. Some lived within the precinct but others stayed at home with their wives and families. In the late eleventh century the Benedictine community at Evesham Abbey (Worcestershire) employed around sixty-five servants, five of whom served in the church. The monks of Battle Abbey (Sussex) had egg-collectors, pigmen and a plumber while the Yorkshire nunnery of Yedingham employed a miller, cowherds and a keeper of geese.[29] The monasteries made use of seasonal workers as well as full-time servants, particularly at harvest when extra hands were needed to gather the crops. Women were part of the working community, even in male houses, and were generally employed as washerwomen. However, the sacrist or the male servants laundered the vestments and the corporals, which were square pieces of linen on which the consecrated elements were placed during the Mass. Women might also be called upon to help gather the harvest, but they were kept at a distance and prohibited from sleeping within the precinct lest this would lead to any indiscretions. Attitudes were often more lax in the later Middle Ages and in 1524 it was alleged that the female cook of Gresley Priory (Derbyshire) had been spotted wrestling with the prior in his chambers; it is hardly surprising that there were complaints about her culinary skills. While servants were essential to the monastery's existence, their presence within the precinct was potentially disruptive to monastic life but could also affect the reputation of the house, for there was a danger that they would disclose the community's affairs to outsiders. Considerable efforts were made to bridle the tongues of servants and make sure that the monastery's reputation remained intact. In some cases lay servants were banned from certain parts of the precinct or made to swear an oath of loyalty and secrecy.

THE WIDER COMMUNITY

In the later Middle Ages it became more common for lay folk to work and even live within the monastery precinct. They might be actively encouraged to rent a shop in the outer court, which could be lucrative for the monastery but was prime property for tradesmen who could capitalize on the pilgrim trade. Professionals sometimes secured lodgings within the precinct. A physician of Cambridge rented accommodation at Ely Cathedral Priory and in 1522 an organist secured lodgings at Buckland Abbey (Devon) in return for an annual payment and his services. It was agreed that for the yearly sum of £2 13s 4d the organist would receive a decent table and a room over the west gate as well as a dwelling house and garden, an allowance of food, drink, fuel and a gown every year worth 12s. For his part the organist was obliged to assist in the choir each day during the Divine Service and teach four boys of the convent, but might choose one to wait upon him as a servant. He was also to instruct any of the boys or monks of the house who wished to learn music or the organ.[30] From the late fifteenth century the larger monastic houses in England might engage professional singers and cantors to enhance the liturgical performance on important occasions. In some cases these cantors wore several hats. At the Cornish priory of Tywardreath the cantor officiated as the prior's barber and sometimes escorted him on his business trips.[31]

Other laypeople might choose to live within the monastery precinct as a corrodian. This meant that in return for a gift of land or property to the community they received accommodation and daily allowances of food, drink, fuel, lighting and perhaps also clothing. The terms, however, varied and not all corrodians lived within the confines of the abbey. Arrangements of this kind could be highly lucrative for the monastery and facilitate their possession of a desirable plot of land. But not every corrodian was profitable and communities might instead be burdened with retired royal officials imposed upon them by the king. This caused contention between the monks of Dieulacres (Staffordshire) and Edward II (1307–27) when the community challenged the king's right to send a corrodian to their house to be provided with food and lodgings. The jury found in favour of the abbot but to little effect, for Edward's successors continued to send corrodians to the abbey regardless.[32] From the thirteenth century the Carthusians admitted a class of outsiders to live within their precincts who were known as *donati*. They were not regarded as members *per se* and did not take vows but were nonetheless subject to the authority and discipline of the prior and procurator of the house. Upon their arrival they agreed to abide by the rules of the house and those who failed to do so forfeited their right to stay. The *donati*'s status is rather vividly conveyed in a contemporary description of them as 'the bowels of the order'.[33]

The Welsh Cistercian abbeys of the later Middle Ages welcomed resident poets or bards as semi-permanent members of the household. In return for their lodgings and generous hospitality at the abbot's table these bards might write poems celebrating their host's generosity. The poet, Tudur Aled (1480–1526), paid tribute to the hospitality of Abbot Thomas Penant of Basingwerk (1481–1522) and his generous patronage of bards. Gutun Owain (1460–1503), who stayed at the abbeys of Basingwerk, Strata Florida and Valle Crucis, wrote more than fifteen poems praising Cistercian abbots.[34] When Guto'r Glyn (1440–93) broke a limb he retired to the abbey of Valle Crucis to recover, which suggests that the bards might have considered these monasteries as a kind of retreat.[35]

VISITORS: THE FLOATING COMMUNITY

An important component of any monastery was the influx of visitors who arrived at the house. They included pilgrims, travellers, patrons and relatives of the brethren, as well as visiting monks. Some houses were inundated with a constant flow of visitors, which could be disruptive but also financially draining. The thirteenth-century monks of Bermondsey Priory claimed that the extensive hospitality they had been obliged to dispense had caused them considerable impoverishment. The priory was only about half a mile off the main London to Dover road and the house would therefore have been a popular stopping-off point for travellers. The monks attributed their predicament also to the conspicuousness of the priory, which was a 'gazingstock' to the king and kingdom; accordingly they could not reduce hospitality without causing scandal or a commotion.[36] Cistercian abbeys were obliged to accommodate members of the Order, particularly abbots travelling to the annual assembly in France. Those coming from Ireland and Scotland often broke their journey at Whitland Abbey in Carmarthenshire, but some stayed for over a fortnight, putting considerable strain on the abbey's finances. In 1220 the situation was such that the abbot of Whitland wrote to the General Chapter seeking its help and advice. Monasteries that faced financial difficulties might be excused from receiving guests until they were in a stable position and able once more to support hospitality. In 1258 the General Chapter of Cîteaux acknowledged the plight of the Welsh abbey of Strata Florida and granted the community dispensation to withhold hospitality for three years.[37]

Monastic communities were regarded as centres of charity as well as hospitality, and were expected to support the worthy poor of the locality. In the thirteenth century visitors to the abbey church at Melrose in Scotland would have likely been greeted by the sight of Adam of Lexington, a venerable monk of the community who spent his days reading the psalter by the church door and offering words of guidance or a blessing to any who wished it. Adam kept a basket of bread at his side which he distributed to the deserving poor. Adam also provided them with milk from cows given to him by visitors whom he had comforted.[38] A number of monasteries sustained Maundy men, who were received daily after the example of the Evangelist and given succour. Abbot Aethelwig (1059–77) of Evesham (Worcestershire) provided for twelve Maundy men, some of whom were lepers. In return for the care they received these men were obliged to observe various religious offices. Each day the almoner of Abingdon Abbey (Berkshire) admitted three poor men for the Maundy, while his counterpart at St Mary's, York, would invite the poor to share his fire in winter when it was icy and exercise charity according to his means.[39] In times of famine and hardship the monastery was invariably seen as a source of refuge for the poor and destitute. When famine devastated Siebengebirge, Germany, in 1190, some 1,500 of the poor in the area found relief each day at the Cistercian abbey of Heisterbach. Abbot Gerard made sure that every day a large ox was cooked with vegetables and personally distributed the bread and meat. The monks allegedly received divine help to support their charitable work, for it was said that the bread miraculously expanded in the oven and the abbey's supply of flour never ran out. The Yorkshire monks of Fountains Abbey similarly tended the local poor during the famine of 1194. Abbot Ralph and his monks set up a refuge camp and for six months provided shelter and spiritual care. They dispensed food, tended the sick and provided head-coverings for those infested with head worms.[40]

Monasteries also welcomed other monks to stay, some of whom were visiting the area and required short-term accommodation, while others had come to undertake research at the house, speak with one of the brethren or observe the monastery's customs, which they could then impart to their own community. These visits were not always harmonious. When John of Harwell, a monk of Neath Abbey (West Glamorgan), stayed with his fellow Cistercians at Whitland (Carmarthenshire) in the late fifteenth century he killed a secular priest in the cloister. John was duly punished for this 'shameful act' and sentenced to imprisonment.[41] Monks who had committed a serious offence might be sent to another house for a temporary period in the hope that the change would cause them to mend their ways. This was often successful but did not always have the desired effect and could instead cause considerable disruption in the house.

A vast array of people were attached to or in some way affiliated to the medieval monastery, whether they resided within the precinct, came to work for the community or were visiting the house. The number of individuals within the precinct could therefore fluctuate considerably, particularly if monasteries were popular pilgrim spots or hosted fairs and markets in their outer courts. While the medieval monastery was intended to be an oasis of solitude it could be a hive of activity that stood at the apex of medieval life.

THE DAILY SCHEDULE

At midnight I rose to give thanks to thee. (Psalm 118)

According to the *Rule of St Benedict*, monks should make a threefold division of their time and engage in liturgical devotion (*Opus Dei*), in reading and contemplation (*Lectio Divina*) and in manual labour which was an act of humility and an antidote to boredom and sloth. The day itself was structured around the seven Canonical Hours that were celebrated in the church (Lauds, Prime, Terce, Sext, Nones, Vespers, Compline) and the Night Office of Vigils or Nocturns as it was also known. Other daily fixtures included the chapter meeting, at which business was discussed and disciplinary matters addressed, and the periods allocated to reading, working, eating and sleeping. Each week the Maundy was carried out, which was the ritual washing of the monks' feet after the example of Christ washing the disciples' feet and in accordance with John 13.14–15 ('If I then, your Lord and Master, have washed your feet, you also should wash one another's feet. For I have given you an example that you should do as I have done to you'). When precisely each of these activities took place varied throughout the year, for the monk's day was measured by the sun. It began at daybreak with the celebration of Lauds and concluded at dusk with the final Office of Compline. This meant that the monk's day was much shorter in winter than in summer with the celebration of Lauds at around 8 a.m. rather than 4 a.m. and Compline around 4 p.m. and not 9 p.m. On account of the longer working day in summer and the two periods allocated to work, the monks were served a light supper in addition to dinner and enjoyed an afternoon siesta known as the *meridian*. The daily schedule was different on Sundays and feast days when more time was spent celebrating the liturgy and no manual labour was carried out; any extra time was spent reading or in private prayer. There were differences also between Orders. Whereas the Cistercians, who were intent to uphold the original tenets of the *Rule*, religiously observed the weekly celebration of the Maundy, this was all but abandoned by the Benedictines, who argued that it was now redundant since the monks washed their own feet. As a token gesture they moistened three fingers and simply touched the instep. The Cistercians, however, dismissed this as an excuse, arguing that there would be no need for the brethren to wash their own feet if the Maundy was properly observed.[42]

A notable distinction between the Benedictines and the new reformed Orders was their attitude to manual labour. From the ninth century the Benedictine liturgy was elaborated to such an extent that there was little time left for work, which was virtually made obsolete. Most of the Cluniac's day was taken up with the liturgy, which was notoriously excessive and ostentatious. Whereas the *Rule* had prescribed that the 150 Psalms should be celebrated over the course of a week, the Cluniacs recited these in a single day. The Cistercians reacted against these developments and, seeking simplicity and authenticity in all aspects of monastic life, pared the liturgy down and made time for manual work which was once more an integral part of the day. One period was allotted to work in winter and two in summer, but at harvest time the monks spent their entire day in the fields and celebrated the Hours as they worked. The Cistercians' dedication to manual labour set them apart from their Benedictine counterparts and was seen as a defining feature of the Order. The Benedictines, in contrast, considered this as outdated, quirky and even inappropriate. Peter the Venerable, abbot of Cluny (1122–56), was struck by the Cistercians' devotion to labour and marvelled at how they were able to sustain this hard work on such an austere diet. But Peter believed it was unbecoming that monks, 'the fine linen of the sanctuary, should be begrimed in dirt and bent down with rustic labours'.[43]

The two Orders also differed in how they spent the period between Vigils and Lauds. Whereas Benedictine monks generally returned to bed after Vigils and rested until daybreak when Lauds was celebrated, the Cistercians, who were 'sterner and more stricter with themselves',[44] stayed awake and either read in the cloister or spent the time in private devotion. They argued that the extra sleep made monks groggy and sluggish for the rest of the day and feared that the brethren would rush the last part of the Office in their haste to return to bed.[45]

MEASURING TIME

The monastic day was measured by the sun, with duties officially beginning at daybreak and ending with the celebration of Compline at sunset. All activities were to be carried out during the daylight hours, apart from the Night Office of Vigils. This arrangement meant that the length of the day and when precisely each activity was carried out varied depending on the time of year and the geographical location of the house. By the later Middle Ages attempts were made to standardize the day and impose uniformity of practice. For example, in 1429 the General Chapter of Cistercians stipulated that the sacrist should wake at 2 a.m. to sound the bell for Vigils, regardless of the time of year.[46]

Timekeeping was the sacrist's responsibility. He might ring a bell or strike a wooden board (*tabula*) to announce to the community when they should rise, assemble for the Office or gather for a meeting. The entire schedule depended on the sacrist making the correct signal at the correct time and he needed some kind of an alarm to help him. Prior to the invention of the mechanical clock various methods were employed, including the cock crow, although this would not have been early enough to wake the monks for Matins. Candle clocks and sundials were also used, as well as the stars. A fascinating tract written in the eleventh century reveals how the sacrist, or whoever was responsible for timekeeping in the monastery, would stand at a designated spot and know from the position of a certain constellation whether it was time to sound the bell for Vigils, light the lamps in the cloister or tend to other duties. For example, on 25 December the monks were required to rise earlier for the Night Office since this was an important liturgical occasion. The sacrist knew to rouse the monks when the Twins were lying almost over the monks' dormitory and Orion was above the Chapel of All Saints. This would have been c. 10 p.m., whereas the monks would normally have risen at around 12.35 a.m.[47]

Another popular and fairly reliable method of timekeeping was the water clock. This was set to sound a bell at a specific time to notify the sacrist when he should rouse the brethren or signal the Hour. The oldest account of a simple water-driven alarm in Europe is in a tenth- or eleventh-century manuscript from a Benedictine house in the Pyrenees. The clock did not have a dial as such but a bell-striking mechanism – a weight on a rope turned an axle that hit a bell on a rod, sounding the alarm.[48] By the twelfth century the water clock was fairly widespread throughout Europe. There was certainly a water clock at Bury

14th c depiction of Abbot Richard Wallingford of St Albans building his clock,
British Library, Cotton Claudius E. IV, f. 201.

St Edmunds (Suffolk) in the twelfth century, for an account of a fire that broke
out in the church in 1199 describes how the brethren ran to the clock for water
to help extinguish the flames. The water clock was seemingly used in a number
of Cistercian houses of the time. The customary of the Order sets out how the
sacrist should set the clock in winter to make it sound on weekdays before Lauds,
unless it was daylight, and to use this as a signal to wake himself before Vigils
so that he could then light the church in preparation for the Office.[49] Water
clocks were not, however, the most reliable means of telling time, particularly in
northern climes where the water was likely to freeze.[50]

Timekeeping in the monastery and indeed throughout Europe was revolution-
ized in the late thirteenth century with the invention of the mechanical clock.
This meant that the day was no longer measured in twelve parts according to
the canonical day but in twenty-four equal hours. By the late thirteenth century
a number of houses had a mechanical clock. The earliest known one was at
Norwich Cathedral Priory, certainly by c. 1273–4 when there is a reference to
its repair. Other examples include the mechanical clock that stood over the
rood screen at the Augustinian priory of Dunstable and those at Christ Church,
Canterbury, Ely, Exeter and St Paul's, London.[51] These clocks were extremely
expensive and little is now known about their design. The first Norwich clock
was replaced by a larger and more elaborate one in 1321–5. The sacrist's rolls
record the financial arrangements for the construction and installation of this
clock and reveal that it had a large astronomical dial of iron plate that was ornate
and gilded, a model of the sun and moon, wooden sculptures and a procession
of monks. The community engaged various craftsmen to construct this clock,
including carpenters and smiths, masons, plasterers and bell-founders, but the
process was fraught with difficulties and expense. Robert of the Tower was made
responsible for building the main dial and ruined the clock. His successors fared
no better and when Roger Stoke was eventually put in charge he had to go to
London in person to supervise the engraving.[52]

The Norwich clock is the earliest known example of a great mechanical clock,
but one of the most noteworthy is the astrological clock built by Abbot Richard
of Wallingford, who presided over the great abbey at St Albans from 1326 to
1336. Richard, whose father was a blacksmith, had himself studied astronomy
and mathematics at Oxford and upon his election to the abbacy at St Albans
channelled his energies and resources into designing and building an impressive
clock for his community. When Edward III (1327–77) visited St Albans he
remarked on the poor state of the abbey buildings and suggested that the abbot
should not perhaps have indulged himself on such a large and costly project when
other necessary work was required. Richard was unfazed by the king's remarks
and replied that his successors could easily repair the buildings but only he could
accomplish this clock. Richard used the professional clockmakers Roger and
Lawrence of Stoke to help construct his timepiece; Roger had previously built a
clock at Norwich. The abbot did not live to see his masterpiece completed. It was
finally finished some twenty years after his death and was an impressive piece
of engineering. The St Albans clock no longer survives as it was destroyed at the

dissolution of the monastery in 1539 but a description by a sixteenth-century visitor to the abbey reveals that the clock stood in the south transept of the church; it had bells, dials and wheels and showed the tides at London Bridge. The clock was not simply intended as a timepiece but calculated the daily rotation of the heavens. It showed the course of the sun, moon and stars, creating a model of the heavens, and has recently been described as a 'celestial theatre as much as a timepiece'.[53]

Claustral life in this figurative Paradise was highly regulated and gave a rhythm and routine to every aspect of the monk's day as well as his night. The time for prayer, contemplation and daily work was carefully defined; the monk's behaviour and very thoughts were closely monitored. What was it really like for these men to live in the medieval cloister and subject themselves to the observances of the Order?

Our food is scanty, our garments rough; our drink is from the stream and our sleep upon our book. Under our tired limbs there is a hard mat; when sleep is sweetest we must rise at a bell's bidding . . . self-will has no scope; there is no moment for idleness or dissipation.[1]

2

The Severity of Monastic Life (1):
Diet, Sleep, Clothing and Bathing

Poverty was one of the three monastic vows and required the monk to give up his personal possessions. From then, all that he needed, including his clothes, belonged to the community. The abbot or one of his deputies would periodically search the monks' dormitory to make sure that nobody was hoarding any personal items. However, poverty did not mean destitution. The Carthusians were particularly concerned to guard against this extreme lest it resulted in begging and thus dependency on the world they sought to shun. This chapter explores the real meaning of poverty for the monk and how it affected him in his daily life in the cloister.

The monastic life properly lived was a hard one. Upon entering the monastery the monks had to cut ties with their families, friends and the outside world, and take vows of chastity. They were subject to severe restrictions regarding their diet and clothing and might suffer greatly from lack of sleep as well as the cold for few places in the monastery were heated. Moreover, the regulation garb was not designed for northern countries since St Benedict had compiled his prescriptions with the Mediterranean climate in mind. Communities might take steps to guard against the cold. For example, on Good Fridays and other occasions when the monks were required to process barefoot, they would wash their feet in warm water after the ceremony and wear their day shoes. If the abbot considered it too cold to go barefoot he might allow the brethren to wear their shoes instead. In winter the sub-sacrist of the Augustinian priory of Barnwell (Cambridgeshire) ensured that those ministering at the altar had warm hands by bringing them live coals in iron dishes.[2] Some monasteries requested exemptions on account of the harsh conditions they faced. In 1245 the monks of Dunfermline Abbey in Scotland received papal dispensation to wear caps in church, given the severe cold in those parts. Similar concessions were granted to the York Cluniacs at Lenton Priory and the Benedictines of Ely and Abingdon.[3] While the church was perhaps the coldest spot in the monastery, the refectory could also be unbearably chilly. In the sixteenth century the canons of Butley Priory, Suffolk, complained that

their refectory was so cold they suffered from chilblains in winter.⁴ By the later
Middle Ages it was not uncommon for communities to light a fire in the refectory
to keep the winter chill at bay.

For many who entered the religious life the austerity was testing and might
prove too much of a challenge. Waldef (d. 1159), prior of the Augustinian community at Kirkham in North Yorkshire and son of Earl Simon of Northampton,
was pushed to the limits when he entered the Cistercian abbey of Warden in
Bedfordshire. Despite his Augustinian training Waldef found the Cistercian way
of life gruelling, particularly the tasteless food, scratchy clothing and onerous
manual labour. Waldef contemplated returning to his former priory but sought
and received the strength from God to persevere. He went on to preside over
Melrose Abbey (1148–59) in Scotland and was posthumously venerated as a
saint.⁵ Not everyone managed to stay the course or progressed to lead as eminent
a life as Waldef. The difficulties experienced by newcomers in adapting to the
severity of claustral life, and the doubts and conflicts they encountered, are
considered later in this chapter; the help and encouragement they might receive
from within the community is discussed in Chapter 6. Even the great ascetics,
such as Bernard of Clairvaux, acknowledged that, for most, extreme austerity
could be injurious to their spiritual and physical well-being. Still, this was not
an excuse for laxity for there was a marked difference between working to one's
limits and shirking. Bernard had no time for detractors. He railed against monks
who feigned illness to enjoy a respite from monastic observance and, while their
fellow brethren endeavoured to pursue their monastic vocation and continued 'to
wallow in blood and gore', shamelessly retreated to the infirmary to enjoy better
food, a cosy bed and time to chat and rest.⁶

FOOD AND DRINK: THE MONASTIC DIET

The body, but not the soul is fattened by frying pans.⁷

According to the *Rule of St Benedict* monks should eat once a day in winter but
might take a light supper for sustenance from Easter until mid-September, when
their day was much longer. At dinner the brethren were offered a choice of two
cooked dishes known as *pulmenta*, which were cereal or vegetable based but
might include a little egg, cheese or fish. A third dish of fruit or vegetables was

served when available and would often be comprised of home-grown produce. No meat was permitted except to the sick and food was to be kept simple and flavoured with salt or home-grown spices; later, however, it became more common to introduce exotic spices such as cumin and saffron. The monks of Abbey Dore in Herefordshire had their own saffron garden, as did the monks of Norwich Cathedral Priory. In addition to these dishes each monk received a daily allowance of bread and a measure of drink, which might be ale in England but wine in the southern regions of France. On special occasions, such as feasts and anniversaries, the community's diet was supplemented with additional dishes known as pittances. These treats might consist of small portions of fish, eggs and other delicacies that were not normally enjoyed on a daily basis, or better quality foods such as fine white bread in place of the coarse grainy black bread, and spiced wines rather than ale. From the twelfth century pittances were less of a rarity and for the Benedictines became an integral part of their diet and a way to introduce variety and new dishes into the monastery.[8]

A FRUGAL DIET

Black bread and plain water, mere greens and vegetables are assuredly no very delectable fare: what does give great pleasure is when, for the love of Christ and the desire of interior delight, a well-disciplined stomach is able to satisfy itself with such fare and be thankful.[9]

It was not intended that monks should starve or suffer excessively through want of food. Indeed, those who went to this extreme were unlikely to be fit for the rigours demanded by the daily liturgical round. Rather, the restrictions imposed on the monastic diet, like those imposed on other aspects of their life, were a way to master the senses and suppress physical desires such as greed, lust and torpor. This would ensure that the mind stayed focused on lofty matters and was not a servant to bodily wants. While rich and highly flavoured foods would likely overwhelm the senses and distract the mind, overindulgence would lead to sluggishness, with monks fit for sleep rather than work. As Bernard of Clairvaux warned, anyone who attended Vigils before having fully digested his food would yield a groan rather than a tone.[10] However, an important reason for abstaining from food and particularly meat was the belief that this was an effective way to curb one's carnal desires and keep the libido in check, a vital consideration if chastity was to be preserved.

Some of the great ascetics observed a rigorous dietary regime and exercised indifference as well as abstinence, but most monks were expected simply to show a sensible attitude to food and drink and practise moderation. Concessions were granted to novices, who were often introduced gradually to the restrictive diet, and also the sick and infirm, who were permitted a little meat to nourish and fortify them. They had to eat this in a separate room since no meat was allowed in the refectory. Still, every monk was entitled to some relief from the ascetic diet, both to sustain him physically and boost his morale. St Benedict ruled that each member of the community might on occasion dine at the abbot's table and enjoy a more appetizing spread. The abbot of Abingdon (Berkshire) was permitted to invite to his table whomsoever of the monks he wished when he was entertaining guests. In some cases this led to allegations of favouritism, with complaints that a few of the monks were regular diners at their abbot's table yet others rarely, if ever, enjoyed this privilege. In 1394 the Cistercian monks of Hailes Abbey (Gloucestershire) were reprimanded for taking liberties and using their invitation to the abbot's table as an opportunity to skip the Offices of Collations and Compline, to gossip 'uselessly' and drink to excess. They were warned to reform their ways or lose this privilege for a month.[11]

THE PROHIBITION OF MEAT

> Strong meat of four-foot beasts the Rule denies; so flesh of bird that runs or bird that flies they long for, not as tasty but as rare. But when they cook it, no-one dwelling near perceives the smoke, too conscious of the act. The meal all done, no vestige of the fact remains, for lest the chicken-bones be found crying, 'We're here' they're buried underground.[12]

The consumption of flesh-meat by all but the sick was prohibited in the *Rule of St Benedict* but some 800 years later was given papal sanction. In 1336 Pope Benedict XII permitted Benedictine monks to eat meat on four days of the week so long as this was outside the fast season and was not served in the refectory. A special chamber called the *misericord* ('mercy') was often the appointed place for these carnivorous feasts.[13] To make sure that the monks did not take advantage of this concession, it was ruled that no more than half the community should eat outside the refectory at a given time. A century earlier there were reports that at Bury St Edmunds (Suffolk) no more than six of the monks dined in the refectory while the rest indulged themselves in private chambers.[14]

The sanction of meat-eating by the papacy should not be seen as a volte-face. Rather, it was an acknowledgement of the reality of the situation and an attempt to at least control current practices. Before the end of the twelfth century Benedictine and Cluniac monks had been regularly eating meat in special chambers but also bending the rules governing meat-eating in the refectory by distinguishing dishes of pre-cooked meat, such as rissoles and meatballs, which they ate in the refectory, from those that were cooked for the first time and were eaten outside.[15] Evidently, as far as these monks were concerned it was fine to eat bubble and squeak in the refectory but not a sirloin roast. In the late twelfth century Gerald of Wales alleged that the monks of Christ Church, Canterbury, found a way around the prohibition of meat on Fridays by making a soup from it.[16]

The Cistercians, who emerged as part of the late eleventh-century reform movement, at first held out against the eating of meat and as in all aspects of their daily life sought to observe the *Rule of St Benedict* to the letter. Inevitably changes soon crept in and from the late twelfth century some of their critics suggested that they surreptitiously indulged in forbidden fowl while publicly professing their abstinence. The twelfth-century satirist and archdeacon of Oxford, Walter Map, remarked on the curious fact that while the Cistercians kept hundreds of pigs and certainly sold the bacon, they neither sold nor disposed of the feet, heads and legs – 'What becomes of them, God knows'.[17] Such reports were mere speculation but there is tangible evidence for the eating of meat in Cistercian monasteries from the 1220s, when the General Chapter of the Order formally reprimanded these offenders. Thus, while the Order did not officially tolerate meat-eating until the early fourteenth century, it was clearly not uncommon before then.[18] The Carthusians, who were renowned for the severity of their life and unwillingness to bend, stood firm against these changing attitudes to meat-eating and prohib-ited this even to the sick. They associated the eating of flesh with the Great Flood and maintained that standards in the monastery would fall if the brethren were permitted to eat meat – the monks would be tempted to feign sickness in the hope of receiving a meaty treat and might deliberately delay their recovery to prolong this indulgence. The Carthusians were accused of inhumanity by some of their contemporaries, who argued that to withhold meat to the sick was actually injurious to their health. The Carthusians strongly countered these allegations and one fourteenth-century monk of the Order who wrote a treatise in their defence remarked that Carthusians were actually healthier than the Benedictines but also recovered more quickly, since they were not tempted to spin out their illness.[19] Interestingly, when the Carthusian bishop, Hugh of Lincoln (d. 1200), suffered illness in his latter years he initially resisted the doctors' advice to take a little meat to aid his recovery. The archbishop of Canterbury and other eminent men urged Hugh to reconsider and eventually, concerned that he should not offend these reverend persons, Hugh conceded but asked specifically for pigs' feet since he had read that the Holy Fathers had permitted this to the sick. However, Hugh had not tasted flesh for many years and could only manage a mouthful of the meat; he similarly struggled to eat the small birds that were brought to him. The incident aptly conveys how Hugh was prepared to modify his ideals but only to a certain extent and within known boundaries.[20]

MODIFICATIONS TO THE *RULE*: IDEALS IN PRACTICE

Benedict's prescriptions were only ever intended as a model, a starting point that communities might later modify in accordance with their growing needs and the demands of the time. In some cases the modifications were considerable while in others there was little regard for the original tenets. The new reformed Orders that emerged in the late eleventh century sought to return to basics and impose a dietary regime that followed closely the requirements of the *Rule*, but the very fact they were marked out for their rigorous policy is an indication that at this time the monastic diet varied. Thus, whereas the twelfth-century Benedictines were known for their liking for fine dining and a tendency to overindulge, the Cistercian and Carthusian monks were renowned for the severity of their diet and strict abstinence from meat. Guibert of Nogent, a Benedictine monk writing at the turn of the twelfth century, remarked on the sparseness of the Carthusian diet that was evidently quite different to his own, and noted that their wine was diluted to such an extent it was basically water.[21]

The harsh dietary regime was clearly an aspect of life that monks and especially newcomers found particularly challenging and in some cases intolerable. One twelfth-century monk of the Cistercian abbey of Rievaulx complained that the food cleaved to his mouth 'more bitter than wormwood'.[22] The *Exordium Magnum*, a Cistercian text compiled in the early thirteenth century by a German monk, Conrad of Eberbach, tells of one nobleman who joined the White Monks at Clairvaux (Langres) and found the diet gruelling, especially the pottage (a kind of pease pudding), which occasionally caused him to retch. The nobleman considered leaving the monastery and raised his concerns with the abbot but at the next meal he found the loathsome peas to be rich and flavoursome, tastier even than meat. The novice concluded that the abbot must have taken pity on him and arranged that some bacon fat be put in his dish but was assured that this was not the case. The cooks swore they had simply flavoured the beans with salt and water and served everyone the same dish. At this point the novice realized that God had come to his assistance and miraculously made these foods seem delicious. Indeed, the next day he found that the beans were once more tasty and thereafter confessed that often he derived more pleasure from eating pease pudding than he had previously from dining on fat stock and game.[23]

Throughout the course of the Middle Ages some monks observed the full rigours of the monastic diet and even took this to extremes. Inevitably there were many more who struggled with these strictures, modified practices or disregarded the rules. The Cluniacs in particular were parodied for their gluttony. Gerald of Wales (d. c. 1223) recounts his experience as a guest at the table of Baldwin, Archbishop of Canterbury, when he was seated beside a Cistercian monk, Serlo, who had previously been a Benedictine. After dinner the conversation turned to the gluttony of the Black Monks, provoking Serlo to declare that one had a greater chance of entering heaven as a black dog than a Black Monk.[24] Parodies of this kind are inevitably rather one-sided, offering only a partial insight into the reality of the situation. Similarly, visitation records and statutes represent only one side of the story since they are concerned with recording abuses rather than cases of satisfactory behaviour. There are, however, other sources of evidence for what was eaten in the monasteries. The sign lists that were drawn up to teach monks how to communicate in the cloister without speaking generally include a number of signs for foods and drinks that were commonly served and can therefore offer an insight into what was regularly enjoyed in the cloister. In some cases these lists were derivative and do not necessarily reflect what was eaten at a particular house at a given time. But communities might modify these lists by adding or deleting signs in accordance with their own needs. The monks of Christ Church, Canterbury, for example, introduced a sign for oyster at a time when shellfish was rarely eaten elsewhere. Communities might also change a sign to one that was more meaningful to them. Thus, while the Cluniacs signed for milk by imitating a suckling baby – the little finger was placed on the lips – the German monks of Hirsau mimicked the milking of a cow by tugging the little finger of their left hand.[25]

Monastic accounts and obedientiary rolls are an important source of evidence for the types of foods eaten in the monastery, revealing what the monks bought but also, and importantly, what was grown in the orchards and nut-yards and sold if there was a glut. In the late fourteenth century the gardener of Abingdon Abbey (Berkshire) sold apples, grapes, pears, nuts and cider; the Cistercian monks of Kinloss (Moray) sold cabbages.[26] Some of these records date from the late twelfth and the thirteenth centuries, but most are from the fourteenth. They record purchases monastic officials made and in some cases gifts received, such as the sealfish Abbot John Greenwell of Fountains (1442–71) was given by the prior of Newminster Abbey. Fragments of seal and porpoise were found during excavations at Norwich Cathedral Priory, which suggests this was also a delicacy enjoyed elsewhere.[27]

Collectively, these sources suggest that, in the larger houses at least, the monks had a relatively rich, varied and meaty diet. In addition to the staples of eggs, beans, fruit and vegetables – home-grown when possible – the monks ate plenty of fish and a variety of meats. The fourteenth-century accounts for the cellarer of Battle Abbey (Sussex) reveal that the monks there enjoyed mutton, lamb, pork, veal, kid, suckling pig, poultry and game, as well as a wide variety of fish including herring, mackerel, cod and salmon. The fourteenth-century obedientiary and manorial rolls for Norwich Cathedral Priory show similar purchases – the monks ate pork, mutton and beef on those days when meat was permitted, and on fish days might have cod, eel, roach, herring or whiting. More unusual delicacies served at the prior's table included eel tarts.[28] From the fifteenth century, oysters were eaten.[29] Excavations at monastic sites such as Fountains Abbey in Yorkshire have found similar evidence of cockle, mussel and oyster shells, as well as beef, pork, venison and mutton bones.

Not all of the purchases recorded were eaten by the monks, as some were intended for their guests and members of the household. It is likely, for ex-ample, that the swans, cygnets, dolphins, eels and other exotica listed in the accounts of Battle Abbey were for the community's guests rather than the monks since the amounts recorded are relatively small and would not have fed all the brethren. The abbot of Fountains purchased similar delicacies for his household and guests in the fifteenth century, and the bursar's records show that he served venison, partridges and quail, as well as figs and walnuts. Battle was in a wine-importing area and the cellarer's accounts indicate that a large and varied amount of wine was bought by the community. This would have been served on special occasions but also offered as treats (pittances) or to the bloodlet.[30]

For many the monastic life meant the guarantee of a reliable source of food and drink. It was the superiors' responsibility to provide their communities with sufficient provisions and guard against discontent. A number of communities complained of inequality when it came to dining and claimed that while their abbot or abbess feasted sumptuously in private chambers he or she stinted on the community's provisions. The abbess of Campsey Ash in Suffolk was evidently just as mean with herself as her nuns and subjected everyone to burnt lamb and skinny oxen; even the guests complained. A common criticism in the later Middle Ages concerned the quality of ale. This might even be cited as justification for an excursion to the local tavern. In 1515 the ale served to the monks of Ely Cathedral Priory was allegedly so bad it was declared unfit for pigs. The prior of Ely was ordered to improve the quality of ale so that the monks had no cause to go into town. The serving of substandard ale in the monastery sometimes led to the arrival of entrepreneurs who set up stores within the precinct, such as the married lay women who in 1534 sold their beer to the nuns of St James, Canterbury. The number of complaints made by monks in the later Middle Ages about the quality and quantity of their food and drink suggests that they were less tolerant than their predecessors and, like their secular counterparts, had greater expectations when it came to their diet. Thus the sub-cellarer of St Augustine's, Canterbury was advised to vary the monks' diet, lest they were bored with the choice of food, and to ensure that the produce was fresh. He was warned not to serve stinking fish since the brethren should not be fed 'from the refuse of the people'.[31] It would seem that by this time food was no longer simply to sustain the monks but to entice the eye and please the taste buds.

GLUTTONY AND RESTRAINT

Do not look on wine when it glows and sparkles in the glass. It goes down smoothly but in the end it will bite like a snake and spread venom like a serpent. (Proverbs 23.31–2)

Abbot Norreys of Evesham (1190–1213) allegedly 'surpassed all English monks in their winebibbing and lechery' and exploited his position to enjoy 'an abundance of choice foods' (Isaiah 66.11). He was not alone. The late medieval Welsh bards praised the hospitality of their native Cistercian abbots whose tables, they

Monk (cellarer) drinking from barrel, late 13th c, British Library, Sloane 2435, f. 44v.

claimed, were usually spread with sumptuous meats and fine wines served in silverware.[32] For most the relative harshness of the monastic diet was one of the most challenging aspects of claustral life and might even cause hallucinations – Caesarius of Heisterbach (d. c. 1240) tells of one monk whose longing for wine was so great he saw small cups of wine in the choir.[33] The monastic diet may have been frugal but the monks were not to starve. They were to show restraint and self-control, for gluttony was not simply a matter of how much one ate but when and how. This meant not eating before the accorded time and showing indifference to whatever was served, regarding food simply as sustenance. Few, however, would have been as strong-willed as Bernard of Clairvaux (d. 1153), who reputedly on one occasion drank olive oil, mistaking it for wine or water. While his companions were astonished and no doubt sickened at what they had witnessed, Bernard himself seemed oblivious.[34] Jocelin of Brakelond, a monk of Bury St Edmunds, describes how his own abbot, Samson (1182–1211), always accepted whatever was placed before him and had never sent back a dish of food. This prompted Jocelin to test the abbot by setting before him a broken black plate of unappetizing food. Samson, however, did not even raise an eyebrow and ate what he had been given without a murmur. Jocelin was then ashamed of his actions and tried to change the dishes but Samson insisted that they remain.[35]

SLEEP

The body does not enjoy the luxury of a bed nor the bed that of a crimson coverlet, nor the face that of a pillow, nor the chest that of a soft cotton sheet. Instead of a bed there is given a pallet, instead of a crimson a cell-wall, instead of a pillow a pile of dust, and instead of soft cotton, sackcloth.[36]

Adam of Lennox, a thirteenth-century monk of Melrose Abbey in Scotland, was reputedly so holy that he was never seen to enter or rise from his bed during the twenty years he was a member of the community. It was alleged that the straw over which his sheets were placed remained in the same position throughout this entire period. Adam, of course, occasionally slept but did so either sitting or lying prostrate before the altar of the Blessed Mary, where he spent most of the winter nights playing his harp and singing songs in her honour.[37] Sleep, like food, was regarded as a physical need and self-deprivation was a mark of holiness, showing one's mastery over the senses. But it was also considered an important weapon in the war against evil since it was thought that the devil preyed on monks while they slept and were at their most vulnerable. For Bernard of Clairvaux (d. 1153) sleep was a waste of time but also potentially dangerous as the sleeper who was dead to the world might also be dead to God. Bernard himself was said to have survived on very little sleep and often spent the night in vigil. For Bernard's contemporaries his ability to go without sleep was 'beyond human endurance'.[38]

Few monks would have been as devout or resilient as Adam and Bernard. Nor were they expected to exercise this level of control, but were advised to sleep lightly so that they could waken easily and be ready for the day. Sleep was to refresh the body without smothering the soul and the monk was to avoid carnal sleep at all costs and regard it as an 'abhorrence'.[39] Even those who sought to enjoy deep slumbers had little opportunity to do so for every monk was required to rise at midnight to celebrate the Office of Vigils. Some communities then returned to bed and rested until Lauds, which was celebrated at daybreak and marked the start of the monastic day. Others remained awake lest the spiritual impetus was lost and spent the time reading in the cloister or in private prayer. Newcomers as well as established members of the community often found the lack of sleep a real challenge and the obligation to rise at midnight especially gruelling. Richard Fox, Bishop of Winchester (1501–28), clearly appreciated the difficulty of rising during the night and advised the nuns in his diocese that those who were up first should rouse the others by making a soft and sombre stirring with their mouths or feet, but might knock upon the bedstead of any who were sluggards.[40]

Various monastic officials were made responsible for maintaining vigilance during the Offices, and would periodically shine a lantern in the face of any monk who was sleepy or slothful and rouse those who drifted off.[41] An effective way to encourage alertness was through the telling of *exempla* to warn of the perils that befell anyone who nodded off during the Office. A thirteenth-century collection by a Cistercian monk, Caesarius of Heisterbach, records a number of these rich and colourful tales. He tells how one habitual snoozer received his comeuppance when the image of the crucified Christ came down during Vigils and struck him with an almighty blow on the cheek; the offender died three days later.[42] Monks might develop their own strategies to stay awake. One monk of Villers-en-Brabant (Belgium) would chew on a peppercorn to stop himself from falling asleep while Dom Arnold, a monk of Himmerod (Germany), would stop his mind from wandering by moving his fingers under his cowl and playing the cords on an imaginary harp.[43] A few fell asleep even before they reached the church and in some houses a reliable monk was sent to search the dormitory and latrine block before Matins, to check that nobody was still in bed or had fallen asleep on the privy.[44]

The sick and perhaps anyone who was exhausted by heavy labour or had returned from a long journey might be granted permission to remain in bed while the others rose for Vigils. The abbot or senior officials might also be permitted to rise a little later on account of their seniority but in some cases this privilege was abused. In 1394 the monks of Hailes Abbey (Gloucestershire) were instructed that everyone should rise together for the Night Office, to quell accusations of favouritism.[45] The stress and strain of holding office might however lead to sleep deprivation. Matthew of Rievaulx, who officiated as precentor of the Yorkshire abbey in the late twelfth and early thirteenth century, complained of exhaustion and insomnia from leading the Night Office for a month.[46]

CLOTHING

'They that wear soft raiment are in kings' houses' (Matthew 11.8); such things become not a monastery.[47]

The monks' garments, like their diet, were to be simple and functional but their clothing had also symbolic meaning. Black was the colour of humility while the habit, according to one twelfth-century monk, was angelic and the cowl the sign of perfection which protected the monk from evil while he slept.[48] Chapter 55 of the *Rule of St Benedict* permitted each monk two tunics and two cowls. This allowed for washing but also night-time wear since the monks originally slept in their habits; nightgowns were introduced in the later Middle Ages. An apron-like garment (the *scapula*) was worn for work and other items included shoes, stockings and a belt. Each monk carried on his person a needle, so that he could make minor repairs to his garments. He also had a pen and a knife, which was removed before going to bed lest he injured himself while sleeping.

CHANGING FASHIONS

For their name arose from the fact that, as the angels might be, they were clothed in undyed wool, spun and woven from the pure fleece of sheep. So named and garbed and gathered together like flocks of seagulls they shine as they walk with the whiteness of snow.[49]

Benedict's prescriptions for clothing were intended for monks living in Mediterranean countries. Modifications were later made on account of the Northern climate and changing fashions, and also in the name of vanity. Some monks took great pride in their clothing, seeking out the finest fabrics and wearing fur-lined garments and brightly coloured robes. Others, notably the Cistercians and Carthusians, reacted against this extravagance and sought to return to the more simple style of clothing espoused in the *Rule of St Benedict*. The Cistercians' concern for simplicity prompted them to break with tradition and wear habits of undyed wool rather than the traditional black garb. This earned them the nickname the White Monks or Grey Monks but also generated hostility from some Benedictines, who saw this as the Cistercians' proclamation of superiority over themselves; the Cistercians themselves denied this and maintained they were simply declaring their commitment to poverty. The Cistercians also broke with contemporary practice by refusing to wear trousers, since Benedict had nowhere permitted this in his *Rule*. Their stance was considered rather quirky and made them the butt of ridicule, for it had become commonplace for monks in the West to wear trousers on account of the climate as well as for reasons of modesty. The Carthusians were similarly renowned for their austere clothing which was rough and dirty – an antidote to pride. They were also noted for their decision to wear hair shirts next to their skin. Yet the Carthuisan wardrobe was fairly extensive, if basic, for the monks lived in bleak conditions and needed skins and layers of clothing to keep warm and dry. In addition to the customary razor and comb that all monks carried the Carthusian had a number of writing implements, since much of his time was spent alone in his cell copying and mending books.[50]

The monks were expected to wear their habits with modesty and received extensive instruction on how precisely they should do so. Novices at Cluny were shown how to arrange their clothing properly so that their habits did not touch the ground when they bowed to pray, and learnt that in choir they should gather the sleeves of their habits and collect these on their lap.[51] It was common for senior monks of the house to carry out routine checks to make sure the brethren did not slip into slovenly ways. At Christ Church, Canterbury, the sub-prior of the house remained behind after Compline and watched to see that the monks had their hoods up and nobody was walking irreverently. Elsewhere it was the task of the prior or of senior monks of the house. These officials also checked that the brethren had folded their garments neatly in the dormitory and reported anyone who had left his clothes untidily.[52] Rules governing the way in which monks were to wear their habits were not just to preserve decorum but to ensure modesty was practised at all times. It was imperative that the monks always shielded their nakedness. Accordingly, they were to sleep fully clothed and cover their heads when sitting on the privy, avoiding eye contact with other members of the community. There was evidently quite an art to changing clothes and preparing for bed while remaining fully covered. The monks received detailed instructions on how precisely to do so from their novice-master, who would then carefully observe them dressing and undressing in front of others, to make sure they had indeed mastered the technique.[53]

THE PROVISION AND CARE OF CLOTHES

All clothing technically belonged to the community rather than the monks themselves since the monastic vow of poverty prohibited individuals from having personal possessions. The monks therefore had use rather than ownership of these garments, which remained part of the common stockpile managed by the chamberlain of the house. Clothing was washed by the resident lay community or servants but in some cases was done by the monks or nuns themselves. In Gilbertine houses the nuns and lay sisters washed their own clothes and also the canons', who passed their dirty laundry to the women every month through the revolving door that separated the male and female communities.[54] In most cases washerwomen were employed since laundry was regarded as women's work, although the washing of the liturgical vestments was done either by the sacrist and his helpers or male servants. The laundry was generally hung out to dry or air in the cloister and shoes might be hung from a tree. One sacrist of the London Charterhouse would hang the corporals to dry on the lavender borders, presumably to infuse these linen cloths with a pleasant smell.[55] At Cluny, the dry clothes were folded and set on benches around the cloister so that each monk could collect his pile of garments and bring them to the dormitory. Anyone who failed to do so was punished at Chapter the following day.[56]

The monks were expected to look after their clothing and keep it in good repair. Each monk carried a needle and thread so that he could carry out minor repairs himself but more extensive work was done by a tailor, who might reside within the monastery precinct. At Cluny, the monk's name was sewn into his garment lest there was confusion when a repaired item was returned. As an added precaution two custodians remained in the dormitory to make sure there were no quarrels over mix-ups or the loss of clothing.[57] Clothes were periodically renewed. In the thirteenth century the monks of Westminster Abbey received new stockings and boots either on Palm Sunday or the Feast of All Saints; if any visiting abbot happened to be staying with the community he was given the same. There was a similar system at Durham and the monks received new boots each year at Easter. St Cuthbert (d. 687) was reputedly so removed from worldly matters that he did not take off his boots from one Easter to the next; the cloister must have been rather ripe on this occasion.[58] At Cluny the monks received a new frock and cowl every year at Christmas and a new hide garment once every three years. The chamberlain left these items on the monks' beds while they were dining in the refectory.[59] Whenever a monk died his clothing and bedding often passed to the guestmaster for use in the hospice; the Carthusian monks passed their old hide coats on to the lay brothers.[60]

BATHING AND SHAVING

It was important that the monks kept themselves clean and presentable, yet did not pander to personal vanity. Washing was therefore a part of the daily timetable in the monastery but was subject to restrictions. Upon rising for Lauds at daybreak, which marked the start of the monastic day, the monks washed their hands and combed their hair before entering the church. They also washed their hands before entering the refectory for meals, which was symbolic as well as practical. Each Saturday the brethren's feet were washed at the Maundy, a ritual in memory of Christ's washing the disciples' feet.[61] Some monks plunged themselves into icy baths to cool their passions and bridle their lust but bathing as such was considered a luxury and subject to restrictions. The Gilbertine nuns were warned not to wash their feet unless they had dirtied them in the marshes or mire and might wash their heads only seven times a year; the abbot of the Cistercian monastery of Pilis, Hungary, was reprimanded in 1225 for bathing on a Sunday and since he had shaved himself in the bath on this occasion.[62] Bathing might, however, be prescribed to ease pain and aid recovery and was a concession often granted to the sick and infirm. Aelred of Rievaulx's biographer, Walter Daniel, emphasized that the numerous baths Aelred took were essential to ease the elimination of urinary stones and prevent certain death should one become stuck. He stressed that these were in no way a luxury but a gruelling ordeal – on one occasion Aelred endured forty baths and was so exhausted by the evening he looked 'more dead than alive'.[63] It was vital that whenever the brethren washed or bathed they exercised modesty and shielded their nakedness; the Gilbertine nuns were instructed to cover themselves with linen.[64] While there were tight regulations governing when monks should wash and how they should do so modifications might be made if necessary. Thus in 1379 the monks of Norwich were accorded the right to bathe whenever they wished, seemingly in response to their complaints about the lack of tubs for bathing and shaving.[65]

Whenever the monk made his profession and was formally received as a member of the community, he was given the tonsure as a visible sign of his monastic status. Thereafter he, like his fellow brethren, was periodically shaved in the cloister. This was a communal affair and usually took place before an important date in the liturgical calendar, in preparation for these holy celebrations. In the twelfth century Cistercian monks were shaved seven times a year, namely at Christmas, just before Lent (Quinquagesima), at Easter, Pentecost, the Feast of the Blessed Mary Magdalene (22 July), the birth of Mary (8 September) and All Saints (1 November). By the later Middle Ages the monks might be shaved more regularly, perhaps every two weeks in summer and every three in winter. Shaving did take place outside these communal sessions. If, for example, a monk had eaten meat he was shaved as part of the purification process and as an outward manifestation of his atonement. The monks did not shave themselves but in pairs or else one member of the community was specially appointed to the task. In some cases there was a pecking order and the senior monks were shaved first when the razors were sharper and the towels drier.[66] Later, it was common for monasteries to engage professional barbers to reduce the number of accidents.[67]

The physical hardships of the cloister were demanding and could take their toll on the monk's health and well-being, but the monastic life also tested the brethren emotionally for they were required to cut ties with their families, friends and worldly distractions.

For no one after he has become dead to the world and has entered the cloister, ought on any account, even in intention, to return to worldly affairs.[1]

3

The Severity of Monastic Life (2): Family Ties, Health and Sickness

SEVERING TIES

Eadmer of Canterbury (d. 1124), who was a monk of Christ Church Cathedral Priory, recounts the story of a young monk of his house who was wont to receive thirty shillings a year from Archbishop Lanfranc. This was paid to him in six instalments, each of which he discreetly passed on to his mother when she visited the monastery. On one particular occasion the exchange was evidently too subtle for the monk unwittingly dropped the pouch to the ground and returned to the cloister. When he later learned what had happened the monk was alarmed since he believed that the archbishop would punish him for his carelessness. Lanfranc instead showed compassion and gave his young charge seven shillings to pass on to his mother at their next meeting, but warned that he should not reveal this to anyone else.[2]

It has been suggested that Eadmer was recounting his own experience at Canterbury and that he was in fact the monk in the story. Whether or not this is Eadmer's personal testimony it offers an unusual and important insight into the nature and regularity of family visits in post-Conquest England – the young Canterbury monk evidently expected his mother to visit about six times a year. The account also indicates that responsibility for one's kin might continue from within the cloister and did not necessarily cease when one entered the monastery. How, then does this accord with the belief that monks were dead to the world and severed all links with their family, friends and external affairs?

FAMILY VISITS

Eternal bitterness fills those whom the sweetness of the world allures, and perpetual bliss pervades those whom the sweetness of God attracts.[3]

Whenever a monk entered the cloister and took vows of stability he committed himself to the service of God. He was part of the brotherhood of Christ and his place was now in the monastery; he could not strictly speaking leave without the abbot's permission. If the monk was to remain focused on his spiritual goals it was vital that he was not distracted by external affairs. But he did not sever all links with the outside world. It was generally accepted that monks would receive occasional visits from their families and perhaps also friends. However, it was important to make sure that these visits did not unsettle the community or drain the monastery's coffers. For this reason rules were often made regulating just how often relatives might visit each year and how they should be received. Thus the Beaulieu Abbey account book, compiled in around 1270, stipulates that the monks' families might visit once or twice a year, staying for two nights on each occasion and leaving on the third day after they had eaten. Anyone who wished or needed to stay longer had to secure permission from the abbot and was seemingly then liable for the extra costs incurred.[4] While the number of visits permitted to relatives would have varied from house to house and among Orders, two nights several times a year seems to have been fairly common and there were similar arrangements at Abingdon and St Swithun's, Winchester. Female houses, and monasteries that had few resources or were struggling financially, might restrict guests to one night or even withhold their hospitality. The Carthusians imposed more severe restrictions on family visits for they sought to withdraw more fully from the world; it was not until the late nineteenth century that relatives were permitted to visit for two days and speak with the monks for an hour on each day.[5]

Before a family meeting took place permission was required from the abbot or prior. These meetings were in theory closely regulated and were to be conducted in an appropriate place to cause least disruption to communal observance. Meetings often took place in the outer parlour, which was part of the west claustral range. It was particularly important that meetings with female relatives – or any women for that matter – were closely monitored lest scandal arose and tarnished the monastery's reputation. In the thirteenth century the monks of Bury St Edmunds (Suffolk) were warned that nobody should meet with female relatives or strangers either at the green door, the cross or any other secret places. Moreover, they were not to meet at dinner or supper, during the post-dinner siesta or when they were served their drinks.[6] Still, it was difficult to control these encounters and throughout the Middle Ages there were problems with monks meeting and entertaining females in private chambers. This elicited a response from Henry V (1413–21), who stipulated that no monk in his kingdom should take any woman to a private room to speak, eat or drink, not even if she was his mother or sister. Brethren might only meet at the gatehouse in the presence of witnesses and must, of course, have the abbot's permission.[7] The Cistercians initially prohibited all women from their precincts but in time relaxed their stance. In the later Middle Ages concessions might be granted to female relatives. In 1437, for example, any of the monks' sisters or mothers who had travelled a long distance to visit their kin at Hailes Abbey (Gloucestershire) might stay the night; all other women were forbidden to do so.[8]

While family might arrange a visit at any time of the year, and would likely try to visit if their monk relation was ill, they often came to the monastery on festive occasions. At Abingdon Abbey (Berkshire) it was common for the monks' relatives to visit the abbey on the Nativity of Mary (8 September), which was the abbey's patronal feast and attracted a large number of visitors from the locality. They received refreshments on both the Vigil and the day of the feast. It was not just the monks' immediate family who visited the monasteries on these festive occasions. Richard, a sub-prior of Norwich Cathedral Priory in the twelfth century, welcomed his aunt and uncle to the monastery on the Feast of Holy Trinity. During her visit Richard's aunt, who suffered from a long-standing ailment, sought relief from her afflictions at the shrine of St William.[9] There are other examples of monks' families seeking the help of the resident saint. The prior of Norwich's nephew brought his infant son to the monastery to be healed by St William and at Wilton Abbey (Wiltshire) a disabled kinsman of one of the nuns would lie at the shrine of St Edith, hoping to secure relief from his pain.[10]

What kind of care did the monks' relatives and friends receive during their stay? The monastery accommodated a number of visitors within the precinct, either in a guesthouse or in the abbot's quarters. Others secured lodgings outside the monastery and stayed with locals or in a hostel. Irrespective of where they stayed the monks' relatives would have eaten at the monastery or received provisions from the cellarer of the house. The thirteenth-century account book of Beaulieu Abbey (Hampshire) suggests that relatives and 'special friends' fared reasonably well there, receiving conventual bread, good conventual beer, pottage (a kind of soup) and pittances.[11] In the early fifteenth century the cellarer of Westminster Abbey set aside about 200 gallons of ale each year for the use of the monks' parents and sisters when they visited, while in the fourteenth century the sub-cellarer of St Augustine's, Canterbury, gave each monk a small gift of food and drink four times a year that he shared with his friends when they visited or, if he preferred, sent to them as a gift.[12] Relatives were not always welcomed as warmly as they ought to have been and in 1219 the monks of Abingdon were warned to receive family with respect when they visited; a similar enjoinder was issued to the monks of Bury St Edmunds in 1234.[13]

HOME VISITS

> *Do not visit your relations, they do not need your advice or help in any way,*
> *nor can you receive any advice or help from them regarding your intention*
> *and profession which you could not find in the cloister. The intention of your*
> *way of life is different from their way of life. . . . What have you in common*
> *with them?*[14]

It was one thing for the monks to receive visits from their families but quite another for them to break their vow of stability and go on a home visit. Anselm, as prior of Bec and archbishop of Canterbury (d. 1109), was emphatic that monks should never leave the cloister, not even if there was a family crisis. When Henry, a monk of Christ Church, Canterbury, sought to return to his native Italy to rescue his sister from bondage, Anselm begged him to stay and show his commitment to the monastic life.[15] Most, however, adopted a less rigid stance and conceded that monks might occasionally secure leave of absence to attend to important family matters. The twelfth-century life of Abundus, a choir monk of the Benedictine abbey of Villers-en-Brabant, presents his brief excursion home as a meritorious act and a testimony to his worthiness since on this occasion Abundus rescued his sister from an arranged marriage and settled her in the local convent.[16] Attitudes differed from Order to Order and also over time, and what was permitted in one monastery was prohibited in another. The Carthusians strictly forbade their monks from leaving the cloister to visit their family or for any other reason, and also discouraged relatives from visiting the monastery. Yet in the twelfth century the Grandmontine monks were seemingly accustomed to visiting their families, even though this was not formally approved until 1222. However, they always travelled in pairs. Matthew Paris (d. 1259), who was a Benedictine monk of St Albans (Hertfordshire) in the thirteenth century, suggests that at this time it was possible but not common for monks to return home. He explains that any monk of St Albans might leave the abbey to visit his family and friends providing he first secured permission from the abbot. But this was only granted in exceptional circumstances, presumably if a relative was sick or dying, or if he had a funeral to attend. Moreover, the monk was subject to constraints. Leave was granted for only a short period and he was to travel with a companion, for this was not to be regarded as an opportunity to gallivant around the country.[17] By the later Middle Ages there was a change in attitudes and leave of absence was considered a right more than a privilege; still, it was not to be abused. According to Henry V's reforms of 1421 for the Benedictines in England, monks might visit their kinsfolk and friends once a year at the most and their abbots were expected to provide them with an escort of 'honest secular persons'.[18]

Female communities were subject to greater restrictions regarding their claustration and more rigid regulations governed their meetings with family and friends, both within the precinct and at home. Gilbertine nuns were permitted to meet their parents, siblings, children and near kinsfolk once or twice a year, either at the gate of the great gatehouse or at the little window of the cloister, which was essentially a small slit. These visits took place in the presence of two witnesses.[19] Similar restrictions were enforced in Cistercian nunneries. Until the mid-thirteenth century the nuns conducted their meetings with visitors through a timber-barred gate but later might receive visitors in the outer hall or another suitable place. These restrictions were not always heeded and there were complaints of guests entering the claustral area, the infirmary and even the choir of the church.[20]

Like their male counterparts, nuns might secure permission from their superior to leave the confines of the monastery either to conduct business on behalf of the community or to visit their families and friends. Initially these visits were subject to tight scrutiny – Gilbertine nuns were only allowed to visit their relatives if this was considered essential and before leaving had to provide details of their precise route. They were only permitted to stay overnight in case of illness or necessity.[21] There is evidence that attitudes were more relaxed in the later Middle Ages, when a visit home was considered the norm rather than a concession but was nonetheless subject to restrictions. In the fourteenth century the Yorkshire nuns of Rosedale Priory were permitted to leave their monastery once a year for up to fifteen days, to visit friends or relatives. There was evidently some room for negotiation since Mary Ros, the prioress of the house, secured licence to visit her father twice a year for eight days on each occasion.[22]

THE TIES THAT BIND

It was difficult for the monks to shake off their family ties entirely and the monks' thoughts and fears would inevitably turn to their relatives. Moreover, they were actively encouraged to think of their kin since prayers for relatives, alive and dead, were a daily part of communal worship and private devotion. When Bernard of Clairvaux was a novice at Cîteaux (Burgundy), he recited the Seven Penitential Psalms for the soul of his mother each day.[23] The monks might fear greatly for the spiritual welfare of their families, who lived in the world and accordingly were not guaranteed salvation; after all, the monk considered the claustral life as the only true path to salvation. This was evidently of such concern to one twelfth-century monk of Villers-en-Brabant that he sought help from the Virgin and asked her what stage his relatives were at in Purgatory.[24] Fear for their family's souls prompted some to encourage their relatives to take the habit and secure their place at the heavenly table. A touching example concerns Gundulf, a monk of the Norman abbey of Bec, who was transferred to William I's new monastery at Caen in 1066 and subsequently settled his mother in the neighbouring convent that had been founded by William I's wife, Matilda.[25] While the two would scarcely have had any contact it was evidently important for Gundulf to know that his mother was near at hand and provided for physically and spiritually.

The monk's relatives might continue to influence his decisions in the cloister and even from the grave. John Homersley (d. 1450), a monk of the London Charterhouse, claimed that on one occasion after the celebration of Compline his dead mother and father appeared to him with three spirits and spoke comforting words about the life hereafter. They urged John to speak with them but he, remembering how the Desert Fathers had been duped 'by mocking visions', ignored them, realizing that they were spirits seeking to deceive him.[26] William Wendover, a monk of the Cistercian abbey of Meaux in Yorkshire, was transferred to the London abbey of St Mary Graces at the behest of his father, who secured permission from King Edward I (1272–1307) for his son's removal to the royal foundation. William was duly appointed prior of the London house. It is not clear why precisely William's father initiated this transfer – perhaps he considered St Mary Graces a more prestigious house. Nor is it apparent if William was reluctant to leave the Yorkshire monastery, but interestingly he sought to return to Meaux after the death of his parents some eleven years later.

There, he officiated as prior, then porter and finally in 1399 William was elevated to the abbacy of the house.[27]

FAMILY WITHIN THE CLOISTER

It was not unusual for members of the same family to join the community and as previously noted the monk might actively encourage his relatives to join him in the cloister and secure their salvation. When Bernard of Clairvaux entered the monastery of Cîteaux (Burgundy) in around 1112, he was joined by four of his brothers, an uncle and a cousin; later, his father and youngest brother entered the community. In double foundations where the male and female communities were separated, family members were not permitted to have contact. According to Gilbertine legislation no canon or lay brother of the Order who had a female relative in the community might visit or speak with her, not even if she was his mother; anyone who disregarded this was liable to be excommunicated.[28] The presence of one's relatives within the cloister could be a comfort but did not always make for easy relations. When Bernard, the young abbot of Clairvaux, was working miracles his uncle and brother, who were both monks of the house, taunted him and undermined these wonders lest Bernard would be puffed up by pride. While they acted out of love for Bernard and, as the *Vita Prima* states, they played the part for God of thorns in the young abbot's side, their words were harsh and often reduced Bernard to tears.[29] Family alliances might generate hostility within the community, breeding resentment and perhaps complaints of nepotism. Two brothers who were senior monks of Norwich in the late Middle Ages antagonized a number of the brethren with their ostentatious ways and particularly their flamboyant manner of dressing. One of the brothers, John, took pride in wearing fine clothes and fancy footwear and even hoisted up his habit in front of the junior monks to show off his shoes to the prior.[30]

HEALTH AND WELL-BEING

Brethren sometimes fall into a state of weak health from the irksomeness of life in the cloister, or from long continuance of silence; sometimes from fatigue in the choir or extension of fasting; sometimes from sleeplessness or overwork.[31]

In 1442 it was conceded that the prior of Hailes or his deputy might occasionally lead the monks into the fields to take recreation 'in a manner seemly for religious'.[32] This would have given the brethren an opportunity to enjoy fresh air and freedom, and shake off the torpor of claustral life in a controlled and safe environment. Hence the community was warned that on these excursions nobody should wander off on his own or sneak into a tavern in the town. The relentlessness of monastic life could take its toll on the mental and physical well-being of the monks. The compulsion to rise each night to celebrate Vigils in a cold church, the constant round of liturgical duties and the austere living conditions might lead to physical and mental exhaustion. Stomach complaints were common on account of the harsh diet. The Cluniacs frequently suffered back problems from ringing notoriously heavy bells, but were prone also to congestion and coughs for their liturgical demands were excessive; indeed the monks might be required to recite over 200 psalms a day. Abbot Peter the Venerable of Cluny (d. 1156) was bothered with catarrh, which affected his chest and voice, and prevented him from preaching.[33] Poor lighting, dust and the celebration of the Night Office meant that a number of monks suffered eye strain and even blindness. The sacrist of St Augustine's, Canterbury, made sure that the older monks had plenty of light.[34] Caesarius of Heisterbach (d. c. 1240) describes the apathy suffered by a number of monks and known as *accidie*. He explains that this weariness or depression might distract the monk or cause him to be lazy, angry or even cowardly, but might lead some to despair and even drive them to take their lives.[35]

It was often the greatest zealots who were most vulnerable and it is hardly surprising that Aelred of Rievaulx and Bernard of Clairvaux, two of the great twelfth-century ascetics, suffered severe health problems caused by a life of austerity. Aelred's numerous ailments included colic and he was wont to pass stones the size of beans. Bernard suffered serious gastric problems and would vomit up undigested food.[36] Those who pushed themselves to extremes were vulnerable to mental breakdown. Baldwin, a thirteenth-century monk of the Cistercian abbey of Rittersheim, was overly fervent in his devotion and suffered severe headaches as a consequence. One night he rose before Matins and while the brethren were asleep in the dormitory he tied the bell rope in the church around his neck and jumped. The sound of the bell ringing alarmed the sacrist, who immediately cut Baldwin down and resuscitated him. Alas, the lack of oxygen had caused irrecoverable damage and Baldwin's reason was never restored.[37]

PREVENTATIVE MEASURES

*All of us, because we are monks, seem to have stomach troubles and so we
have to follow the Apostle's advice and take some wine.*[38]

The monastic life was not meant to be easy, but it was not to be overly severe. It was important that the monks were strong enough to fulfil their duties and that morale was maintained. For this reason it became common for monks to have some kind of respite from claustral life to prevent ill health and depression. This might mean a walk in the fields, a seat in the vineyard or even a spot of archery. It was not uncommon for monks to have a break away from the monastery on one of the community's manors, where they could convalesce or simply recharge their batteries. This was particularly desirable if the monastery was situated in the town, for it was considered important to escape the dirty urban air and enjoy the peace and tranquillity of the country.

Bloodletting (seyney) was regarded as an important way to prevent sickness. The monks were regularly bled in groups to keep them in optimum health and ensure they could serve God efficiently. However, it was important that not too many of the monks were bled at once and enough remained to sing the Office and perform the various claustral duties. Carthusian monks were routinely bled five times a year, after the octaves of Easter, on the feasts of St Peter and Paul, and in the second week of September, the week before Advent and the week before Lent. Elsewhere the monks were bled up to nine times during the year and perhaps more, since anyone who was sick might receive an additional session to cure him.[39] The process itself often took place in the warming-house or a special seyney room within or beside the infirmary. At Ely Cathedral Priory this was seemingly adjacent to the Black Hostelry and cellarer's house. Some communities had their own seyney houses; a sixteenth-century map of the Cistercian abbey of Ten Duinen (Belgium) shows the seyney house near the chapel of St Mary, in the west corner of the precinct.

Jocelin of Brakelond's chronicle of Bury St Edmunds (Suffolk) reveals that the regular bloodletting sessions were often a chance for the monks to gossip and exchange news. They were also an opportunity to enjoy a more relaxed regime, for the monks were to be served more nourishing food and allowed a little meat to aid their recovery from the bloodletting process. Further, they might sleep in the infirmary, which was warmer and more comfortable than the monks' dormitory and where a little conversation was permitted. The late thirteenth-century ordinances of Barnwell Priory (Cambridgeshire) instructed the master of the infirmary to make sure that anyone recovering from the bloodletting process was comfortable, happy and free from worries. Dice, chess and other such games were prohibited since they might lead to strife.[40] On account of these post-treatment perks most monks were not averse to being bled and saw this as a welcome relief from the rigours of the cloister. Some even feigned illness so that they could request a bloodletting session and enjoy the benefits this brought. It was for this reason that restrictions were imposed at St Augustine's, Canterbury, and it was ruled that the monks were only to have blood let once every seven weeks.[41] But there were also dangers in having blood let too often. It was said that Bishop John Kirkby of Ely (d. 1290) went mad as he was bled too many times by his barber.[42]

CARE OF THE SICK

> *Before and above all things, care must be taken of the sick, that they be served in very truth as Christ is served; because He hath said, 'I was sick and you visited Me' (Mt 25.36). And 'As long as you did it to one of these My least brethren, you did it to Me' (Mt 25.40). But let the sick themselves also consider that they are served for the honour of God, and let them not grieve their brethren who serve them by unnecessary demands.*[43]

It was inevitable that members of the community would periodically suffer from ill health. It was thus vital that the monastery provided proper care to nurse them back to strength, so that they could once more play a full part in claustral life. In accordance with the *Rule of St Benedict* a monk was assigned to care for the sick in a special room – the infirmary. Here, they were kept warm and comfortable and received everything they required in the way of food and drink. The sick were therefore exempt from the normal dietary restrictions and were allowed to eat meat, fish and any other treats and delicacies that would aid their recovery. While these indulgences were permitted they were nonetheless regarded as a breach of the *Rule* and once the monk was fully recovered he was required to seek absolution for his excesses. Those who were ill were often allowed to relax the rules regarding clothing. The prior of St Benet of Holme (Norfolk) was exempted from wearing sandals since he suffered from ulcerated varicose veins, while David Winchcombe, a monk of Hailes Abbey (Gloucestershire) in the mid-fifteenth century, was permitted to wear linen

Abbess Aelflaed and a nun cured by St Cuthbert's girdle, late 12th c, British Library,
Yates Thompson 26, f. 48v.

on account of his ailments.[44] The sick usually carried a stick as a sign of their weakness and in many cases as a necessary prop, but they also covered their heads to show that they were in a state of penitence.

Any monk who was unwell did not generally go to the infirmary in the first instance but stayed in the cloister and participated as much as he could in communal life. If this proved too much he then sought permission to go to the infirmary. At St Augustine's, Canterbury, in the fourteenth century, monks who received permission to go to the infirmary collected a fat capon and wine from the cellarer and candles from the sacrist before making their way to the infirmary, where they stayed for at least eight days.[45] The rules for admittance to the infirmary differed from house to house. In the late thirteenth century any monk of Westminster Abbey who suffered physical or mental fatigue was permitted to go to the infirmary, yet a fellow sufferer at the Augustinian priory of Barnwell (Cambridgeshire) had to remain in the choir.[46] Monks at St Albans (Hertfordshire) who felt unable to follow the full round of monastic observances, yet were not considered sufficiently ill to go to the infirmary, stayed in a halfway house called the Oriel.[47]

The abbot or prior usually visited the sick each day and offered the brethren emotional comfort. The abbot of Abingdon (Berkshire) called into the infirmary every morning and also when he returned from a journey; the kitchener of the house visited the sick each morning and at dinner to check what they would like to eat.[48] At St Augustine's, Canterbury, the prior and custodians visited the sick at specific times throughout the day, namely after private masses, following meals and after the Office of Compline.[49] As prior of the Norman monastery of Bec, St Anselm (d. 1109) was committed to the care of the sick, whom he tended with love and devotion. One monk whose afflictions prevented him from controlling his limbs was refreshed by grapes that Anselm crushed in his own hands for the man to drink.[50] Rest and relaxation were considered important to recovery and the sick were not expected to rise to celebrate the Night Office. In some houses they were sent treats and delicacies both to fortify them and to boost their morale. The sick were also permitted to talk a little to each other to raise their spirits, but were not to jeer or play contentious games, since it was essential to preserve a tranquil environment. The infirmarer of St Augustine's, Canterbury, would arrange to play soothing music for the sick in the infirmary chapel if he thought this would lift their mood; he might ask one of the monks or servants to play a harp sweetly, but was careful that the noise did not filter into the hall or cells of the infirmary.[51] Fresh air was considered beneficial and the sick were often encouraged to sit or walk outside to aid their recovery. In the early thirteenth century the sacrist of Bury St Edmunds bought the vineyard across the river from the infirmary, and enclosed it for the comfort of the infirm and those undergoing the bloodlet.[52]

The infirmary was set apart from the claustral buildings and was often to the east. It was generally on one level so that monks who were weak or injured did not need to negotiate stairs as they would have to do when accessing their dormitory on the first floor. The monk infirmarer who was in charge of the sick slept in the infirmary so that he could readily tend the inmates and also maintain discipline, for while the sick were exempt from the full rigours of the cloister they were nonetheless subject to restrictions; for example, they were to remain silent after Compline. The infirmarer was usually helped by monk assistants and perhaps lay servants. At Abingdon Abbey two monks were assigned to help the infirmarer carry out his duties.[53]

The infirmary was not just a place for the sick to convalesce. Older members of the community who were no longer able to take a full part in claustral life were often accommodated here, away from the common toil. They were known as the 'old stagers' (*stagiarii*). At Bury St Edmunds the west part of the infirmary was reserved for these long-stay inmates, who did not require special attention as such but could rest in a warm and relatively comfortable environment, and receive nourishing food. The *stagiarii* included men such as Thomas, who was the oldest member of Norwich Cathedral Priory and suffered from a long-term illness. By the later Middle Ages these *stagiarii* were often extremely well provided for in the infirmary and essentially had their own private rooms there. In the mid-fifteenth century the infirmarer of Bury spent 4s 2d on special meals for these inmates and their friends. The brethren were not always as tolerant as they ought to have been towards these elderly members of the community, who might bore them with their tedious reminiscences. In the late thirteenth century the canons of Barnwell Priory (Cambridgeshire) were reminded to show these older folk due respect but the old stagers were also warned to behave more appropriately – they were not to recount 'silly tales of old with foolish hilarity or laughter after the fashion of secular men'. The old canons were evidently wont to indulge in a tipple or two and engage in too much conversation and were instructed to shun drinking and take their siesta in silence.[54]

I have sought to cast out from the field of my heart anything idle or weedlike, cultivating it instead with the plowshare of silence and sowing it with the best of meditations for seed.[1]

4

The Sound of Silence (1): The Silence of the Cloister

The cloister stood at the heart of the monastery and was the focus for communal life. Yet this was a place of solitude that provided a tranquil environment for the monks to meditate and contemplate their path to salvation. Conversation was therefore restricted and work was to be conducted with the minimum of fuss; necessary communication was carried out using a system of signs. The quietness of the cloister had also symbolic significance and evoked the eternal silence of God. Silence was not, however, absolute. Bells sounded throughout the day while music emanated from the church. There was noise from the monks going about their daily chores, of animals, and not infrequently of workmen carrying out repairs. It was permissible to break the silence in exceptional circumstances, for example if a fire broke out, a monk died or there was a theft. On the night of St Etheldreda's (23 June) 1198 the cloister at Bury St Edmunds resonated with noise and confusion when the shrine of St Edmund caught fire and was engulfed by flames. The master of the vestry, who discovered the fire, sounded the gong to raise the alarm and cried to the brethren for help.[2]

The cloister was not always a haven of tranquillity and this chapter explores the real meaning of silence in the monastery. It considers the restrictions imposed on conversation, the use of sign language and the daily sounds that were part and parcel of claustral life.

CONVERSATION

For it belongs to the master to speak and to teach; it becomes the disciple to be silent and to listen . . . coarse jests, and idle words or speech provoking laughter, we condemn everywhere to eternal exclusion.
(Rule of St Benedict, *ch. 42*)

Meditation and contemplation were the cornerstones of monastic observance but if the monk was to remain focused on lofty affairs it was imperative that he was not distracted by gossip or disturbed by the sound of others talking. There was also a risk that discussion would lead to arguments or even conspiracies, generating strife and discontent within the community. Conversation was therefore strictly controlled in the claustral area and forbidden entirely in the church, where the monks communicated using signs and bells. Talking was prohibited in the refectory and dormitory, and in some houses all forms of communication were banned in the dormitory lest this should lead to inappropriate behaviour. The abbot and prior were exempt from these restrictions and were allowed to speak to any monk in any part of the precinct. Senior officials might be granted similar concessions so that they could talk to workmen or guests. The sacrist, for example, was permitted to speak quietly with visitors to tell them about a relic or miracle.

There were certain times of the year when the regulations governing silence were more strictly imposed, for instance during Lent and periods of penitence. The monks were not to speak at all when standing huddled around the fire in the warming house or when working lest these gatherings should turn into gossip sessions. They were advised to sing the psalms when working, to stave off the inclination to chat. Conversely, there were times and places where the monks might legitimately engage in a little appropriate conversation. Any monastic official who wished to speak with his assistants or members of the community about duties relating to his office might do so briefly in the parlour – either the inner parlour on the eastern range or the outer parlour on the western side of the cloister. Monks who were recovering from bloodletting and were allowed to talk a little to regale each other might be allowed to do so in the outer parlour. Another place where conversation was permitted but closely regulated was the chapter house, where the community gathered each day for a meeting. Only one monk was allowed to speak at a time here and had to address the entire Chapter, for private conversations were forbidden and all discussion was to pertain to the monastic life.[3]

There was a rather mixed attitude to talking in the cloister itself. Whereas the Cistercians forbade any conversation here, except with the abbot, prior or a senior official, the Grandmontines seemingly paid little heed to the rule of silence and were satirized for their wagging tongues. The Cluniac monks were permitted to indulge in a little 'private conversation' here each day after the chapter meeting, but according to the twelfth-century Cistercian, Idung of Prüfening, this was a grave mistake for these occasions often degenerated into rowdy gossip sessions. Idung compared the Cluniac cloister to a tavern full of drunks, where arguments were at times so vehement that the wooden board had to be struck to recall the Chapter.[4] The Carthusian monks, who spent most of their day alone in the solitude of their cells, used signs sparingly when they met as a community but on Sundays and feast days they were permitted to speak for an hour in the cloister and might be joined by visitors. The monks were also allowed to talk with each other for consolation if a member of the community died, but were warned not to speak too much on these occasions lest this interfere with their study. Moreover, they were forbidden to gossip or argue, which was blasphemous in the mouth of any religious but heinous in the mouth of a Carthusian.[5] Yet the cloister could function as a forum to counsel and succour the brethren as well as guests. Anselm of Bec (d. 1109), who was described as an 'indefatigable talker', inspired and regaled his monks during the periods when conversation was permitted. When abbot of Bec, Anselm visited the monks of Christ Church, Canterbury, and captivated the English community with his words on the life and habits of monks, 'setting forth the wonderful things which had not been heard before this time, with reason and eloquence'. Anselm spoke in private to the more intelligent members of the community about profound issues relating to sacred and secular books, and diligently answered their questions.[6] For Anselm and others conversation was a vital way to edify and enthuse the monks, helping them progress on their spiritual journey, and might also win converts to the monastic life. Conversation clearly had a place in the cloister and rightly used could aid rather than impede monastic observance.

'LET CONVERSATION BE OF THE CLOISTER'

Death and life are in the power of the tongue. (Prov. 18.21)

What did monks talk about during their periods of conversation? All discussion was meant to relate to the monastic life and might concern theological issues, matters regarding the running of the monastery or instruction on obedience and humility. The monks would likely discuss whatever was uppermost in their own thoughts or of concern to the house, such as the election of a new abbot. This was the case at Bury St Edmunds in the late twelfth century, when the community had to appoint a successor to Abbot Hugh (1157–80). Jocelin of Brakelond, who was a monk of the house, explains that this was on everyone's minds when the community gathered for the routine bloodletting, a time when monks 'are wont to reveal the secrets of their hearts, each to each, and to confer with one another'. On this occasion the brethren exchanged views on the qualities they required in their new abbot and on who, in their opinion, would be the best choice. Interestingly, one candidate was dismissed by the monks on account of his speech. As Jocelin vividly explains, 'it was said that he had dough or pig-food in his mouth when he had to speak'.[7]

Inevitably, not all conversation was about monastery affairs and discussion might turn to worldly matters with monks reminiscing about their lives before entering the cloister. William of Newburgh, an Augustinian Canon of this Yorkshire priory, recounts how Wimund, an old monk of the neighbouring Cistercian abbey of Byland, had retired to the monastery after a life of piracy and adventure and would relate his misfortunes to anyone who would listen. William had himself often seen Wimund and heard the old monk's account of how he secured the See of Man, of his reign of terror, eventual capture and subsequent blinding and castration. Yet Wimund remained unrepentant and belligerent; he maintained that if he could only see and had even the eye of a sparrow, he would wreak revenge and 'his enemies should have little occasion to rejoice at what they had done to him'.[8]

SOUL FOOD

> At table the monks should not only take food, but with their ears feast on the
> Word of God. No one should concentrate entirely on eating, but attend to the
> Word of God so that only the mouth takes food while the ears take the Word.
> If one receives less nutritious food than others, his joy should be greater. Those
> who bear deprivation with zeal are truly blessed.[9]

The refectory was one place where silence was strictly enforced because the monks were meant to feast their spirit while nourishing the body and listen to an edificatory reading as they ate. It was important to keep all noise to a minimum lest this should distract the brethren or prevent them from hearing the reader. The monks of St Augustine's, Canterbury, were warned that anyone eating nuts should open these quietly with his knife and not his teeth so as not to disturb the reading.[10] A little conversation was permitted if an important guest happened to be dining with the community. Otherwise all necessary communication was made by signing. The monks were to be sparing in their use of signs, although this was clearly not always the case. Gerald of Wales, who was a guest at Christ Church,

Canterbury, on the Feast of Holy Trinity c. 1180, remarked on the excessive gesticulating that he observed in the refectory on this occasion, comparing it to a dumbshow. He tartly concluded that the monks would cause less disruption if they simply spoke in moderation.[11] Bernard of Clairvaux complained of monks who laughed and gossiped during meals, which should be a time to feed the spirit and satisfy rather than oppress the body and senses.[12]

The use of signs and gestures by monks as a silent form of communication has a long history, but the monks of Cluny were the first to develop a comprehensive system, which was then adopted and adapted by other Orders, who modified the list to suit their own needs.[13] Some of these lists are extensive and include a number of signs for everyday objects and actions; as such they can offer a vivid insight into the sights and sounds of the cloister. The descriptions of how precisely these signs should be made reveal something about the mental associations the monks made and what had meaning for them. For example, to make the sign for a pillow the monk bent his fingertips as if to fly and then raised his hand before placing it under his cheek, as is commonly done when sleeping. To indicate something bad he spread his hands over his face, mimicking the claws of a bird dragging something to it and ripping it.[14] The descriptions are often graphic since the manuals were intended to instruct, but they suggest that communication in the cloister could be quite a theatrical performance. A striking example is the sign the monk made if he wished to go to the privy – he first made the sign for the *reredorter* by grabbing his habit with his forefinger and thumb and shaking it lightly against his groin; he then signalled to his superior that he wished to go there.[15] It is not perhaps surprising that Gerald of Wales compared Canterbury's refectory to a dumbshow.

Signs were intended to communicate necessary information only and were not to be overused or wrongly used. To deter monks from engaging in private and inappropriate conversations all signing was to be done openly and not beneath the sleeves. Some monks found ways to circumvent this regulation and signed instead with their feet and toes.[16] Most signing was done with the hands. Gestures made by winking or nodding were often restricted or even prohibited, especially in the dormitory lest this provoke inappropriate behaviour. The monks of Cluny were only allowed to use hand signals in their dormitory and were absolutely forbidden to communicate by winking. Their novices were not seemingly taught signs made with the eyes, which was perhaps regarded as a rather risqué form of communication.[17]

THE SOUNDS OF THE CLOISTER

The silence of the deep of the night reigns even in the middle of the day. . . .
The only sound that can be heard is the sound of the brethren at work or
singing their Office in praise of God.[18]

The silence of the cloister was relative. Various noises resounded throughout the
monastery and were part and parcel of communal life. The sound of the monks
going about their daily business infiltrated the cloister. Singing radiated from the
church when the community performed the liturgy or practised their harmonies
to perfect the 'Angels' Office'. There was also the hum from brethren reading
aloud, for silent reading was at this time uncommon and even discouraged,
since it was thought to foster inattentiveness. Accordingly the novices of Christ
Church, Canterbury, read 'in a loud voice' every morning in the cloister as it was
believed this would focus the mind.[19] Although silence was not absolute it was
important to prevent excessive noise and ensure that all activities were carried
out discreetly. Hence the monks of Cluny were to sharpen their knives in the
cloister only during periods when conversation was allowed. In 1442, a group of
monks at Durham who were practising their singing in the chapter house were
evidently disturbing their fellow brethren for they were asked to move to a more
secluded spot where they would cause less disruption.[20]

THE MONASTERY BELLS

Some sounds were essential to monastic observance. The striking of bells and
beating of boards throughout the day regulated daily life and were a necessary form
of communication within the cloister. They conveyed instructions concerning
the daily routine, signalling when the community should rise, attend an Office or
prepare to eat. But they also announced the exceptional, proclaiming the arrival
of an important guest or the death of a monk. The sacrist was largely responsible
for signalling to the brethren when they should rise, attend the chapter meeting,
celebrate the various Offices or gather in the refectory. It was vital that he did so
at the correct time or the entire day would be thrown into disarray. The prior
often shared the task of timekeeping. In Cistercian houses it was his job to sound
the gong to summon the brethren to work and ring the bell calling them to the
refectory; at Christ Church, Canterbury, the prior sounded the bell on various
occasions to call the monks to drink.[21]

The choice of bell or device that was sounded and how precisely it was struck carried a specific instruction to the community and resonated with meaning. For example, while one of the large bells in the church was rung to summon the monks to the major Hours (Lauds, Compline, Nocturns/Vigils), a smaller one called them to the minor Hours (Prime, Terce, Sext, None(s)); a little bell in the refectory, the *skilla*, summoned them to eat or drink. A full peal of bells was rung to announce the arrival of an important guest whereas the death of a monk was signalled by a series of strong, rapid blows to the wooden board. It was therefore vital that the sacrist was well versed in their use. The monks of Bury St Edmunds exploited the significance of sound to voice their opposition to Abbot Samson (1182–1211), who had merged the community's resources with his own. The monks rang an exceptional peal of bells on the anniversary of Abbot Robert (1102–7), who was credited with separating the abbatial and conventual revenues at Bury, thereby according the celebration greater status than was customary and making their feelings crystal clear.[22]

The sound of bells carries and was therefore an effective way to summon those working in remote parts of the precinct. Yet this could cause problems between neighbouring monasteries, which might be disturbed and confused by each other's bells. This was the case in twelfth-century Yorkshire when a group of Savigniac monks moved to Old Byland (Byland on the Moor), just over a mile from the Cistercian abbey of Rievaulx. The Rievaulx monks soon complained that the newcomers' bells were discordant with their own and causing confusion, since the two communities followed different schedules. This prompted the Savigniacs' removal to a new location. Some deliberately sought to disturb their neighbours by ringing their bells vehemently and at inappropriate times. When the vicar of Winchcombe was embroiled in an argument with the local abbot, he vigorously rang the bells of the chapel of St Peter's precisely when the monks of the abbey were celebrating the Office, hoping that this would cause them considerable disruption.[23]

ANIMALS, WORKMEN AND VISITORS

The sounds of dogs barking, hens clucking or even a billy goat cavorting through the church are probably not what we would associate with the medieval cloister. Yet the noise of these and other animals would have been integral to the monk's aural world. Livestock was essential to the monastic economy and while many of the community's sheep and cattle were kept on their manors or granges, others stayed in the outer court of the monastery and must often have been audible in the claustral area. On occasion they actually roamed around the cloister. At the Yorkshire nunnery of Swine, chickens and hens wandered about the choir, cloister and chapter house, while sheep pastured in the cloister at Norwich in the sixteenth century. Such behaviour was considered inappropriate and disruptive to monastic observance, and both communities were warned to reform their ways.[24]

The keeping of domestic animals as pets was discouraged since they could cause considerable disturbance and distract the community from their duties. Moreover, it was feared they would deprive the poor of alms, as the animals were generally fed scraps intended for the needy.[25] Nevertheless, by the later Middle Ages it was not uncommon for monks, and particularly nuns to keep lapdogs and birds in the cloister and even bring them into the church. In 1387 the nuns of Romsey (Hampshire) were reprimanded by their bishop for bringing birds, hounds and rabbits into the church while the nuns of Abbaye aux Dames in Caen allegedly brought squirrels into their choir. Abbess Alice Walerand (1290–8) of Romsey was warned against keeping a number of dogs and monkeys in her chamber.[26] These prohibitions were clearly difficult to enforce and in many cases there was a tacit acceptance of pets in the monastery and an attempt to control rather than curb the practice. Thus in the first half of the fifteenth century the prioress of St Helen's, Bishopsgate (London), was allowed to keep one or two of her many dogs while in 1520 the head of Flixton (Suffolk) was permitted to keep one favourite pooch.[27]

There are examples of more unusual animals finding their way into the cloister. The community at Battle (Sussex) evidently had a monkey in the thirteenth century, for the cellarer's accounts record the payment for its chain. Unfortunately it is not known where the animal was kept or for how long it had been in the monks' possession.[28] The monks of Bury St Edmunds (Suffolk) raised a billy goat that would cavort around the monastery and even ventured into the church. One day it broke a leg but undeterred ambled around on the remaining three and was ultimately cured at the shrine of St Edmund in the abbey church. A black pig once stormed into the chapter house at Norwich at night and duly leapt on top of one monk who was seeking relief at the saint's shrine. There was quite a commotion as the monks chased the pig out of the chapter house and drove it from the cloister. Some members of the Norwich community believed that the pig was the devil in disguise.[29] Monks were explicitly forbidden to keep hawks and hounds and were prohibited from indulging in hunting and other worldly pursuits. Not everyone heeded the ruling and steps were taken to enforce it. Hence anyone conducting a visitation of a Cistercian abbey was reminded to check that no hawks or hounds were kept at the abbey or on its granges.[30]

It was not just the monks and nuns who brought their animals into the cloister but also their boarders. In 1440 the nuns of Langley Priory (Leicestershire) complained that Lady Audeley, who stayed at the house, was followed into the church by a convoy of twelve dogs. They claimed that the dogs made such a din that it terrified the nuns and seriously impeded the psalmody. In the same year the nuns of Legbourne Priory (Lincolnshire) declared that they were kept awake at night by the birds belonging to their boarder, Margaret Ingoldesby, who bought her feathered companions into the dormitory.[31] Guests who arrived with a fleet of beasts and birds or used the monastery to kennel or stable their animals might cause serious disruption. Moreover, the care of these animals could be extremely expensive. When William of Longchamp, bishop of Ely and chancellor of England, conducted a lightning tour of the religious houses in the kingdom in 1190 he reputedly swept through the country with a vast entourage of men, dogs and birds, crippling any house where he stayed for even a night.[32] Queen Isabella of England (1308–58) caused the prior of Christ Church, Canterbury, considerable concern when she deposited her pack of hounds at the priory and departed for France. The queen seemingly left instructions that the animals should be dispersed among her friends but to the prior's horror they remained at Christ Church. This prompted him to write a series of frenzied letters to her advisors urging the immediate removal of the hounds which, he claimed, were a significant cost and inconvenience to the house.[33]

Despite the potential noise and disruption animals might cause in the cloister and irrespective of measures to keep them out they remained an important part of monastic life. A striking testimony to the great fondness for animals is a fifteenth-century effigy of an abbess of Wherwell Abbey (Hampshire) showing her with a dog at her feet. Affection was often mutual and Jocelin of Furness (fl. 1199–1214) tells a touching story of the love and devotion one horse showed to its abbot, Waldef of Melrose (d. 1159). The horse, who was jokingly called 'Brother Grizzel', was sensitive to his rider and if Waldef happened to doze off while riding, Brother Grizzel would pick his steps carefully and slowly lest he trip. However, once the abbot was awake the horse galloped swiftly to catch up with his companions. Brother Grizzel was allegedly so devoted to Waldef that he

showed displeasure if he had to carry another rider and upon the abbot's death
was distraught and simply wasted away through sadness.[34]

BUILDING AND REPAIR WORK

*The court echoes to the sound of pickaxes and stonemasons' tools as the
guesthouse is knocked down. At this very moment nearly all is demolished.
May the Most High provide for the rebuilding.*[35]

The rebuilding of the great abbey of Cluny under Abbot Hugh the Great (d. 1109)
lasted three decades and throughout this period the precinct was a hive of activity.
Ox-ploughs brought stones to the abbey, there were masons carving on site and
workmen with pulleys and ropes. Monastic observance continued amid this
chaos although Abbot Hugh took steps to lessen disruption and stipulated that
all work should stop when the monks were celebrating the Hours and hearing
Mass in the choir.[36]

The construction and upkeep of the monastic buildings was a vast project. It
could take many years and perhaps several generations to complete the church
and claustral buildings, which then required maintenance and renovation.
Building and repair work was effectively an ongoing process. Some of these tasks
would have been carried out by members of the community but workmen were
often engaged and would have been a common presence in the cloister. The very
sight of workmen wandering through the cloister, the sound of hammering
and chiselling, and the need for the monks to relocate on occasion while a
particular building was repaired would have disturbed and in some cases severely
impeded monastic observance. Attempts were made to minimize disruption
and at Abingdon Abbey workmen were forbidden to pass through the cloister
inappropriately attired and were not to wear cloaks or boots. In summer the
Office of Collations was delayed if workmen happened to be in the church.[37]

VISITORS AND INTRUDERS

*From receiving guests cheerfully the reputation of the monastery is increased,
friendships are multiplied, animosities are blunted, God is honoured, charity
is augmented and a plentiful reward is promised in heaven.*[38]

Hospitality was integral to monastic life. It was expected that, in accordance with
Christ's teaching in Matthew 25.34–40 and as stipulated in Chapter 53 of the

Rule of St Benedict, the monastery would extend a warm welcome to whoever requested its kindness. This applied to the weak and infirm as much as the great and the good. There were various reasons why visitors sought hospitality from the monks and while some simply stopped off to break a journey, others came specifically to attend a meeting, celebrate a feast or visit the shrine. In some cases medical help was sought – Robert Bouteuylleyn, a founder of Pipewell Abbey (Northamptonshire), claimed it his right to have four bleedings at the house each year, while the people of Moray in Scotland flocked to the abbey of Kinloss where the monastery's gardener from Dieppe was renowned for his skill at dressing wounds.[39]

Through extending hospitality the monks could hope to secure their own salvation and a place at the heavenly table. But the presence of these outsiders might interrupt monastic observance and lead the brethren astray. To ensure that the community was not unduly disturbed by the arrival of visitors the guesthouse was usually located well away from the claustral area, often to the west of the precinct. Moreover, guests had to obtain permission if they wished to meet with a member of the community. Visitors to the Augustinian priory of Barnwell (Cambridgeshire) were warned to speak in a low voice whenever they were in the parlour and the community was in the cloister, so that the brethren would not be disturbed by their laughter and conversation.[40] The cloister itself was subject to close surveillance and access to outsiders was restricted. In 1232 the monks of Bury St Edmunds were reminded that external custodians should monitor the cloister more carefully and watch the doors of the parlour and cellar.[41] Guests were expected to conduct themselves with propriety in the cloister and were not permitted to enter unaccompanied or unannounced; nor were they to enter inappropriately attired, for example barefoot or simply in drawers. Any guests visiting St Mary's, York, who wished to see the claustral offices were shown around by the guestmaster (hosteller) when the brethren were not in the cloister.[42] At Abingdon (Berkshire), the hosteller showed visitors into the church to pray only if the monks were not in the choir, and otherwise brought them to pray in the vestry.[43] Most houses prohibited outsiders from entering the cloister when the monks were eating, sleeping, shaving or at their chapter meeting where the community's private affairs were discussed. Each day after the last Office of Compline had been celebrated the cloister doors were locked and nobody was admitted until after Prime the following morning. Women faced greater restrictions than men and were generally forbidden from entering the cloister, even with a monk as escort. Some exceptions were made, particularly in the later Middle Ages when patrons or their relatives might secure special licence. In 1336, for example, permission was granted to the wife and daughter of the patron of Meaux (Yorkshire) to enter the monastery between Prime and Compline, although it was stressed that they were not allowed to stay the night.[44] In some cases the prohibition was simply ignored and women entered the cloister regardless of any restrictions.

Despite the various rules and regulations it was impossible to shield the monks completely from external disruption and there were times when guests caused commotion and also damage. Festive occasions invariably drew large crowds of visitors and the monastery might be inundated with outsiders. The pressure of numbers descending on St Denis, Paris, prompted Abbot Suger (1122–55) to expand the church there. Suger explained that the narrowness of the church forced the women to run to the altar on top of men's heads, posing a danger to the monks celebrating the Eucharist.[45] The appeal of a particular shrine might cause a number of visitors to flock to the monastery and this too might present problems for the community. The monks of Norwich Cathedral Priory complained that they were greatly disturbed by the number of pilgrims who passed through their cloister to visit the shrine of St William in the chapter house. The saint was duly translated to the south side of the High Altar in the church, but this also proved troublesome since the pilgrims now impeded the processional route. St William was finally moved to the northern side of the altar, where there was more room and less likelihood of disruption.[46]

By opening its doors to outsiders the monastery exposed itself to unruly behaviour and even criminal conduct. In 1195 the monks of Bury St Edmunds were greatly disturbed by a group of knights staying at the abbey on their return from a tournament. After dinner, when the monks were trying to enjoy their afternoon siesta, the rowdy visitors wreaked havoc. First, the knights sent into town for drink and disturbed the community with their carousing. They then ridiculed the abbot and broke through the monastery gates to enjoy what revelry the town had to offer.[47] The Palm Sunday procession at Øm, in Denmark, was brought to a dramatic standstill by a group of local women who confronted the monks and stripped down to their underwear. Queen Christina (d. 1170) had incited the women against the monks, prompting this act of defiance, but their behaviour did not go unpunished and the priest's house where they had stored their clothes was burned to the ground.[48] In the thirteenth century, the

Cistercian abbey of Ford(e) in Dorset was invaded by a band of Cluniacs from Montacute Priory (Somerset) seeking the body of the renowned hermit, Wulfric of Haselbury. The Cistercians locked the intruders inside their church but the Cluniacs responded to the challenge and pushed the corpse through the window to several of their men who were waiting outside. A spectacular tug of war ensued as the venerable body was shoved back and forth through the window. The final victory went to the monks of Ford, who buried Wulfric's body secretly in the western part of their church to prevent any future attempts at theft. A similar incident occurred in Yorkshire between the nuns of Swine and the monks of Meaux over the body of Amandus Stewart, who had bequeathed his body with a gift of land to Meaux community. The nuns hoped to secure the land by taking the body. Accordingly, they seized the corpse from Meaux and had it reburied in their own cemetery.[49]

The various restrictions imposed on outsiders were not simply intended to prevent disruption to claustral life but were a way to ensure that the community's affairs remained private and that no scandal was spread. This was vital if the monks were to retain their credibility and, crucially, ensure continued support and benefaction. In some cases these measures were imposed to prevent ridicule. In 1394 Abbot Herman of Stratford ruled that no seculars should be admitted to the dormitory at Hailes Abbey (Gloucestershire) lest they laugh at the simplicity of the monks' bedding.[50]

FIRES, FLOODS AND FALLING MASONRY

On the night of St Etheldreda's day . . . part of a candle burnt out on the dais, which was covered with hangings, and began to ignite all about it above and below, so that the iron walls glowed all over with fire. . . . Around the same time the clock struck for Matins, and the vestry master, on getting up saw the fire and ran as fast as he could and beat upon the board as if someone was dead, and shouted in a loud voice and said that the shrine was on fire.[51]

The monastery of Bury St Edmunds was thrown into disarray in June 1198 when a candle above the shrine of St Edmund fell, setting alight to all around it. Fortunately the fire was detected in its early stages by the vestry master, who was rising to waken the brethren for Matins. He beat loudly upon the board in the cloister to alert the monks to the danger and cried out that the shrine was on fire. The community responded quickly to the fearful alarm and rushed to the fire, which had by this time engulfed the shrine with the flames extending almost to the beams of the church. Jocelin of Brakelond, a monk of the house, vividly conveys the terror and pandemonium that he witnessed and describes how the young monks ran to fetch water while others hurried to save the reliquaries, beating back the flames with their hoods. The damage was extensive but miraculously the shrine remained intact. Blame was attributed to the carelessness of the shrine-keepers who had simply patched up the two candles by putting wax on wax and had left rags lying around the shrine, which were a fire hazard. But the reputation of the entire monastery was at stake for as keepers of St Edmund the community had a duty to protect the shrine. The monks were concerned that news of the fire should not be made known and therefore sought to conceal this from the pilgrims who were due to arrive the following morning to celebrate St Etheldreda's Day. They covered the scorch marks with wax, summoned a goldsmith to join the metal sheets and told the visitors that a candle had fallen over and burnt three towels. The pilgrims were not so easily fooled. Indeed, some would have heard the commotion the previous night and probably also the vestry master's cry that the shrine was on fire; moreover, they would surely have been able to see and smell evidence of what had really transpired.[52]

Fires, falling masonry and flooding caused by accident or through negligence occasionally interrupted the solitude of the cloister, striking terror among the community and sometimes causing fatalities. Shoddy workmanship and carelessness were often to blame. The collapse of the great tower at Abingdon (Berkshire) in 1091 was attributed to builders undertaking the extension of the church who had carelessly joined the new work to the old tower. The tower fell down during the celebration of Vigils but luckily there were no casualties for the prior had had the foresight or perhaps Divine Prompting to move the community from the church to the chapter house shortly before disaster struck. There were several near casualties and the monks were severely shaken by the incident. The chronicle of the house describes how a great cloud of mortar fell with the tower, extinguishing the lights and leaving the monks in a state of darkness and despair – 'those present threw themselves to the ground awaiting nothing save death'. A disaster of even greater enormity struck St Albans (Hertfordshire) in 1323 when two of the huge columns in the abbey church crashed down one after the other, causing a tremendous racket and quite a spectacle; those present in the church at the time were 'struck dumb' by what they had seen and heard. However, there was worse to come for when the crowd gathered to look at the debris the entire wooden roof above the columns collapsed, together with part of the southern side and almost all the adjoining cloister. As at Abingdon poor workmanship was blamed for the incident.[53]

Similar catastrophes occurred elsewhere, although not of this magnitude. In the mid-thirteenth century the bell tower above the nuns' dormitory at Wherwell Abbey (Hampshire) collapsed 'through decay'. The nuns were inside at the time but luckily nobody was injured. Abbess Euphemia (d. 1257) was clearly concerned to avoid any further incidents of this kind at Wherwell; she therefore had the tower rebuilt and also stabilized the presbytery of the church since this was in danger of falling down. Bell towers could be particularly hazardous and the monks of St Augustine's, Canterbury, were warned to avoid ringing a peal that required four bells since this caused their tower to shake.[54]

Disasters could often be prevented by ensuring that buildings were properly maintained. Communities were invariably reminded of the importance of this at visitation. It was also vital to remove fire hazards and exercise vigilance. The importance of the latter was emphasized by the abbot of Hailes (Gloucestershire) in 1437, when he was preparing to leave on a journey to Rome. The abbot urged his sub-prior to attend to matters of safety during his absence and to make sure that all fires were kept under control. He was warned to keep vigil until the eighth hour, the time when all candles should be extinguished in the dormitory, for bedtime reading could be perilous. This was likely the cause of the fire that broke out at Westminster Abbey on the Feast of St Crispin (25 October) in the early fifteenth century. The fire began in the ninth hour of the night and burned down the dormitory. The culprit was George of Norwich, a novice of the house who later succeeded to the abbacy.[55] It was not just the monks but visitors who had to be monitored lest their carelessness led to disaster. At Barnwell Priory (Cambridgeshire) the servant of the guesthouse was instructed to stay awake until visitors had finished eating so that he could extinguish their fire and ensure the safety of the house. A number of accidents were caused by pilgrims bringing candles to shrines in the monastery church. An incident of this nature occurred at Durham Cathedral in the twelfth century when a man visiting the shrine of St Cuthbert unwittingly started a fire at the foot of the tomb from the candle he had brought. This could have been catastrophic but fortunately St Cuthbert intervened, saving the hangings and bejewelled shrine from the flames.[56]

Little could be done to safeguard the community from earthquakes, lightning and floods, which could be perilous and wreak havoc. Few houses would have escaped an attack of this kind at some point in their history but some fared worse than others. The monks of Meaux Abbey in Yorkshire lost men and beasts in a great flood of 1253 and were badly shaken in 1349 when an earthquake hit Yorkshire and blew them from their choir stalls. The monks of La Grande Chartreuse, north of Grenoble, lost six monks and a novice in an avalanche of 1132 which destroyed the monastery buildings; one monk was unearthed after twelve days but died soon thereafter.[57] Guibert of Nogent (d. 1124) recounts how lightning struck his abbey of Saint-Germer de Fly (Picardy) on three occasions in the late eleventh century. The first assault was particularly vicious and resulted in the deaths of three monks of the house who, curiously, remained sitting after they had been struck. Others were so badly injured that they were anointed immediately in case they should die, but the entire community was greatly shaken – and singed. Guibert vividly describes how the flames penetrated some of the monks' habits, singeing the hair beneath, and exited through their socks and sandals.[58]

Monks, like the rest of society, were at the mercy of nature but might receive Divine Help in their time of need. Such was the case at the royal abbey of St Denis, Paris, which was hit by a severe storm around 1140. Building work was underway in the church at the time and the force of the wind caused the arches that were under construction to sway precariously, for they were unsupported by scaffolding. The bishop of Chartres, who was celebrating Mass in the church, was greatly alarmed and in the hope of averting disaster made the sign of the cross in the direction of the arches. This was not, evidently, in vain, for miraculously the rather fragile arches survived the storm, even though many of the solid buildings were destroyed.[59] While these disasters could cause considerable distress and damage to the monastery, the cost of repair was often extensive. Moreover, the monks might be deemed liable for damage to a neighbouring property. The Augustinian Canons of Barnwell found themselves in this predicament in 1287 when fire destroyed the tower at their priory, wrecking the stonework, clocks, windows and bells, but sparks carried in the wind also set fire to neighbouring houses which they then had to repair.[60]

ACCIDENTS AND EMERGENCIES

If anyone has a nosebleed or an attack of vomiting he should hurry into the cloister, followed by the brother who is responsible for tending such casualties . . . [who] continues to serve him there until he has washed up and can return to choir . . . If the regular assistant has not noticed that someone is vomiting or bleeding, one who does should signal to him.[61]

The monks and nuns of the Middle Ages were as susceptible as their secular contemporaries to trips, tumbles and nosebleeds. Lack of food and sleep likely made them more prone to fainting and bouts of nausea than their lay counterparts, and accidents and ailments were fairly commonplace in the monastery. The monastic books of customs often set out precisely how such incidents should be dealt with, for they were to cause minimum disruption to communal life. This was especially important in the church and refectory, where the preservation of silence and decorum was imperative. It was usual for a brother to be specially appointed to tend these casualties efficiently and discretely. The twelfth-century Cistercian customary is particularly detailed and reveals the exact procedure for dealing with any brother who had a nosebleed or vomited in choir. The brother responsible for tending these casualties escorted the sufferer from the choir and ministered to him in the cloister. Once the monk had recovered the pair returned quietly to the choir. If the priest celebrating Mass happened to have a nosebleed he did not leave the church but was brought two bowls of water and tended on the spot.[62] It was surely not uncommon for monks to faint in choir, particularly during Vigils when they were tired, cold and probably hungry. In the event of this happening the monk did not leave the church but moved to the *retrochoir*, the area immediately behind the monks' stalls that was occupied by old and infirm members of the community.

Measures were taken to prevent accidents, which could be injurious but also disruptive. When a nun of Chicksands Priory (Bedfordshire) who was hurrying to the kitchen tripped over a piece of wood, her fellow sisters rallied around and carried her to the infirmary, where they tried everything to treat the blackened foot and even put it in traction.[63] Tombstones around the cloister walks that were uneven or jutted above the surface were also potential stumbling blocks, especially from the late twelfth century when lay burial there became more widespread. It was to prevent accidents of this kind that in 1194 the Cistercian General Chapter ruled that the slabs of these graves should be made level with the ground.[64] The monks of Cluny were warned to wear gloves when working in the kitchen so that they would not burn their hands when moving the cauldron on the fire.[65] The brethren were also warned against being overzealous in their devotions for this was showy but also potentially dangerous. The Cistercian monk, Caesarius of Heisterbach (d. c. 1240), recounts how one nun genuflected overenthusiastically in choir and injured her knee. While recuperating in the infirmary she was visited by the Virgin Mary, who reprimanded her undisciplined movements and warned that in future she should be modest and discreet in her prayers.[66]

DEMONIC DISRUPTIONS

Occasionally, the peace of the cloister was shattered by instances of madness – or demonic possession – whereby a member of the community became violent and abusive and had to be restrained. This behaviour was not simply noisy and disruptive but could evoke fear and terror among the brethren. There was a striking incident of this nature at Christ Church, Canterbury, in the late eleventh century when Aethelweard, a monk of the house, was assisting Archbishop Lanfranc (1070–89) at Mass and was suddenly invaded by the devil. He grabbed the prelate by the shoulders but Lanfranc calmly restrained him, finished the service and then ordered that Aethelweard be removed from the cloister to the infirmary and bound with chains. There, Aethelweard remained incarcerated for several days but continued to terrorize the community with his ranting and raving and gnashing of teeth. He taunted the brethren, threatening to reveal their sins and secrets, and caused them considerable alarm. They believed that this was in fact the devil speaking and claimed that the demon could be seen moving within Aethelweard in the form of a tumour, running around like a little cat or a dog. Aethelweard became increasingly abusive, but was eventually relieved at the tomb of St Dunstan in Canterbury Cathedral, under the watchful eye of Aelwin the sacrist. Eadmer, who was a monk of Christ Church, attributed some of the blame for this incident to his own community, for he maintained that the monks' luxurious living had made them vulnerable to the devil's attack, but concluded that the incident had at least instigated necessary reform.[67]

There was a similar occurrence at Ely in the twelfth century when the devil allegedly invaded a young monk of the house during the celebration of

Compline. The community was startled by the severity of their brother's rage and his master, Siward, pursued him with a board. Yet the monk continued to rave and blaspheme throughout the night. Eventually he succumbed to sleep and, as the chronicler of the house graphically explains, he 'ejected his tormentor through his foul orifices'. This, however, brought foulness of another kind into the monastery, for such was the stench arising from the privy that the air here and, indeed, elsewhere, was putrid,

> . . . the polluted exhalation spread itself through every nook and cranny, and scarcely anyone escaped its vapour. And this uncleanness was no less extreme than the former madness . . . one horrible because of the going out of his mind, the other astonishing because of the effluvium of his stomach, as if that most evil spirit was either totally being changed into excrement or, on being ejected, was taking the latrines themselves with him.[68]

Clearly it was not simply the sound and sight of these demonics that could cause disorder for their very smell could be offensive.

While the monks were 'dead to the world' and the cloister was in theory a solitary place, silence was relative. Conversation and indeed communication per se may have been restricted or prohibited but a variety of noises permeated the monastic day and night, some of which were vital to claustral life and regulated monastic observance.

*When you go to sleep always take with you in your memory
or your thoughts something that will enable you to fall asleep
peacefully and sometimes even help you to dream; something also
that will come to mind when you wake up and renew in you the
previous day's purpose. In this way the light will be shed on the
night for you and it will be as the day, and the night will be your
illumination in your delights [Ps 138.11ff.]. You will fall asleep
peacefully, you will rest in tranquillity, you will wake up easily
and when you rise you will have no difficulty in returning with
your wits about you to what you have not wholly laid aside.*[1]

5

The Sound of Silence (2): The Silence of the Night

William of St Thierry's (d. c. 1148) advice to monks on how to enjoy a peaceful and restorative night's sleep (p. 101) was well intentioned but the night was often a fearful and menacing time in the monastery. The sacrist of Norwich Cathedral Priory was petrified on one occasion when he was preparing to rouse the brethren for Matins and heard a strange noise emanating from the chapter house; his hair allegedly stood on end in fright and the terrified monk insisted that from then on a light should always burn in the chapter house during the night.[2] Unfamiliar noises heard in the silence and darkness of the monastery could be alarming, particularly when one was surrounded by saints and relics and felt vulnerable to attack from the devil. Moreover, in the silence and solitude of the night there was opportunity for reflection and introspection, and the monks might be plagued by fears, worries and doubts. Not least, the imagination could play tricks on the mind and it is hardly a coincidence that most of the visions and visitations experienced in the monastery occurred at night when the recipients were drowsy, perhaps jumpy and prone to vivid dreams. Each of the three visions Thomas of Monmouth had in 1150 of the late Bishop Herbert of Norwich occurred after Matins, when Thomas had returned to bed to rest before Lauds.[3]

The fears and worries that plagued the monks at night and the forms of visions they experienced can reveal much about their beliefs, attitudes and very psyche. These and nocturnal disruptions of a more earthly kind are explored in this chapter.

THE TEMPTATIONS OF THE NIGHT

We must take care that nothing be done at night that will be shameful to hear in the morning.[4]

Devil attacks monk, British Library, Cotton Cleopatra, C. XI, f. 25.

If monks were to sleep peacefully and enjoy the restorative night's sleep that William of St Thierry recommended, it was important that they first confessed their sins and freed their minds of guilt. By doing so the monks also armed themselves against the devil who, it was believed, would seek to ensnare them at night when they were at their most vulnerable. For the canonist, William Durandus (d. 1296), the dormitory itself represented a clean conscience since the monk came here after his day in the service of God.[5] Yet the dormitory presented the monk with various opportunities to sin. He might be tempted to engage in private conversations with his companions, to entertain inappropriate thoughts or behave indecently. It was therefore vital that rigid rules were implemented. Hence speech was forbidden and contact of any other kind was regulated.

The sheer size of the dormitory would have helped to prevent physical contact and communication but strict regulations were enforced to ensure that modesty was preserved at all times, even when sleeping. The monks were taught how precisely to dress and undress without exposing any flesh and were even instructed on how to get into and out of bed in an appropriate manner. The monks of Cluny were warned that their cowls should remain up until the blankets covered their elbows. Even in the heat of summer only their heads, feet and arms might be exposed while sleeping.[6] These measures were also intended to safeguard the monks from demonic forces. It was thought that both angels and devils surrounded the brethren at night as they slept, and should any monk be lying immodestly he would repel the good and draw the evil.[7]

A light burned in the dormitory throughout the night to help monks find their way to the privies, which were often located at the far end of the dormitory. But this was also to deter them from engaging in illicit conduct. Most houses took extra precautions and appointed one or more senior members of the community to patrol the dormitory throughout the night, noting any misconduct, which was reported and punished at Chapter the following day.[8] These roundsmen were also concerned about matters of safety and would check that no monk had left a candle burning by his bed. This could be a serious fire hazard and was the cause of several significant conflagrations – a fire at St Peter's, Westminster, in the fifteenth century burned down the dormitory. It was to avoid instances of this nature that the Augustinian Canons of Barnwell Priory (Cambridgeshire) were forbidden to read in bed with a candle.[9] There were additional checks on the monks' behaviour. They were reminded that God, who was omniscient and omnipresent, saw everything that they did, even in the dark. The Cistercians had an extra incentive to conduct themselves with modesty at night, for they believed that the Virgin Mary, who was patron saint of the Order, was wont to patrol their dormitories while they slept and bestow her blessing on those whom she considered worthy. Immodesty could have serious consequences. Mary allegedly averted her eyes and withheld her blessing from one monk who was not fully clothed as he slept; a lay brother who exposed himself was said to have been kissed by the devil disguised as a nun and died several days later.[10] Stories such as these that were circulated among the brethren would likely have had a powerful impact on the community and encouraged them to control their thoughts and deeds at all times.

NOCTURNAL VISITATIONS

The enemy tries to deceive in sleep those religious whom he cannot entrap
when awake.[11]

The devil was always at work in the monastery but was particularly active at night, when he preyed on the monks as they lay sleeping and unguarded, endeavouring to lead them from the path to salvation. He would try to inveigle his way into their minds, tempting them with thoughts of worldly delights to instil in them dissatisfaction with the hardships of the cloister. Novices were most vulnerable to his wiles and from the moment they pledged their life to the cloister might be hounded by the devil, who hoped to lure them back into the world. When Ida the Gentle decided to dedicate her life to God at the convent of La Ramée (Brabant), the devil plagued her relentlessly for a year and a half. Ida, however, remained steadfast and successfully withstood his wiles by taking refuge in Christ and receiving the Eucharist frequently.[12]

The devil did not simply try to infiltrate the brethren's minds but might launch a physical attack which could strike terror, inflict pain and disrupt the entire community. This could take various forms and affect any of the senses. A nun of Hoven (Germany) was tormented by several demons who tried to remove her from her bed. She managed to repel them by invoking the Virgin's help and crossing herself but was left shaken and fearful (a bolder nun who was similarly attacked boxed the demons' ears). In her distress the nun ran to the bed of another and broke the silence to explain what had happened. Her companions sought to comfort and protect her by reading from the beginning of St John's Gospel and the following morning the nun was fully recovered.[13] The entire community of Rievaulx (Yorkshire) was thrown into disarray in the mid-twelfth century when the devil 'seduced' two monks of the house, who 'bellowed like bulls' in the dormitory. They wakened the house with their groans and sighs, spreading terror throughout the monastery 'in a reverberation of sound'.[14] The devil might appear in the guise of a bird or a beast, striking terror and inflicting pain. A monk of Dunfermline Abbey who was resting in his bed in the dormitory was startled when two shaggy dogs, one red and one black, sprang into the room. The first leapt on top of the monk and seized him by the throat, almost strangling him, but fortunately St Margaret, the resident saint, came to his rescue and repelled the dogs with her staff. A novice of Dunfermline had an equally frightening experience. One night when he was trying to sleep he saw a huge flock of crows entering the dormitory. The most terrifying of the group swooped towards him and placed a small object, like a stone, on his throat, leaving him completely paralysed. The attack had a profound impact on the rest of the community, who were deeply alarmed at what had happened. They carried their brother to the infirmary where St Margaret visited him and effected his cure.[15]

Anything bad, whether illness, madness, malevolence or even malodour, was considered to be the work of the devil. A striking example relates to Prior Roger of Durham (1137–49), who had a rather unpleasant brush with a demon who was seeking to lead Godric, the hermit, into temptation. As Roger was helping the holy man to withstand the devil's wiles, the angry demon wreaked his revenge on the prior by paying him a personal visit and delivering a loud, smelly fart. This was reputedly so rank the odour lingered in Roger's nostrils for three days.[16] Conversely, sweet odours were associated with saints and angels and considered evidence of their presence. When one nun who was recovering in the infirmary from an injured leg smelt a sweet odour around her bed she knew at once it was the Virgin who had come to cure her.[17]

It was not only demonic forces that walked at night and monks were just as likely to receive visions and visitations of a saintly kind. While saints often came to the community's rescue and like St Margaret repelled the demons or effected a cure, they frequently visited to instruct, chastise or even to punish. In some cases this resulted in physical pain and even death. In the mid-twelfth century the late bishop of Norwich, Herbert de Losinga (d. 1119), 'visited' a monk of the cathedral priory, asking that he relay a message to the prior of the house. When the monk failed to carry out his wishes Herbert visited him for a second time and shook the monk so hard that he left a thumbprint on his body. Richard of Norwich fared worse at the hands of the resident saint, William, who repeatedly asked Richard to bring to his shrine the candles he had stashed away. When Richard neglected to do so the saint, impatient and angry, struck the monk with a tremendous blow to the forehead, leaving him in considerable pain.[18]

The night could therefore be a fearful time in the monastery since demons and also saints were wont to visit the brethren, attack the vulnerable and chastise the guilty. Stories recounting the various experiences monks and nuns had with these other-worldly visitors would no doubt have influenced how the community interpreted their own strange dreams and any untoward noises they heard. The circulation of these tales would also have been an important way to instil good behaviour, encouraging the monks to confess their sins and act with modesty and decorum lest they too were subjected to such a visitation.

WORLDLY DISRUPTIONS

Monks should always be given to silence, especially, however, during the hours of the night. (Rule of St Benedict, *ch. 42*)

When Alice (d. 1250), a young nun of La Cambre (Belgium), contracted leprosy she was moved out of the common dormitory to a hut. Here, she felt lonely and fearful, particularly at night, for having entered the convent at a young age Alice was unused to sleeping by herself and missed the reassurance of knowing the other sisters were with her in the darkness and solitude.[19] Not everyone would have found the communal sleeping arrangements as comforting and at times the presence of so many others sharing the dormitory would have been disruptive and intrusive, and stood in the way of a good night's sleep. Measures were taken to try to minimize disruption and as far as possible to preserve the silence and decorum of the dormitory. It was important that the monks showed consideration for their fellow brethren. Accordingly, if anyone needed to rise before his companions he was to be careful not to waken the others. The brethren of Barnwell Priory (Cambridgeshire) were warned that while they were permitted to rise early to prepare for Mass, they should not then waken the others, who might sleep until the bell sounded for Lauds. At Westminster Abbey and elsewhere, those who snored or talked in their sleep were liable to be removed from the dormitory. Odo, who was the abbot of the Sussex house of Battle from 1175 to 1200, suffered a long-standing stomach disorder and elected to sleep outside the common dormitory to spare the monks the offensive 'emanations'. Odo was allegedly so embarrassed by his condition that he refused to have any companion within ear or eyeshot.[20] It was not simply the sound of monks snoring, sleep-talking or coming and going to the privy that might disturb the others but the cries from anyone struck with pain or experiencing a nightmare. In the mid-twelfth century the novices of the Burgundian house of Cluny were startled in their sleep by the screams of one of their companions having a nightmare. Monks of Norwich (Norfolk) were woken from their slumbers when a member of the community cried out in agony for he suddenly had an excruciating pain in his right eye. Rather surprisingly, the monk only seemed to waken his neighbours and did not disturb the entire dormitory; perhaps the brethren were trained to wail *sotto voce*.[21]

LACK OF SLEEP

Look at your coarse woollen blanket and bedcovers and compare your bed
to the grave, just as if you were entering it for burial. . . . If you can sleep, all

is well; if you cannot, experience has proved that if you say the Athanasian
Creed seven times or the Seven Penitential Psalms, you will fall asleep.[22]

Matthew of Rievaulx, who was precentor of the Yorkshire abbey in the late twelfth and early thirteenth century, complained of insomnia and exhaustion as a result of rising early for a month to lead the Night Office. Matthew was not alone and a number of monks suffered from insomnia and sleep disorders as a consequence of their duties and the communal sleeping arrangements. Then, as now, sleeplessness was taken seriously. The Cistercian, Stephen of Sawley (d. 1252), acknowledged this as 'a punishing affliction' and suggested various remedies to help sufferers. He advised any monk struggling to sleep to look at his coarse woollen blanket and bedcovers and think of his bed as a grave that he was entering for burial. If this failed to bring relief a sure remedy was to recite seven times the Athanasian Creed or the Seven Penitential Psalms.[23] The hermit, Wulfric of Haselbury, engaged the assistance of the whole community to help a young monk of Ford(e) Abbey (Dorset) overcome his severe insomnia. The brethren were instructed to recite the Lord's Prayer three times for their sleep-deprived brother, who was successfully cured.[24]

The communal sleeping arrangements did not simply interfere with the monk's rest but also with his privacy. Benedict had stipulated in his *Rule* that the entire community should sleep together in the dormitory, but by the twelfth century a number of abbots had moved to a private chamber or suite of rooms. By the later Middle Ages others had followed suit – the prior and also chief officials might have their own rooms and the dormitory itself was sometimes partitioned to make individual cubicles that could be locked. The monks' dormitory at Westminster Abbey was divided into cubicles certainly by the mid-fourteenth century when blue muslin curtains acted as partitions; by the late fifteenth century buckram was used.[25] Similar modifications were made in the infirmary, where individual cells might be made to provide senior members of the community with a private chamber or allocated to older monks in their retirement. While modifications of this nature were widespread they were not necessarily legitimate and in some cases steps were taken to reform what was regarded as an abuse of the *Rule of St Benedict*. The Cistercian General Chapter issued and reissued legislation to control this practice, fearing that it would give rise to feasting, carousing and the hatching of conspiracies. In 1394 the Cistercian monks of Hailes Abbey (Gloucestershire) were warned that all the brethren should sleep together and not in private chambers as they had evidently been wont to do.[26] But the desire for privacy was clearly strong and ultimately the authorities had to be satisfied with controlling rather than curbing the practice. For example, they conceded that monks might have private cubicles in the dormitory so long as these were not locked.[27] This growing desire for privacy in the monastery was part of a more general trend and laypeople similarly sought to have their own private chambers. It was both a cause and a consequence of the break-up of communal living in the monastery but, as has recently been suggested, it likely afforded greater opportunity for private reading and devotion.[28]

The monk's conduct and even his thoughts were closely monitored during the day and night. As we shall see, he was required to adhere to the observances of the Order at all times, for his was a life of obedience and subject to the enforcement of monastic discipline in all its forms.

Your infirmary . . . is the cell [cloister] . . . the treatment which has begun to bring you healing is obedience, true obedience. . . . A man who is on his way to a destination will quickly arrive at it if he keeps to one road, the straight road . . . wandering does not lead to any end. Stay put then and do not change your course of treatment but apply the remedy of medicinal obedience until you arrive at the goal of perfect health.[1]

6

A Life of Obedience

The monastic life was founded on obedience – to God, to the *Rule of St Benedict* and to the superior of the house. Through obedience and self-abnegation the monk attained unity and communion with his fellow brethren. Obedience was also the way to true freedom, for this alone enabled one to progress on the road to salvation and enlightenment. Disregard for the rules or the will of the abbot was considered a serious offence and one that required punishment if the miscreant was to be absolved and continue unfettered on the path to Redemption. Any members of the Gilbertine Order who refused to yield to the rules and died without having amended their ways were buried as a guest and outsider.[2]

Obedience was to come from within. The monk's conscience was to be his guide so that he would be shamed from committing wrongs and encouraged to confess his sins before being accused. However, the brethren needed help and support to remain steadfast and resist temptation, particularly novices, who were most vulnerable to the wiles of the devil. The abbot, novice-master and senior members of the community might all help to regale the brethren and help them in their fight against evil, but measures were also implemented to enforce obedience and restrict the opportunity to stray. Senior officials were wont to carry out checks around the monastery and external inspections were periodically undertaken by ecclesiastical officials and representatives of the Order. This chapter considers the various ways in which obedience shaped the monk's life, how discipline was enforced and the nature of the punishment that was meted out.

OBEDIENCE TO THE ABBOT

This is the virtue of those who hold nothing dearer to them than Christ;
who . . . as soon as anything has been ordered by the Superior, receive it as a
Divine Command and cannot suffer any delay in executing it.
(Rule of St Benedict, *ch. 5*)

The governance of the monastery depended upon the will of the abbot, who had absolute authority and was to be obeyed in all matters. His command was to be treated as the will of God and acted upon without delay or resistance. Nothing could be done without the abbot's knowledge or permission, and anyone who defied his word would be punished. Anselm of Bec/Canterbury (d. 1109) underlined the importance of this to a certain prior called Hugh, whose turbulent relationship with his abbot prompted him to consider resigning from office. Hugh sought Anselm's advice on the matter and was urged to persevere unless his abbot agreed to his resignation. If the abbot withheld his permission Hugh was instructed to put aside personal rifts and 'bear the burden, even unprofitably in obedience'; should the arguments continue Hugh ought to remain silent.[3]

The only occasion when Hugh or indeed any monk might legitimately defy his abbot was if the prelate's wishes ran counter to the *Rule of St Benedict*. The monk might then seek dispensation from his bishop, archbishop or even the Pope to sanction his opposition. It was not always easy or wise for monks to challenge their abbot's unorthodox ways and as one monk of Bury St Edmunds (Suffolk) concluded, the monk's 'supreme' duty was to remain silent and shut his eyes to the irregularities of his superior. Thus, although the justiciar of England, Ranulph de Glanville, reprimanded the Bury monks for not resisting their abbot when he acted contrary to God's will, they held that it was often wiser and in fact safer to keep quiet, for those who opposed the abbot might end up in chains or even exiled. Hence it was better for monks to die as confessors rather than martyrs.[4] Not everyone was prepared to remain silent. Andrew Gragy, a monk of Balmerino Abbey (Fife), was compelled to seek royal help against his abbot, Robert Forrester (1511–c. 1560), who sought to seize the abbey's lands at Gadvan (Dunbog), which Gragy administered in his capacity as 'master' of Gadvan. James V of Scotland (1513–42) wrote to the Pope on Gragy's behalf, explaining the monk's predicament and concern, since it was dangerous for the brethren to litigate with their superiors. James requested that the Pope free Andrew completely from his abbot's authority and give him a hearing.[5]

LET CONSCIENCE BE YOUR GUIDE

For you will be driven to correct even all your thoughts as if they were open to his gaze and visited by his rebuke, when you consider that he is watching.[6]

Obedience to the abbot, to the *Rule of St Benedict* and the monastic way of life was ideally to be self-motivated and the monk was to be judge of his own actions. William of St Thierry (d. 1148) compiled a list of recommendations advising novices on how best to lead an observant and disciplined life. Every morning the novice was to take account of the night and draw up an agenda for the day, while each evening he was to reflect on the day that had passed and lay down a rule for the night ahead. Crucially, he was to blind himself to worldly matters and remain focused on himself. The novice was advised to draw up a timetable and allocate spiritual and bodily exercises to each hour, paying particular attention to the morning hours when he was free of external concerns, and the evening hours when the day's tasks had been finished and there was little to hinder him from his devotions. At these times he was to stand before God and see clearly the reasons for joy and sorrow in what he had done and feel true repentance for his sins.[7]

Through self-awareness the monk would experience genuine remorse, leading him to confess his wrongs and seek absolution. This was critical since it was only through confession and contrition that the brethren could be truly pardoned and progress on their spiritual path. Anyone who failed to confess his sins was accused by his brethren in Chapter so that he could then atone for his wrongs. But having concealed his sins the monk was guilty of a second and often more serious crime for which he had also to make amends. The importance of confession is made clear in an example relating to a monk of Winchcombe Abbey (Gloucestershire), who had committed the sin of fornication on the eve of the Feast of St Kenelm (16 July). This was a grave offence at any time but particularly heinous before an important feast, when it was vital that the brethren had been absolved of any wrongs and were clean and chaste for the celebration. Had the monk simply confessed he would have been duly punished and pardoned in time for the feast. As he concealed his crime and, worse, presumed to carry the Psalter of Quendrada, Kenelm's sister, in the procession, his guilt was revealed, for the Psalter stuck onto the monk's hand and was only released when he admitted to his offence.[8] A twelfth-century nun of Sempringham who did not reveal her culpability in starting a fire at the house similarly received her comeuppance and was forced into confession. The accident occurred one evening when the nun was walking though the convent kitchen. When she tried to light a second candle from the one she was carrying, she caused it to fall onto the ground, where it set light to straw that had been gathered for the following day. The

Monk receiving the tonsure, British Library, Cotton Cleopatra, C. XI, f. 27v.

nun, however, was not concerned for she believed the fire would simply burn itself out and gave the matter little thought. Alas, she was gravely mistaken – the candle started a great conflagration which caused considerable damage to the monastery. The next day the master of the Order questioned the community to discover the cause of the incident but the nun remained silent and said nothing of her culpability; in doing so she doubled her offence, for it was one thing to have accidentally started a fire but quite another to deliberately conceal her fault.

The nun duly received her just deserts. She was struck with a severe pain that she attributed to her guilt and was compelled to confess and seek absolution.[9]

These stories and others like them were intended to remind monks and nuns of the importance of confession and admitting their sins. It was acknowledged that nobody was infallible and anyone could make a mistake, but to deliberately conceal one's errors was deemed reprehensible and would be severely punished. William of St Thierry (d. c. 1148) underlined the importance of this when he urged monks to show their 'ulcer' to the doctor (their abbot) and hide nothing from him so that they might be healed.[10] The brethren could confess either at the daily chapter meeting that was attended by the entire community or privately to their abbot or a senior priest of the house. Private confession was generally conducted in the cloister or in the chapter house, after the others had left. A compassionate abbot, who was a good listener, could greatly help the brethren unburden themselves. But the abbot might also find this a humbling and even moving experience. Abbot Guibert of Nogent (d. 1124) described how the candour of his monks, who 'opened their hearts' to him at confession, brought him closer to them than any others he had known.[11] While the monks were encouraged to confess regularly so that they could be absolved, they were advised to be concise. Confession was not an excuse for conversation. In 1440 the Carthusian monks of Hull Priory (Yorkshire) were reprimanded for making overly wordy confessions; they were reminded to be more succinct and avoid 'wives' tales'.[12]

It was vital that the monk accepted his punishment gracefully and sought to amend rather than defend his ways and resist correction. This is clearly underlined in Archbishop Lanfranc's (d. 1089) constitutions that were implemented at Christ Church, Canterbury, and elsewhere in England. They stipulate that serious action should be taken against any monk who sought to justify his wrongs or answered his abbot or prior in a rebellious way. In the first instance force was used against these miscreants. The rebel was seized violently by several of the brethren and either carried or dragged to the prison, where he was punished appropriately in the hope that this would cause him to rescind and accept his guilt. Such being the case, the community was notified at the chapter meeting and the offender brought before them to receive punishment for his original crime. Depending on the severity of his conduct the offender appeared either clothed in his habit or barefoot and stripped from the waist up, 'like a fugitive monk'. If the offender refused to atone and remained 'full of diabolical pride', spiritual aid was employed and the entire community prayed for their brother; if the abbot believed there was no hope for correction he might elect to keep the monk in confinement or in the last resort could expel him from the monastery.[13]

SUPPORT FROM WITHIN

I know the malicious jealousy of the devil who is grinding his teeth, wasting away with envy at the thought that you are escaping from his hands, nay rather from his jaws. So I am certain he will attempt to deceive you in countless ways, by showing you either the hardship of the service of God which you have chosen or the delights of serving himself through love of the world which you have relinquished . . . By God's Grace I hope I can guard you against all his sly tricks – which abound in fallacy and folly.[14]

A knight who entered the Cistercian abbey of Clairvaux (Langres) was progressing well in the monastic life when suddenly he became half-hearted in his devotion and was disruptive in the cloister. The abbot blamed himself for the novice's behaviour, regarding himself as a poor shepherd who had allowed the wolf to carry off the sheep when he should have offered protection from the devil's wiles. He spoke to the novice, hoping to steer him back onto the path to salvation through 'soothing, cherishing and caressing'. The abbot faced little resistance, for the novice readily confessed his sins and showed remorse for his behaviour but felt unworthy of remaining in the monastery and contemplated leaving. The abbot, however, convinced him to stay by offering to take responsibility for the novice's wrongs, and he was duly rewarded for his actions. This was revealed to the novice in a vision in which he entered heaven and saw not one but two couches awaiting his abbot who, like Christ, had laid down his life for his flock.[15]

Monks often needed help and support to resist temptation and adhere to the rules of the Order. It was ultimately the abbot's responsibility to shield his flock from the devil and help them stand strong against his wiles. The abbot therefore combined the roles of protector, father and disciplinarian. He was a figure of authority but also someone from whom the monks could receive help and support. Abbot Richard of Fountains (1139–43) was known for his skill in comforting the sad and 'finding out the hidden causes of the sickness of a conscience'.[16] Other members of the community might similarly encourage and regale their companions, and help them resist evil. A nun of La Ramée (Belgium), 'in grip of a certain vice', sought spiritual direction from her companion, Ida, who was prone to fits of ecstasy and considered by the sisters to have special insight. Ida's advice enabled the nun to overcome her wickedness and progress, once more, on the path to salvation. Monks of the Cistercian abbey of Himmerod (Germany) who were disruptive and antagonistic towards the others were counselled by Walter Birbech, the guestmaster of the house, who was a former knight. Walter showed empathy to these troubled brethren and shared with them his own fears and failings and the difficulties he experienced in resisting temptation.[17] This was particularly important, for it was crucial that the monks realized they were not alone in their struggle and that they, like others, could overcome the battle against evil.

Newcomers were especially vulnerable to doubts and temptations, which were regarded as tricks of the devil. They were forewarned of this by their abbot, novice-master or mentor so that they would be on guard and prepared for resist-ance. Anselm, abbot of Bec and archbishop of Canterbury (d. 1109), outlined to novices the various ruses and temptations the devil was wont to employ to lure them away from the cloister. In doing so he sheds light on the kinds of doubts and anxieties that commonly afflicted monks and the general restlessness newcomers invariably felt upon entering the cloister. Anselm explained that the devil would likely cause the novice to remember the delights he had once enjoyed but would no longer experience, to question if he would be able to suffer the rigorous demands of the cloister for the rest of his life and whether this decision had been a flippant one. He might prompt the novice to think he could lead a religious life in the world and did not actually need to remain in the monastery. But the devil was a master of subtlety who employed many ruses and he might instead encourage the novice to believe the monastic life was after all the best choice and that any sins he committed were natural and inevitable in the young and would be cancelled out by virtue of his monastic status. Anselm thus urged novices and in fact all members of the community to be vigilant and resist any feelings of restlessness or discontent, especially at the start of their vocation.[18]

It was crucial that each monastery established an efficient support system to provide monks with the help and nurturing they required to withstand evil and adhere to the rules of the Order. Discipline was also maintained through surveillance. Most houses assigned senior members of the community to carry out regular checks around the monastery and report any incidents of wrongdoing.

These officials or 'roundsmen' (*explorators*) generally conducted their inspections at regular intervals and followed a fixed route, but random checks were also carried out and would have been an effective deterrent, limiting the opportunity for misconduct.[19] At Abingdon Abbey (Berkshire), the prior and sub-priors of the house were chiefly responsible for carrying out these inspections. After Compline, which was the last Office of the day, the prior remained behind to watch the monks leaving the choir and make sure everyone was present and had his hood up. Thereafter he conducted his rounds of the monastery, beginning in the guest parlour on the western range and working his way around the church and adjoining buildings, completing a circuit of the abbey. The prior checked to make sure that everybody was where he ought to be and acting appropriately, but also that doors were locked and the monastery was safe and secure for the night. In some houses a thorough search of the dormitory and toilet block was made before Matins by a responsible member of the community to check that no monk was still asleep in the dormitory or had dozed off on the privy.[20]

These roundsmen were the eyes and ears of the convent and might eavesdrop on conversation while they were patrolling the monastery. In Victorine houses the roundsmen were seemingly on constant duty, although no checks were made during the chapter meeting or at Collations, when the cloister door was locked. The roundsmen were warned to walk slowly, solemnly and in silence when conducting their checks and must have been a formidable presence. They were not, however, permitted to speak but gestured to offenders, although they might stamp their feet to rouse sleeping monks or elbow them in the ribs. The roundsmen had no power to admonish the reprobate and were simply to report the crime and leave it to the abbot or prior to pass judgement. It was vital that those who were appointed as roundsmen were models of discretion and would act fairly and justly when carrying out their duties. Hence nobody was to report anyone out of malice or personal spite, or close their eyes to the misconduct of a friend.[21]

FEAR AND COMPASSION

In order to mould his leaf into a suitable form the goldsmith now presses it, and strikes it gently with his tool, and now even more gently raises it with careful pressure and gives it shape. So, if you want your boys to be adorned with good habits, you too, besides the pressures of blows, must apply the

*encouragement and help of fatherly sympathy and gentleness. . . . The
weak soul which is still inexperienced in the service of God, needs milk –
gentleness from others, kindness, compassion, cheerful encouragement, loving
forbearance and much else of the same kind.*[22]

The abbot had a difficult role, for he was to enforce obedience and command
respect from the brethren yet show compassion to and love for his flock.
Attitudes towards punishment varied considerably. While some favoured a harsh
approach and reprimanded offenders severely as a deterrent to their companions,
others were gentler in their correction. Gilbert of Sempringham (d. 1189),
founder and master of the English Order of Sempringham (Gilbertines), found
a middle way. He would initially deal harshly with miscreants both to test them
and discourage others, but once he was sure that the offender's remorse was
sincere Gilbert would show forgiveness and compassion, and weep with the
repentant.[23] Anselm of Canterbury (d. 1109) was a fervent proponent of the
gentle approach and felt that true victory was achieved only when the monk
felt guilt and remorse; it was therefore essential to incite self-reproach if future
misconduct was to be avoided. This attitude was in keeping with the spirit of the
Rule of St Benedict, which compared the abbot to a physician who should in the
first instance apply 'soothing lotions, ointments of admonitions, medicaments
of the Holy Scriptures'. Should this fail he might resort to 'the blows of the lash'
or even excommunication, but if this too was ineffective a stronger medicine was
required and the abbot and brethren should pray so that God might Himself
heal the brother. If, and only if, all these methods failed the miscreant was sent
away from the community, lest he infect the entire flock.[24] Anselm's treatment of
Henry, the cellarer of St Neots, which was a dependency of Bec in England, shows
how he implemented his beliefs. Anselm, who was at this time prior of Bec and
thus Henry's superior, was devastated when he heard ill reports of the cellarer's
conduct in England – Henry had allegedly taken to drinking in the local taverns
and was accused of using foul language. Anselm responded with grief rather than
anger and offered Henry the opportunity to mend his own ways. Thus he simply
prohibited Henry from going into taverns and drinking until he was drunk but
warned the cellarer that if he did not then reform his ways he would have to do
penance according to the judgement of the archbishop of Canterbury, the bishop
of Rochester or the monks of St Neots. If Henry actually refused to alter his ways
he was to leave England and return to Anselm at Bec, where he could be guided
by their discipline rather than be 'irretrievably lost'.[25]

Anselm advised other prelates to take a similar approach. He urged that they temper the blows with encouragement and compassion and, like a goldsmith, apply gentle pressure when moulding the leaves into beautiful figures. He insisted that extreme measures should only be taken when truly deserved. He begged Anthony, the sub-prior of Christ Church, Canterbury, to be less severe in his punishment of offences and urged him not to treat minor lapses as grave offences, as he was wont to do, or to act on hearsay. Severe punishment should be reserved for crimes that were in violation of the *Rule*. Anselm warned Anthony that harshness could actually have adverse effects on monastic discipline, fostering resentment and rearing unruly beasts. If the superior was to command respect and love, and encourage the brethren to correct themselves 'without any feeling of shame', it was imperative that he disciplined them justly and fairly.[26]

ENFORCING DISCIPLINE

We who are in this vale of tears have to weep. And because we sin every day,
we need daily penance.[27]

It was clearly impossible to prevent all acts of misconduct, but if the monk was to progress unfettered on his spiritual journey it was vital that severe crimes and also minor indiscretions were punished. Disciplinary matters were dealt with at the daily chapter meeting, which was attended by all the monks and presided over by the abbot or prior. Each monk was invited to step forward and confess his wrongs before the entire community. He prostrated himself on the ground, asked forgiveness and awaited judgement. Anyone who did not voluntarily confess was likely to be 'accused' by another so that he could then be punished and freed of his sins. It was essential that any accusations were based on real evidence rather than on hearsay or suspicion. The accused had several options. He might deny all allegations and proclaim his innocence, explain he had no recollection of the offence or acknowledge his guilt and await his fate. The monks were reminded that they were not to bear any grudge against their accuser, who was acting out of compassion and like 'the razor of God' sought to remove their 'unsightly hair' so that they would appear 'more pleasing in the presence of God in the light of the living'.[28]

As the head of the community and the figure of authority it was the abbot's task to judge how each offender should be punished and deliver his verdict to the whole Chapter. The nature of the punishment depended upon the severity of the crime but was usually a beating, fasting or exclusion from communal activities. For example, the miscreant might have to eat by himself after the other brethren had dined. Privileges were commonly withheld as a form of punishment and the offender might be prohibited from sending or receiving letters. Any monk who was to be beaten received his punishment at the chapter meeting in front of the entire community, a warning to the others that acts of misconduct would not be tolerated. Either the offender lay on the ground in his shift and was beaten with a stout rod or sat and was thrashed on his bare back with a bundle of fine rods, like a switch. While this was taking place the rest of the community bowed in a show of compassion but were forbidden to speak or make eye contact with the reprobate. At St Augustine's, Canterbury, a thrashing across the bare shoulders of the prostrated monk was appropriately known as 'stripes'. By the later Middle Ages exclusion was a more common form of punishment than beating – the miscreant would sit apart, covering his head and face in his hands, while the rest of the community bowed their heads in a show of compassion, but neither looked at nor spoke to their shamed brother.[29]

Graver crimes, such as violence, sodomy or conspiracy were punished more severely. The offender was flogged in chapter, as for less serious offences, but would likely receive additional beatings. Archbishop Lanfranc's (d. 1089) constitutions for the monks of Christ Church, Canterbury, reveal that after the monk had been beaten he lay down his knife, drew up his hood and was escorted in silence to a locked room where he was guarded by a member of the community who acted as keeper. This was the only monk with whom the offender had contact during his time of punishment. The keeper led the miscreant to and from the church for the Offices and brought him his daily allowance of food and drink. It was the abbot, however, who decided what precisely the offender should receive to eat, but he would be careful that this was not unduly harsh lest starvation pushed him into a state of melancholy. Monk keepers had an onerous task and were liable to be punished if negligent. In the late thirteenth century the monks of Hailes (Gloucestershire) were warned that if any delinquent monk escaped as a result of his keeper's carelessness, the keeper would himself be imprisoned.[30]

Sin was a barrier to communal life and set the monk outside monastic obedience. During his time of penance the offender was physically removed from the community and was often sent to a locked chamber. Many of these were situated within the infirmary complex, where they were well away from the claustral buildings but also because the monks could be shackled to the beds there, which were more substantial than those in the dormitory. In the late eleventh century, a monk of Christ Church, Canterbury, who was possessed by the devil, shocked the community with his violent and abusive behaviour. He was eventually removed to the infirmary and constrained but continued to rage and exhibited almost preternatural strength.[31] In the later Middle Ages the prison at Durham Cathedral Priory was situated beneath the master of the infirmary's chambers; any monk who committed a serious offence might be shackled there alone for a year.[32]

At the Yorkshire nunnery of Esholt miscreants were incarcerated in a room within the nuns' dormitory. One sixteenth-century nun of the house who was pregnant was imprisoned here for two years. During this time none of the others were allowed to speak with her unless they had special permission. The nun was forbidden to have fish or dairy products and fasted every Wednesday and Friday on bread and water. On Fridays she was beaten before the entire community in the chapter house.[33] Elsewhere it was common for houses to build special prison cells within the monastery. The prison cells at the Cistercian abbey of Fountains in Yorkshire were seemingly located within the abbot's chambers and were uncovered during excavations in the nineteenth century. Latin graffiti was etched on one of the two cells, which suggests they were used by monks rather than lay brothers, who would not have been literate in Latin. The inmate had written the words *Vale libertas* ('Farewell freedom') on the wall, but unfortunately the writing is no longer visible.[34] Statutes for the Burgundian abbey of Cluny offer some indication of the appearance of these prisons, revealing that they had no windows or doors and were accessed only by a ladder. At Christ Church, Canterbury, and also at Durham, a trapdoor was used to let down food to the inmates via a cord.[35]

Just how long a monk or nun might be incarcerated varied depending on the severity of their crime and how disruptive they were to the rest of the community. But practices varied from house to house. Life imprisonment was not uncommon for serious offences and was preferable to expulsion from the Order. In 1226 a monk of Jouy (France) who sought to kill his abbot with a razor was incarcerated for life.[36] Offenders were visually set apart from their brethren while they were undergoing punishment and were also stigmatized when they rejoined the community. Miscreants entered the church with their hoods drawn, and bowed and knelt while the brethren celebrated the Office. In an act of contrition and humiliation they prostrated themselves at the door of the choir at each of the

Hours, so that the monks would have to climb over them when entering and leaving the church.[37] It was the abbot who decided when precisely the offender might be released from his penance and reconciled with the community. His reintegration was formally marked – the monk stripped and was beaten, and was then received back into the community.

Troublemakers and repeat offenders who were a continual disruption to monastic observance were generally removed temporarily from their monastery and sent to another house of the Order in the hope that this would encourage them to mend their ways. In 1218 a Cistercian monk of Foigny (Laon) who had disputed his abbot's sermons and was regarded as an agitator was sent for a spell to an abbey in the Low Countries.[38] In the fourteenth century an unruly and troublesome monk of Worcester Cathedral Priory was sent to the Benedictine abbey at Gloucester and treated as a novice during this process of reintegration.[39] It was seemingly not uncommon for Carthusian monks to be imprisoned at the mother-house of La Grande Chartreuse, north of Grenoble. But their expenses were met by their own community and also the costs of any damage caused. In 1421 the prior of Beauvale (Nottinghamshire) was ordered to bring home one of his reprobate monks, who had been incarcerated for a year at La Grande Chartreuse and had destroyed several parts of the cell where he had been confined; the prior was either to pay the necessary expenses or finance a new prison.[40] Alnett Hales, a troublesome monk of the London Charterhouse, was sent to five different communities in the sixteenth century. He was first removed to Mount Grace but complained bitterly of the cold at this Yorkshire house and also claimed there was a conspiracy against him. Alnett repeatedly wrote to his own prior asking that he be removed to another house. The prior of Mount Grace was seemingly just as happy to be rid of this nuisance and organized Alnett's transfer to Axholme (Lincolnshire). However, he sent Alnett without bedding or adequate resources and the monks of Axholme considered him a burden on their meagre resources. They also regarded Alnett as dead weight since he was apparently too weak to participate fully in communal observances. The community maintained that they were few in numbers and needed someone who could literally sing in return for his supper. Alnett was subsequently transferred to the charterhouse at Coventry (Warwickshire) and finally to Witham (Somerset), where he remained until the Dissolution.[41]

Those who resisted authority were regarded as troublemakers and were often removed lest they should stir others to rebel. An interesting case concerns Osbern, who was a monk of Christ Church, Canterbury, in the wake of the Norman Conquest and the arrival of the reforming archbishop, Lanfranc (1070–89). Lanfranc dealt severely with resistance from the English monks of Canterbury, adamant that he would stifle any opposition to his reforming policies. He regarded Osbern as a chief antagonist since the monk had vehemently opposed Lanfranc's disregard of the native cults and staunchly defended the English saints. Lanfranc subsequently made plans for Osbern's removal to the Norman abbey of Bec. Osbern was not a troublemaker as such, but a passionate defender of the English saints and at Bec he flourished under the guidance of Prior Anselm, who recognized the monk's potential and nurtured his gifts for music and writing. A close friendship developed between the two and when Osbern was ready to return to Canterbury Anselm begged Prior Henry not to crush Osbern through harshness but nourish and guide him through kindness.[42] It was not unusual for offenders to be sent to an affiliated house overseas. This was particularly common amongst the Cistercians, whose abbeys were closely linked within a familial network. In 1228 Abbot Stephen of Lexington, who had been conducting a visitation of the houses in Ireland, wrote to a number of abbots on the mainland asking that they host certain Irish monks who had repented of their wrongdoings but had yet to complete their penance for these crimes. The Yorkshire abbey of Fountains received four of these rebels, who were to stay for two years until their penance was completed. One of the miscreants was Malachy, the former abbot of Baltinglass (Co. Wicklow). Malachy's spell at Fountains seemingly had little long-term benefit, for he was later denounced by Abbot Stephen as 'that perverse and wily fox' and noted for his malice at the General Chapters of 1231 and 1233.[43]

It was generally the offender's own community that was responsible for meeting his expenses while he was staying at another house. In fourteenth-century England this might amount to some six or seven pence a week. Keldholme Priory (Yorkshire), for example, paid the weekly sum of sixpence to Esholt for the upkeep of their nun, Emma of Newcastle, who had been sent there to mend her ways.[44] The miscreant remained answerable to his or her own superior regardless of where he or she was staying, and reports were regularly sent back to their home community with details of their progress and any other matters of importance such as ill health. Good behaviour was often rewarded and those who reformed their ways might be allowed to return early to their own monastery. It was for the abbot or abbess to decide if and when troublemakers should be sent away, but occasionally they faced resistance. A striking case of local hostility occurred in Yorkshire in 1314 when plans were made to transfer two nuns of Swine Priory, Joan Sutton and Juliane Wellenwyke, to Nun Appleton Priory and Rosedale Priory respectively. Both women were well known within the local community and when news of their removal was leaked to the townsfolk an armed mob descended on the priory, threatening violence if the nuns were not allowed to stay. They successfully sabotaged the transfer by picketing the roads and disabling the carts that had been prepared for the nuns' removal, which was seemingly then aborted.[45]

EXTERNAL CONTROL

Discipline is never pleasant, at the time it seems painful but later, for those trained by it, it yields a harvest of peace and goodness. (Hebrews 12.11)[46]

While the abbot or abbess had supreme authority within the monastery, external checks were periodically conducted to assess the state of monastic observance. Delegates or 'visitors' were sent from the diocese or Order to carry out routine inspections, correcting abuses but also offering support and advice. Most houses would expect a visitation from their archbishop, bishop, archdeacon or his deputy, who would leave a set of statutes or injunctions to be implemented following his stay. Some houses were exempt from diocesan authority and were either visited by a representative of the Order or a papal delegate. All Cistercian abbeys were exempt from episcopal visitation and inspections were carried out internally by the Father Immediate of the house, namely the abbot of the house from which the monastery had been founded. He was expected to visit each daughter-house once a year and reprimand the community if necessary but, importantly, offer advice and encouragement. The survival of a number of statutes issued following the visitation of the religious houses, particularly from the later Middle Ages, sheds light on monastic discipline and the nature of wrongs committed by communities. However, it is important to remember that these were reforming documents intended to record abuses and as such give a one-sided perspective of monastic observance.

The register of Hailes Abbey (Gloucestershire), compiled in the fifteenth century, includes a list of questions that the Cistercian reformer should ask

when conducting his visitation and offers an indication of the kinds of abuses
they were intent to correct. The visitor was to check for evidence of backbiting
and conspiracies against the abbot, incidents of disruption to claustral life and
crimes committed by the brethren, especially sodomy but also sorcery or other
'superstitious arts'. Offences of this nature were not exceptional and a monk of
Fountains Abbey who was sentenced to do penance for soothsaying had to wear
a paper scroll on his head with the words 'Behold the soothsayer' (*Ecce sortilegus*);
papers inscribed with the words 'Invoker of spirits' and 'Soothsayer' were fastened
to his chest and back so that his guilt would be known to everyone.[47] The Hailes
register stipulates that the visitor should check that no promotions or ordinations
had been secured unjustly and assess the general state of monastic observance
and the efficient running of the house. He was to make sure, for example, that
the Divine Office was celebrated day and night in both the church and infirmary,
that the brethren observed religious customs regarding dress, silence and the
exclusion of women from the cloister, and that no monk hunted or kept hawks
or falcons in the cloister. The visitor was also to ensure that the brethren were
fulfilling their obligations to the poor and distributing the customary alms,
and, importantly, that they sent the required payments to the mother-house of
Cîteaux in Burgundy.[48]

   These visitations were also an important check on the abbot or abbess, to make
sure that they were behaving appropriately and presiding honourably over the
community. The visitor generally questioned each monk individually to find out
if the abbot was ruling justly, namely that punishment was meted out fairly and
in accordance with the severity of the crime, and that there were no instances of
bribery or favouritism or of inappropriate behaviour. When the bishop of Lincoln
visited Catesby Priory in 1444 the nuns were forthcoming about the indiscretions
of their prioress. The treasuress was particularly vocal and claimed that their
superior was incompetent and careless but also reprehensible – she alleged
that the prioress had pawned the priory's jewels, engaged in several liaisons
and was prone to angry outbursts.[49] Where there was evidence of misconduct
or negligence, the superior was liable to be deprived of office or encouraged to
resign. Abbot John of Wymondham Priory (Norfolk) was persuaded to step
down from office following the visitation of the house in 1492, for the visitor
found the buildings in a disgraceful state and scarcely a semblance of monastic
devotion. John's successor did little to improve matters and seemingly caused
even greater consternation with his violent behaviour – it was alleged that he

threatened two of the brethren with a brandished sword, destroyed musical instruments and was subsequently deposed on account of lunacy. The monks of Tautra Abbey in Norway suffered severely under the mismanagement and violence of Abbot Matthias, who was finally deposed in 1532. It was reputed that Matthias hit some of the brethren in church, causing blood to pour from their noses and mouths and stain the books. This was not apparently an isolated incident and the monks maintained that their abbot used foul language at table and called them Lutherans, heretics and traitors to God.[50]

Any monks or nuns who had been unfairly treated or believed themselves to be victims of injustice could report this at visitation and initiate a case against their superior. In 1447, William Elmeley, a monk of Hailes (Gloucestershire), claimed that the abbot and convent had imprisoned him as an evil-doer without good reason and after he had spent many years living devoutly at the house. A papal mandate was subsequently issued to investigate William's claims and if they were true the monk was to be restored to the community.[51] Some, however, used visitation as an opportunity to fuel a vendetta and deliberately undermine an individual or group within the monastery. Such was the case at Norwich Cathedral Priory in the later Middle Ages, when two rival factions made allegations against each other to the visitor. A group of monks who opposed their precentor, John Sall, sought to defame him and perhaps hoped to secure his deposition by suggesting that he may have dabbled in the black arts.[52] Visitors therefore had to treat claims of this kind with caution lest they were exaggerations or even fabrications intended to indict an individual or settle a score. Accordingly, these colourful and even racy allegations are not necessarily a true reflection of monastic observance.

Not everyone was forthcoming at visitation. Some, whether through loyalty or fear, protected their superiors and revealed nothing of their indiscretions to the visitor. Jocelin of Brakelond (fl. 1200), a monk of Bury St Edmunds (Suffolk), recalls that as a novice he had once asked his master why their prior had covered up for Abbot Hugh (1157–80) when interrogated by the papal legate. The novice-master explained that silence was often wisest, since others who had spoken out against their abbot had been imprisoned or exiled.[53] In some cases the community was threatened into submission. A fifteenth-century prioress of Catesby Priory (Northamptonshire) allegedly whipped anyone who betrayed her to the visitor and threatened imprisonment for any nun who intended to do so. These threats were evidently not heeded and a lengthy list of accusations was compiled against her during the course of visitation; she was accused of negligence, promiscuity and even violence and reputedly was wont to hurl abuse at the nuns and pull their hair.[54]

The nature of misdemeanours committed by the monks, whether minor transgressions or grave offences, is considered further in the following chapter.

If the devil tempted the first man in Paradise, if he presumed to tempt Christ in the desert, what man is there in the world that he will leave untempted?[1]

7

Crimes and Misdemeanours

A thirteenth-century guide for monks walks the reader through the various temptations associated with each of the five senses. Sins related to sight include taking delight in fine clothes, jewels and material goods, watching players and spectacles, and looking at women and other things that inflame desire. Deriving pleasure from rich sauces and spices or showing revulsion at bad odours, including the infirm, are examples of sins connected to smell.[2] The guide sought to incite its monk readers to examine their lives and avoid falling into error, for although the monastery cocooned the brethren from worldly affairs a number of temptations faced the monk in the cloister. This section looks more closely at the types of sins monks committed, from the minor infringements that were regarded as 'light' crimes to those of a more serious nature, for instance bloodshed, violence and disregard for the core vows of chastity and stability.

MINOR TRANSGRESSIONS

No monk was infallible and it was recognized that everyone would at some point commit a minor transgression, whether this was laziness, a breach of silence or simply making a noise while eating. Lateness was a common offence and one that had to be atoned for, even if the offender was only a little delayed. Thus any monk who was late for the Office could not simply slip into the choir and take his place with the brethren but had to make satisfaction for his tardiness. The latecomer would generally have to lower his hood upon entering the choir as a sign of his penitence and make a deep bow to the altar, remaining until the signal was given to rise and return to his stall. Even here the offender was marked out and was to sit if the community was standing and vice versa. Anyone who had not arrived before the end of the first psalm was forbidden to enter the choir. He celebrated Matins or Lauds alone in front of the crucifix and was reprimanded for his tardiness at the chapter meeting.[3]

It was often a reluctance to leave their beds that was the cause of monks' lateness. Following his visitation of Heynings Priory (Lincolnshire), Bishop William Alnwick of Lincoln (1436–49) noted that several of the nuns preferred their beds to the church and were sometimes late to the Night Office of Vigils. In the fifteenth century, the Benedictine monks of Bardney Abbey (Lincolnshire) frequently missed Vigils altogether, for they were wont to stay up at night drinking and playing dice.[4] Latecomers might have a valid reason for their delay. Monastic officials (obedientiaries) were generally excused from some of the Offices if necessarily detained by their duties. At times this privilege was exploited and used as a pretext for absence. In 1234 monastic officials at Bury St Edmunds were reminded that they should not miss the Hours unless necessarily detained by their duties. Senior officials were to attend Matins, Vespers and great Masses unless waylaid by important business, while minor officials were to be present at all of the regular Hours. In the sixteenth century, senior monks of Norwich were reprimanded for taking advantage of their status to skip the early morning Office. This had evidently caused dissension among the junior members of the community who enjoyed no such perk.[5]

The confinement of the cloister could prove difficult to withstand. For some the rejection of worldly delights was too much and they might be tempted to drink and play dice with each other or even their guests within the monastery. Others sought pleasure beyond the precinct and broke free from the cloister in search of fun. A lively example concerns a Cistercian abbey in Wales that unwittingly entertained the king, Henry II (1154–89), who arrived here incognito when he was separated from the royal hunting party. Gerald of Wales, who recounts and likely embellishes the alleged encounter, describes how the king was welcomed warmly by the monks, who were oblivious to their guest's true identity. Had they known their visitor was in fact the king of England they may have behaved in a more decorous fashion to impress such a distinguished guest. But, blissfully unaware that they had royalty in their midst, the monks entertained their visitor to a late-night drinking session, carousing and toasting each other until early the next morning.[6] The king may well have enjoyed his stay – and given Henry's penchant for a party he no doubt had a ball – but this was hardly appropriate conduct for the cloister and was a flagrant breach of the *Rule of St Benedict*, for while monks were expected to be hospitable they were hardly to use this as an excuse for indulgence and decadence. Gerald's account is not entirely trustworthy, for he was a harsh critic of the Cistercians and an acerbic raconteur. Nevertheless,

Nun and friar dancing, 14th c, British Library, Stowe 17, f. 38.

behaviour of this kind was not unknown. It was alleged in the fifteenth century that the nuns of Heynings Priory enjoyed late-night drinking sessions in the priory's guest chamber, particularly when visitors were staying, while the monks of Norwich liked to dance in their guest hall and were wont to frolic through the night until Nones the following day.[7]

In pursuit of fun and frivolity the monks might venture outside the cloister to the local tavern. The abbot and monks of Hailes Abbey (Gloucestershire) were evidently guilty of such misconduct in the mid-fifteenth century and were warned that no member of the community should in future frequent taverns unless he was obliged to go there with a guest.[8] It was clearly acceptable at this time for monks to visit taverns in the name of hospitality and also if the quality of monastery ale was so bad that it drove them out in search of a better brew. It was thus the abbot's responsibility to make sure he provided quality ale for the brethren and thereby gave them no reason to patronize the local tavern.[9]

Nuns were subject to more severe restrictions regarding enclosure, but this did not always prevent them from venturing outside the precinct in search of light relief. One such fun-loving rebel was Isobel Benet, who was treasuress of Catesby Priory (Northamptonshire) in the mid-fifteenth century. It was reported that one night Isobel slipped away from the priory into the town, where she spent the evening singing, dancing and playing the lute with Augustinian friars. Having relished her taste of freedom, Isobel made a similar excursion the following night, but this time partied with the Friars Preachers at Northampton.[10]

DISHARMONY AND DIVISION

Every kingdom divided against itself shall be brought to desolation.
(Matthew 12.25)

In 1199 a serious rift developed between Abbot Samson of Bury St Edmunds and the monks of the house over the treatment of their gatekeeper, Ralph. The argument caused disunity and discordance within the community but also threatened to damage the monastery's reputation within the town. Trouble began when the prior and senior monks of Bury claimed that Ralph was seeking lawsuits against them and argued that his wages be withheld as punishment. Samson, however, took the gatekeeper's part and reprimanded the monks for their actions. The resulting furore was unprecedented, with both parties angry and incensed. Samson imprisoned and excommunicated the ringleaders but withdrew from the community and refused to associate with the brethren lest he hit out against them in anger. Meanwhile, rumours circulated among the townsfolk that the irate monks intended to stab their abbot. The opposing sides were eventually reconciled in a tearful reunion and exchanged the Kiss of Peace, but as far as Samson was concerned this was a matter of forgiveness rather than compromise and he was not willing to rescind on the matter of Ralph. The younger monks once again retaliated but this time the senior members of the community accepted Samson's proposals, believing they should suffer disgrace for the sake of peace. Samson duly got his way; the monks' resistance had been in vain.[11]

Samson of Bury was short-tempered and no doubt a number who entered the cloister were of a similar nature and easily roused to anger. In his capacity as abbot, Samson could withdraw from the monastery until his rage had subsided, using removal as a form of anger management. This was not an option for most monks, who were forbidden to leave the monastery and could not therefore escape the source of provocation. The cloister must at times have been a hothouse of emotions, causing some to snap under the pressure. This perhaps explains the rather extreme reaction of William Downom, a monk of Fountains, who seemingly attempted to poison his abbot, John Greenwell (1442–71), when he refused to eat the pottage William had prepared for him. A London physician was summoned to tend the sick abbot, who fortunately recovered. Following a lengthy enquiry William was expelled from Fountains.[12]

The monks might receive support and counselling from within the community to help them control their emotions and avoid angry outbursts. However, it was important that the brethren exercised self-restraint and controlled their rage. An effective way to encourage this was to punish such outbursts severely and recount stories or *moralia* describing the fate of those who succumbed to their emotions. One such tale concerns a Gilbertine nun of Catley Priory (Lincolnshire), seemingly the infirmaress of the house, who was roused to such anger against one of her sisters that she invoked the devil as she left the infirmary. The nun was immediately struck on the head by a heavy weight and fell to the ground, paralysed. She would have been taken for dead had not the tip of her nose remained pink. While suffering in this state of paralysis the nun had a vision in which she saw the founder of the Order, Gilbert of Sempringham, who rejected her since she had forsaken the discipline of the Order and entrusted herself to the devil. It was only after St Clement intervened and roused the nun to contrition that Gilbert absolved her and she regained her speech and the use of her limbs. Those who heard of the nun's fate were reminded that they should not be easily angered or curse their neighbours but be mindful of their vows and vigilant against the devil's snares.[13]

Violent outbursts might be seen as demonic possession or a sign of sickness. A particularly poignant example concerns the Yorkshire abbey of Rievaulx, where the elderly and infirm abbot, Aelred (1147–67), was viciously attacked by a member of the community. A contemporary account vividly describes how the feeble abbot was sitting hunched over an old mat by the fire, rubbing his limbs, when the perpetrator, 'a bovine creature of criminal aspect, moving in the vilest disorder', raged into the room and hurled abuse at the sickly abbot, whom he then threw into the fire. Yet Aelred held no rancour and embraced his attacker, whom he regarded as ill.[14] Occasionally violence resulted in bloodshed or even murder. In the late fourteenth century there was an assassination attempt at the Cistercian mother-house of Cîteaux (Burgundy) when Peter of Castellione, the former abbot of Pontifroid (Metz), sought to murder the abbots of Cîteaux and Morimund. The perpetrator horrified bystanders when he drew out a sword from beneath his habit and wounded Abbot James of Cîteaux in the face, but fortunately nobody was killed. Peter was imprisoned for the rest of his life and sentenced 'to eat the bread of sorrow and drink the water of affliction'.[15] The Scottish abbey of Kinloss was the scene of a murder in the late fifteenth century when William Butter, a monk of the house, flew into a rage and struck a boy dead in the cloister. William was subsequently sent to Rome to obtain letters of absolution from the Papacy which were duly sent to the abbot of Kinloss, but neither William nor his monk companion returned to the abbey. A serious rebellion in Norway in the mid-thirteenth century resulted in the deaths of the abbot of Hovedøya and several senior officials of the house. The monks who perpetrated this crime removed their abbot's clothing and beat several members of the community, but then took the prior, sacrist and sub-cantor to a remote island and left them to die.[16]

Violence and murder were clearly regarded as serious crimes and punished accordingly, but disregard for the basic vows of chastity and stability were considered just as heinous.

CHASTITY

Of all the struggles of the Christian the hardest battles are those of chastity,
where the strife is daily and victory rare, and . . . the sliding to ruin is speedy;
nor does there remain any remedy except flight from temptation.[17]

Caesarius of Heisterbach (d. c. 1240) explained to a novice of his monastery how Bernard, a monk of Clairvaux (Langres), was liberated from his feelings of lust. Bernard had been so greatly afflicted with the 'stings of the flesh' that he considered leaving the cloister, but his abbot urged him not to be hasty and to give the matter due consideration. That night Bernard had a vision in which he was approached by a terrifying executioner brandishing a large knife. Bernard feared he would be castrated and immediately woke to find that miraculously, he was no longer tortured by feelings of lust; his battle was over and Bernard was able to remain chaste thereafter. The novice who heard this story was greatly comforted to hear of Bernard's afflictions since he also had experienced feelings of this kind but had been too ashamed to confess them. The novice now realized that he was not alone but fighting a common battle and one that he, like Bernard, might win. Caesarius advised the novice to confess his sins, since no wise confessor would despise him for accusing himself in this way but would offer him comfort in his struggle.[18]

Chastity was one of the three central vows but was difficult both to observe and enforce, particularly as it meant controlling one's thoughts as well as deeds. It was a continual struggle for the brethren to exert mastery over their desires and remain dead to the delights of the world, and especially testing for adolescent members of the community. A number of measures were implemented to help bridle the monks' passions and keep temptation at bay. These included the use of cold baths to quench their lust and the prohibition of meat, since eating this was thought to inflame desire. The monks were also forbidden to watch animals mate lest they were aroused and titillated. As a further precaution, any monk who sinned by touching or being touched by another was warned to confess this only to God or a priest lest a weaker member of the community would be shocked – or perhaps, excited – by what he had heard.[19] The struggle to suppress such feelings could cause considerable stress and fear, and drive some to take extreme measures. John Homersley (d. 1450), a pious monk of the Carthusian charterhouse in London, was on one occasion so severely afflicted with feelings of lust that he harmed himself physically, hoping that 'the wounds of the flesh might heal the wounds of the mind'.[20] The devil mounted two vicious and relentless attacks on Hugh of Lincoln's (d. 1200) chastity. The first occurred shortly after Hugh entered the Carthusian monastery of La Grande Chartreuse and the second on the eve of his promotion to Witham Priory (Somerset) in 1179 when the forty-year-old Hugh was advanced in the monastic life and exercised considerable control over his mind and body. This second attack therefore took Hugh quite unawares. On both occasions the devil inflamed Hugh's passions so severely that he feared for his salvation and battled to suppress his passions. During the second assault Hugh had a vision of his former prior, Basil, who seemed to cut open his bowels and remove red hot cinders. This extinguished the burning passions in Hugh's loins, leaving him restored and at peace. Thereafter he was rarely troubled by any stirrings and those he felt were insignificant and easily ignored.[21]

THE TEMPTATION OF EVE

We absolutely forbid women to enter our bounds, knowing that neither the Sage nor the Prophet nor the Judge nor the Host of God, nor even the first man formed by the hands of God were able to escape the caresses and ruses of women . . . it is not possible for a man to hide a fire in his breast or walk on hot coals without burning the soles of his feet, or touch pitch without getting stuck.[22]

Hugh of Lincoln's experience in 1179 made him immune to the longings of the flesh and set him apart from his brethren. Accordingly, when Hugh was elevated to the See of Lincoln in 1186 he, unlike others, could safely entertain matrons at his table. Few, however, were like Hugh and for most monks it was essential that contact with women was avoided if they were to bridle their passions and observe chastity. The Carthusians took a particularly rigid stance over the admittance of women and forbade them to enter their precincts, given that no man since Adam had been able to resist their 'caresses and ruses'. But even where the prohibition of women was enforced the brethren might be tempted with thoughts or visions of beautiful females. Abundus, a novice at the Belgian monastery of Villers-en-Brabant, was on many occasions tormented by the devil, who appeared to him in the form of an attractive naked woman, goading him with 'forward words'. Abundus, however, remained steadfast and, making the sign of the Cross, put the demon to flight.[23]

Some communities were more open to female visitors than others and attitudes varied over time as well as from house to house. But their admission was generally subject to strict controls to keep distraction out of the cloister and temptation at bay. Women were not usually permitted to stay the night within the confines of the monastery in case this led to dangerous liaisons; nor were they allowed to enter private chambers. All meetings with the brethren were to take place in the open and with witnesses, to ensure that nothing untoward occurred and, crucially, to prevent any rumours arising. In 1234 the monks of Bury St Edmunds were warned that no member of the community should meet with female relatives or strangers in any concealed place and were forbidden to speak with nuns or female recluses lest this provoked scandal. All meetings had to take place within the precinct of the cemetery and were to be witnessed.[24] Regardless of what rules and restrictions were imposed, illicit encounters occurred and there are various colourful examples of frolics in the cloister, particularly from the later Middle Ages, for which there is more surviving evidence but perhaps also because attitudes were less stringent. In the late fifteenth and early sixteenth centuries the monks of Norwich were reproached for allowing women to walk around their church and chat idly with the monks, and for permitting them to lodge at the monastery and come and go as they pleased. Several of the servants' wives actually lived within the precinct at Norwich, which led to at least one serious case of illicit conduct – the sub-prior of the house was accused of sleeping with the tailor's wife.[25]

By the later Middle Ages there was likely greater opportunity to indulge in illicit soirées, at least for monastic officials who often had their own chambers where they could entertain women in private. To prevent indiscretions of this nature – or suspicions of liaisons – officials were frequently warned to sleep in the dormitory with the other brethren. When rumours circulated around Norwich that the precentor was entertaining women in his private chamber at night he was advised to return to the common dormitory to end these allegations.[26] Others, however, cared little for the opinions of their fellow brethren and openly flaunted their illicit behaviour. According to one monk of Evesham (Worcestershire), Abbot Norreys (1190–1213) welcomed a steady stream of comely women to his private chambers. In the mid-fifteenth century Richard of Coventre, who was abbot of Balmerino in Fife, was accused of keeping a married woman as his mistress and refusing to repent or give her up. Similar allegations were made in 1421 against a neighbouring abbot, John Stelle of Lindores. A papal enquiry was instigated and the abbot was to be deposed if found guilty.[27] Some sought female companionship outside the confines of the cloister. A notable example is Enoch, abbot of the Welsh house of Strata Marcella, who allegedly ran off with a Cistercian nun of Llansanffrae. According to one version of the story, the abbot had enjoyed dalliances with a number of nuns who subsequently became pregnant; he then eloped with one who was beautiful and well-born and lived for many years as a secular before returning to do penance at his mother-house of Whitland (Carmarthenshire).[28] In the late fifteenth century Thomas Bartone, a monk of Bardney Abbey (Lincolnshire), accused a number of his fellow brethren of committing adultery with the local women and denounced one for fornicating with the wife of the abbey's washerman.[29]

If chastity was to be preserved within the cloister and monks were to bridle their passions it was not simply enough to monitor their contact with women but also with each other lest a glance, gesture or mere touch provoked inappropriate thoughts or deeds. It was particularly important to scrutinize behaviour in the dormitory and the various rules enforced there, as discussed in Chapter 4. Extra caution was taken with novices, who were considered more vulnerable to temptation. They were subject to closer scrutiny and were generally forbidden to go alone to the latrine block at night, in case this prompted untoward behaviour. They were instead to waken their master, who escorted them there and back. In some cases a third monk was brought as a witness. This was certainly mandatory at the Burgundian abbey of Cluny in the tenth century when Brother Odo was reprimanded for escorting a young boy to the privy alone. Odo was warned that in future he should always bring another monk as a witness to prevent any suspicions arising.[30] His experience underlines the real fear of sexual encounters within the community, particularly with the younger members of the community.

LUSTY NUNS

Gerald of Wales (d. c. 1223) told the story of a Gilbertine nun who lusted after Master Gilbert, the founder and master of the Order. Gilbert was a rather wizened and emaciated figure and was hardly much of a heart-throb, but he would have been one of the few males the nun encountered in the cloister and an obvious target for her affections. Gilbert, however, had an effective way to cool her passions. He first preached a sermon on the virtue of incontinence and resisting desire, and then whipped off his cloak, revealing his repulsive body to the nun and her fellow sisters. Indeed, Gilbert turned around three times to make sure that everyone could see him in all his splendour. This apparently had the desired effect and quenched any passions the nun may have entertained for the master.[31]

As Brides of Christ it was imperative that nuns upheld their vows of chastity and particularly important given that any indiscretions could lead to pregnancy and injure the reputation of the house. But clearly this was not always easy and nuns might struggle as vehemently as their male counterparts to contain their passions. Various measures were implemented to protect these Brides of Christ. Access both into and out of the precinct was tightly controlled, so that the nuns could not easily engage in illicit affairs with male visitors or venture outside the confines of the convent to indulge their passions. Still, rules were sometimes broken, not infrequently by abbesses, prioress and other office-holders, for whom it was perhaps easier to break free from the confines of the cloister. Nigel Wireker, a twelfth-century monk of Christ Church, Canterbury, wrote a satirical poem on the religious Orders in which he remarked on the curious fact that although the nuns were all called virgin some were barren, others mothers and the most holy, the abbesses, were the likeliest to bear children. Nigel's barbed comments may well have been influenced by the rumour circulating at this time that the abbess of Amesbury (Wiltshire) had given birth to three children.[32]

Double foundations which housed a male and female community within the one precinct implemented strict measures to segregate the men from the women and prevent in-house liaisons. In Gilbertine houses such as Watton Priory in Yorkshire, the nuns' cloister occupied one part of the precinct and the canons' and lay brothers' another. The church was divided into two so that neither side could see the other. In the early days they might, however, hear each other singing, but according to Gerald of Wales (d. c. 1223), Master Gilbert of Sempringham put a stop to this after one nun and canon literally fell in love with each other's voices. Gerald explains that a Gilbertine nun and canon of the house whose voices far surpassed the rest of the community were so captivated by each other's singing that they arranged to meet secretly that night and eloped over the convent walls. When Gilbert heard of their escapade he ruled that from then on the canons alone should sing the Office. As a further precaution the nuns were to cut their hair short and were forbidden to comb it or care for it in any way; moreover, they were not to wear white or coloured veils. Some communication between the two sides was necessary but was closely monitored. Conversation took place at the small window in the window-house while food that was cooked in the nuns' kitchen was passed to the canons through the larger window; here too the canons handed over their dirty laundry, which was washed by the women.[33] As an added deterrent, severe penalties were imposed on members of the Order who engaged in illicit behaviour. Any nun who was caught with a canon or lay brother of the Order was shut up in a cell, where she effectively spent the rest of her life fasting and in prayer. Nevertheless, liaisons occasionally happened. There was a particularly sensational affair in the twelfth century when a nun of the Gilbertine priory of Watton (Yorkshire) fell in love with one of the male members of the community who had been sent to work in the female quarters. The nun soon became pregnant and was duly beaten up by her sisters, who imprisoned her and then forced her to castrate her lover. Events took a more gruesome turn when one of the sisters thrust the severed parts 'befouled with blood' into the fettered nun's mouth. But all was not lost, for Henry Murdac (d. 1153), the former archbishop of York, appeared to the nun in a vision and miraculously restored her purity. Her fetters subsequently fell away, showing that she was now cleansed and truly liberated from her sin.[34]

Visitation records from the later Middle Ages offer a colourful insight into the escapades, antics and secret trysts that took place between nuns and their male admirers. Not infrequently these were clerics and monks, who might legitimately have some contact with women in their capacity as confessors and spiritual guides. Isobel Benet, who as previously mentioned was treasuress of Catesby

Priory (Northamptonshire) in the mid-fifteenth century, allegedly gave birth to a child fathered by the chaplain of Catesby, while a nun of Swine (Yorkshire) was accused of committing incest with a neighbouring monk of Meaux in 1310. Geoffrey of Eston, who was the sheriff of Bulmer and Cleveland, was evidently well known to the local nuns, for in 1310 he was accused of trysts with nuns of Arden and Keldholme.[35] Extreme measures might be implemented to prevent the nuns from venturing out of the cloister or smuggling guests inside and these indicate the lengths to which some might go to enjoy a dalliance or two. In the sixteenth century the prioress of Esholt (Yorkshire) received strict instructions to tighten security in the house, probably a reaction to the recent pregnancy of one of her nuns. The prioress was warned to provide locks and keys for the cloister doors and make sure they were locked each day immediately after the last office of Compline had been celebrated. The door of the dormitory was to be locked at night so that none of the sisters could escape for a secret soirée with any of the locals. As a further precaution secular men were banned from lodging in any room that opened on to the cloister and the community's alehouse was to be removed.[36]

Divine Intervention might ensure that the nuns did not stray and remained chaste. A striking example concerns one nun who was prevented by Christ and Mary from pursuing a dalliance with a clerk. The nun had lusted after the clerk for some time and agreed to meet with him in private after Compline, when the rest of the community had retired for the night. As the nun was guardian of the church it was relatively easy for her to absent herself from the dormitory and claim she had duties to attend. But she found it less easy to leave the church, for at every door the image of Christ on the Cross blocked her exit. Finally, having exhausted her options, the nun yielded and was filled with remorse at the enormity of her crime. She threw herself before the image of the Virgin in the church and asked for pardon. Mary at first turned away from the nun and then delivered her such a blow to the jaw that she reeled to the ground and remained there until the following morning when the others entered the church. The nun duly confessed her wickedness and acknowledged that the severity of her crime required a harsh medicine, since illicit thoughts and intentions were as worthy of censure as misdeeds.[37]

STABILITY: 'SINNING WITH ONE'S FEET'

The workshop in which we perform all these works with diligence is the
enclosure of the monastery and stability in the community.
(Rule of St Benedict, *ch. 4*)

All monks took an oath of stability when they entered the cloister, vowing to remain constant to the monastic life and to stay within the confines of the precinct. The brethren were not therefore allowed to leave the monastery unless they had special permission from their superior, who granted this only in exceptional circumstances. The violation of stability was considered a grave offence, whether this was simply a brief excursion out of the monastery or desertion of the monastic life. The breaking of a core vow was injurious to the offender's spiritual progression but was also potentially damaging to the reputation of the house and Order. When news of Godfrey Darel's flight from his abbey at Rievaulx reached the ears of the archbishop of York, John Romeyn (1286–96), the prelate sent out a search party to retrieve the fugitive, who was causing mayhem in the community and making a mockery of monastic discipline. It was alleged that Godfrey was wandering around the countryside in secular clothes, deceiving the faithful through sorcery and incantations and further, 'rejecting the Church to the injury of his salvation and the scandal of all orthodox Christians'. The archbishop was concerned that the monk should be retrieved as soon as possible before he caused greater damage to the Church.[38]

It was vital to punish fugitives severely and make an example of these key offenders, both to underline the severity of their crime and to deter others from following suit. Hugh of Lincoln, prior of the Carthusian monastery of Witham (Somerset), firmly closed the door to any monk who left the sheepfold of his own accord, since this showed his unsuitability to Carthusian life but more importantly posed a potential danger to the rest of the community and might fuel discontent among the brethren. When two monks of Witham, Alexander of Muchelney and Andrew of Lewes, 'hissed against the Order' and left the priory complaining of the boredom and severity of life, Hugh refused to receive them back. Alexander joined the Cluniacs at Reading Abbey but soon regretted his decision and wished to return to 'the true Paradise', but was refused re-admittance. In 1151 the prior of the Carthusian mother-house at La Grande Chartreuse, near Grenoble, resigned from office when the Pope insisted that he take back dissident monks; he clearly regarded apostasy as anathema to monastic life and was unprepared to compromise his stance.[39]

Desertion was generally punished harshly, but not everyone was as uncompromising as the Carthusians. Both Anselm of Bec and Canterbury (d. 1109) and Aelred of Rievaulx (d. 1167) welcomed back apostates as long as they showed remorse and were prepared to mend their ways. Anselm urged others to act similarly and consider the miscreant's humility rather than the severity of his crime. He maintained that it was most important to inculcate self-remorse, which was the only true solution. When Theudinis, a monk of Conflans Sainte-Honorine (north-west of Paris), illicitly went to the French court and lingered there, ignoring all orders from his prior to return, the monks of Conflans Sainte-Honorine sought advice from Anselm on how best to deal with the miscreant, and whether in fact they should receive back one who had disregarded his vow of stability. Anselm recommended gentleness, hopeful that this would induce self-correction. He urged Prior Maurice to accept the wanderer should he return, but to make clear to him the severity of his crime and the need for remorse. If, however, Theudinis failed to reform his ways, Anselm would himself take matters into hand and chastise the rebel according to the severity of the *Rule*.[40]

The Gilbertine Order, or the Order of Sempringham as it was also known, punished apostates according to the number of days they had been away from the monastery. Runaways who returned within a week were disciplined in chapter for each day of their absence. They received a reduction in food and the offender took the lowest place in the community. Anyone who remained away for more than a week but less than forty days received in addition fifteen disciplines and was excluded from communion for a year. Those who failed to return within the forty-day period were subject to anathema and would never rise above the lowest rank. In Cistercian houses apostates who had been returned to their monastery were beaten every Friday for a year in the chapter house before the entire community and during this period fasted on bread and water. By the late thirteenth century offenders were to eat their meals off the refectory floor while serving their penance and wear whatever dress the abbot decided.[41]

Various reasons might prompt the monk to consider leaving the monastery and while some simply sought a short excursion away to enjoy the delights beyond the cloister, others considered the monastic way overly harsh and wished to return to the world. The severity of life and the desire to leave the monastery might cause considerable stress and grief. Caesarius of Heisterbach (d. c. 1240) tells of one novice who was driven mad by a yearning to return to the world and in his delirium called out the names of various women with whom he had slept. His fellow brethren sought to cure him by cutting up puppies and putting their warm flesh on his head but, not surprisingly, their efforts were in vain and the novice allegedly died in agony.[42] This was an extreme case but as mentioned previously the hardships of the cloister were challenging for many and caused a number to leave or contemplate leaving the monastery. A few, conversely, broke the vow of stability in search of a more rigorous way of life. As a young monk of Bec (Normandy) in the eleventh century, Lanfranc sought to flee the abbey to lead a harsher, hermit-like existence. This was not a flippant decision and Lanfranc made careful preparations for his future life, eating the roots of thistles to wean himself on to an austere diet. Divine Intervention put a stop to these plans, for Lanfranc's abbot was warned in a vision of the monk's intentions and quickly intercepted him. Lanfranc subsequently settled at Bec, where he later officiated as prior. He was elevated to the abbacy of William the Conqueror's new foundation at Caen in 1066 and was finally transferred to the see of Canterbury, which he held until his death in 1089.[43]

PHYSICAL AND MENTAL BARRIERS

See then how they die, those who depart from God.[44]

Physical and mental barriers were erected to prevent and discourage the brethren from fleeing their monastery. It was noted earlier that those who absconded were punished severely in front of their brethren to deter others from following suit. Moreover, stories were told of the fate suffered by deserters both in this world and that to come. Caesarius of Heisterbach warned of the perils facing absconders. He described how a storm broke out upon the death of one novice who had left his monastery and a murder of crows hovered above the roof of his house, an ominous warning to others of the fate awaiting those who departed from God's service.[45] In some cases incentives were offered to persuade monks to stay. They might be promised better food and clothing while officials struggling with the burdens of their office might be relieved of their duties. The most effective way to prevent desertion was to make the monastery secure and ensure there were no escape routes. Prelates were warned that the cloister should be monitored and also locked; it was also common to lock the dormitory at night and bar the windows. In the sixteenth century there were plans to build a high wall to the south of the church at Esholt Priory (Yorkshire), to stop the nuns accessing the riverside and bridge. Such obstacles could be an effective deterrent and would encourage the brethren to think carefully about any planned escapades. One nun who bumped her head while scaling the convent walls was prompted to reconsider her actions and decided to stay.[46]

THE SIGNIFICANCE OF OBEDIENCE

All who wish to live piously will suffer persecution. (2 Tim. 3.12)

Obedience was the core of monastic observance. It united the community and guided them on their heavenly path to salvation. It was also the only way to true freedom. The abbot's ultimate goal was to instil in the monks self-discipline, making each member of the community responsible for his thoughts and actions. But the brethren needed help and guidance to resist temptation and fight their demons. It was thus vital that rules and regulations were imposed and that punishment was meted out so that the monks could atone for their errors, and progress unfettered by sin.

Paradise is among us here, in spiritual exercise, simple prayer and holy meditation.[1]

8

The Work of God (1): The Communal Life

As a member of the monastic community each monk joined his brethren to participate in various daily activities, chiefly the round of liturgical offices in the church, the periods assigned to devotional reading and manual labour, and the meals taken together in the refectory. Communal living could encourage camaraderie and solidarity among the brethren and foster a sense of belonging. Yet the lack of privacy and confined conditions might lead to rivalries, friction and factions. This chapter considers what it meant for the monk to be a member of the monastic community. It explores how he spent his time with the other brethren and the nature of relationships within the cloister – the fellowship shared, friendships forged, as well as discord, enmities and the hardships of communal living.

COMMUNAL GATHERINGS: 'THE ANGELS' OFFICE'

Seven times in the day have I given praise to Thee. (Psalm 118.164)

The monk's day was structured around the various Offices that were celebrated in the choir. There were seven daytime Hours, the night Office of Vigils and the daily celebration of Mass; on feast days the liturgy was expanded and there were two Masses. The precise time at which each Hour was celebrated varied depending on the time of year, but the length and format differed from Order to Order. The Cluniacs were renowned for their lengthy and elaborate liturgy, which took up most of the monks' time and energy – one contemporary tersely remarked that the Cluniacs used sign language since their liturgical duties left them too tired to speak.[2] The Cistercians reacted against these excesses and were known for the brevity of their Office and their simplicity of style. They denounced overly elaborate singing, arguing that the Office should be celebrated with modesty and decorum. Aelred of Rievaulx (d. 1167) wrote a particularly damning criticism of what he considered histrionics in the choir, and provides a colourful account of these almost theatrical performances:

> Sometimes you see a man with his mouth open as if he were breathing his last breath, not singing but threatening silence, as it were, by ridiculous interruption of the melody into snatches. Now he imitates the agonies of the dying or the swooning of persons in pain. In the meantime his whole body is violently agitated by histrionic gesticulations – contorted lips, rolling eyes, hunching shoulders – and drumming fingers keep time with every single note. And this ridiculous dissipation is called religious observance. And it is loudly claimed that where this sort of agitation is more frequent, God is more honourably served.[3]

In theory each monk was required to participate in the entire liturgical day unless he was ill or legitimately engaged in another activity. Thus, chief office-holders might be excused if they had necessary business to attend. However, it was essential that everyone was present on important occasions such as Sundays and feast days. When the abbot of Beaulieu conducted his inspection of Hailes (Gloucestershire) in 1270 he reminded the brethren that no monk should miss the Sunday service or leave in the middle of the Office unless he had a very good reason for doing so.[4] A bell summoned the community to each Hour and upon entering the church the monks took up their allotted places in the choir, for everyone was arranged according to seniority. This meant that the monks always sat beside the same people in the choir but also in the refectory, at the chapter meeting and in processions. Each Office began with the Lord's Prayer, which was followed by hymns, psalms and chants (canticles). The monk chosen as the priest of the week led the Office while the precentor and his helper encouraged the singing in choir and made sure that the monks were attentive and celebrated the liturgy with due reverence and devotion. The quality of the performance was important and the brethren were warned against sloppiness and negligence. They were to enunciate the words clearly, reflect on their meaning and sing each Office in an appropriate manner; hence, Prime was to be celebrated as a hymn of jubilation and not a dirge. While the monks would have been familiar with the various chants and psalms which were sung each day, they read the words rather than relying on their memories lest they made a mistake, for this was considered a grave offence. However, it was not uncommon for them to recite the Night Office in the dark to spare their eyes from the dim candlelight. This had been the custom at the London Charterhouse but it was stopped by Prior John Houghton (1531–5) after the brethren fluffed their lines one Sunday at Lauds. Prior John reprimanded the community severely for ruining the 'angels' Office' and dishonouring God. He ruled that from then on the candles should never be extinguished at Lauds and that anyone who was singing alone must have a light.[5]

CONDUCT IN THE CHOIR

The monks were to behave with decorum and reverence in the choir, ensuring that they remained fixed on their spiritual exercises and did not distract the rest of the community. In 1518 four nuns of Littlemore Priory, Oxfordshire, were reprimanded for laughing during Mass at the elevation of the Host.[6] It was important that the brethren sat in a decorous and attentive manner. The monks were warned not to sit with their legs apart or crossed; nor were they to swing their legs or stretch them out. Nobody was to fidget, chat or look around at his neighbours and it was prohibited to cut one's nails, whittle or write. At all times the monks were to conduct themselves with discretion. The Augustinian Canons of Barnwell (Cambridgeshire) were reminded to lift and lower the lids of their seats gently and noiselessly using the left hand.[7] Those who behaved immodestly and threatened the reverence of the choir were liable to be punished and perhaps removed. A striking example concerns Ida the Gentle, a twelfth-century nun of La Ramée who was wont to fall into ecstatic trances after receiving the Eucharist. Ida was allegedly 'so full of God' on these occasions that she lost all physical control; she would cry out loudly in the middle of the choir and then fall down, immobilized, unable to speak or move. Ida's turns caused quite a stir, bringing the celebration of Mass to a standstill. The priests were alarmed at Ida's behaviour and the other nuns were curious at her altered physical appearance during these trances and asked Ida why her face changed colour and her eyes flashed. The community acknowledged that Ida's turns were a mark of her spirituality and considered her privy to Divine Knowledge, but her behaviour was nonetheless regarded as disruptive and irreverent and Ida was consequently barred from attending the Eucharist.[8] Ida's was not an isolated case. Arnulf, a lay brother of Villers (Belgium), was periodically overcome with jubilant laughter caused by an inward flow of Heavenly Grace. On such occasions he would leave the chapter meeting and run into the church to be alone and 'dance until the wine of his drunkenness was gradually digested'. This uncontrollable laughter was sometimes an embarrassment for Arnulf since not everyone understood the cause of his raucous and involuntary chortle and some considered it evil.[9] Even the great ascetic, Bernard of Clairvaux (d. 1153), was obliged to absent himself from the communal life on account of serious gastric problems, caused by years of austerity. In his later years Bernard's digestive system had all but ceased to function, causing him to throw up undigested food. But Bernard was so determined to participate fully in the liturgical day he had a basin sunk into the ground beside him in the choir and would vomit into the vessel during the Office. This was not, however, a satisfactory arrangement. The other monks found Bernard's retching offensive and he was eventually compelled to withdraw from communal activities.[10]

BELL-RINGING

It was common for the laity to ring the monastery bells on feast days and other important occasions. In the twelfth century the young men of Durham were wont to ring the cathedral bells at Whitsuntide and were evidently skilled at doing so. The monks themselves often took a turn at ringing the bells and might relish this opportunity to join their companions to let off steam. The monks of St Peter's, Westminster, were accustomed to gather in the church on the Vigil of St Edward's Day (12 October), to ring the bells in the saint's honour. The entire community participated in this event and would pull on the bell ropes with great exuberance and energy. Those who were ill or infirm were excluded, a fact that deeply upset one twelfth-century monk who had an abscess on his arm, the result of an injury he had incurred when giving blood. The monk sat sadly and watched while the rest of the brethren rang the bells with enthusiasm, but was particularly disappointed since he was devoted to Saint Edward and looked forward to showing his dedication to the saint at this annual celebration. Eventually, in his frustration, the monk leapt to his feet, grabbed a bell rope and tugged at this with both hands. The activity caused the abscess to burst and ooze forth gore, bringing relief and release from suffering.[11] While the tale of the monk's recovery was recounted as proof of St Edward's powers, it offers an insight into the manner in which these communal activities were conducted and how they might be relished by the brethren.

MEALTIMES

Let nothing be done [at table] *with tumult or noise. . . . Some . . . fish for their*
pot-herbs with their bare fingers instead of spoons so that they seem to seek in
that same bowl of soup both the washing of their hands and the refection of
their belly. Others dip repeatedly into the dish their half-gnawed crusts and
the sippets which they have bitten and plunge the leavings of their own teeth
in the guise of sops into the goblets.[12]

An important aspect of communal living and a focus of the monk's day was the
time the brethren spent together in the refectory. In winter the community ate
there once a day but in summer, when the days were longer, they dined twice,
enjoying a light supper in the evening in addition to dinner in the middle of the
day. Although mealtimes were communal affairs they were not social activities,
for the monks were prohibited from talking with each other and communicated
sparingly using signs. Their attention was to be focused instead on the spiritual
reading that they heard while eating, that they might feast their souls while
refreshing the body. There was a regularity and ritual to mealtimes. The brethren
washed their hands upon entering the refectory and took their accustomed place
at the stone tables that were arranged in a 'U' shape around the room. They sat
facing inwards and dishes were shared between two or more diners. The abbot
or prior sat at the high table at the far end of the room, where he presided over
proceedings; he might be joined by important guests. The president and his table
companions were served first and shown deference at all times. Meals were to
be conducted efficiently and with the minimum of fuss. Hence, the sub-cellarer
of St Augustine's, Canterbury, was warned that the food should be on the tables
before the monks arrived, so that they were not kept waiting. The cellarer of the
house kept an eye on the proceedings to ensure that everything was in order and
ran smoothly.[13]

The monks took it in turns to serve in the refectory and help in the kitchen.
These chores were rotated on a weekly basis, so that everyone played his part.
It was imperative that the servers and diners alike behaved with modesty and
decorum to preserve an almost reverential tone that was conducive to the
contemplative nature of mealtimes, but also as manners were regarded as a
manifestation of inner godliness and a way to achieve this.[14] The Cistercian
customary instructed diners and servers to bow courteously to each other when
giving or receiving a dish; nobody was to eat noisily or walk around the refectory

while chewing, and the brethren were always to use both hands when drinking. The significance of the latter was made clear to the Canterbury monks, who were advised to use both hands to drink as was the custom in England before the Normans arrived in 1066.[15] Hugh of St Victor (d. 1142) underlined the importance of etiquette and launched a censorious attack on slovenly behaviour at table, which was not only offensive but a potential health hazard, given that dishes were shared. His colourful invective describes how some fished the pot herbs from the soup with their fingers rather than spoons while others dipped half-eaten crusts into the dishes, leaving behind the remnants of their teeth 'in the guise of sops'.[16] Cleanliness was also important in the medieval refectory and the brethren were constantly reminded to keep the table linen clean and orderly. The monks were instructed never to use their napkins to wipe their teeth; nor were they to wipe their knives on the napkins without first wiping them on their bread. Not everyone shared this opinion. Peter Abelard (d. 1142) regarded the latter as an abhorrent practice and criticized monks who wiped their knives and even their hands on the leftover bread that was to be given as alms, to spare the tablecloths. He claimed that in doing so they polluted the bread of the poor, and thus of Christ, in whose name they were fed. When soft fruit was given to the canons of Barnwell Priory it was served in bowls lest the juice stain the tablecloths; if perchance anyone soiled the linen he was to notify the refectorer immediately so that he could have it washed.[17] Meals were functional and once the monks had finished eating they left the refectory and processed to the choir, where they celebrated Grace and continued their daily schedule. Guests might remain behind with the abbot or prior to enjoy a post-dinner drink and a few words of consolation.

WORK

Open-air exercise and work not only distract the senses but also often exhaust the spirit, except in the case of heavy field work where great weariness of body leads to contrition and humility of the heart. Frequently too the tiredness it causes makes an impact which elicits stronger feelings of devotion. The same is often seen to happen when fasts and vigils and all practices which involve affliction of the body are undertaken.[18]

St Benedict made a threefold division of the monk's time and anticipated that the brethren would spend about six hours of each day engaged in manual labour. This was an act of humility and an antidote to restlessness and boredom since idleness was the 'enemy of the soul'. Moreover, it was believed that the break away from prayer and meditation would refresh the monk, who could then return to his spiritual observances reinvigorated. By the twelfth century the attitude to manual labour varied considerably among the different Orders. Whereas the Cluniacs had all but abandoned it in favour of an elaborate liturgy, the Cistercians made manual work a central part of their day and engaged in heavy labour. They would gather in the parlour each day after the chapter meeting to receive their tools from the prior and might be required to chop wood, garden, grease boots or perhaps help with decorating. This could at times be precarious and lead to accidents. A monk of Newminster Abbey (Northumberland) fell from his ladder while whitewashing the dormitory but fortunately was saved by the resident saint.[19] At harvest time all the brethren were required to help in the fields and would generally celebrate the Office as they toiled but on other occasions they might sing psalms or recite the Psalter as they worked, edifying the soul while engaging the hands. At Cluny any monk who was working in the bakery was forbidden to sing the psalms lest his saliva fell into the dough.[20]

The various chores were generally distributed among the brethren on a weekly rota, so that everyone took his turn and there were no complaints of favouritism. Anyone who had a special talent might use this for the good of the house. At St Albans (Hertfordshire), the new guesthouse that was constructed in the thirteenth century was exquisitely painted by one of the monks, Brother Richard.[21] Work did not necessarily mean heavy labour and the monks might illuminate manuscripts or copy books. The Carthusians, who spent most of their time alone in their cells, borrowed and copied books for their own consumption but also to disseminate outside the monastery and in so doing 'preached with the pen'. It was common in the nunneries for the women to spend their time embroidering. Goscelin of St Bertin (d. c. 1099) remarked on the wonderful needlework he saw at Barking Abbey (Essex).[22] Several Yorkshire communities worked in silk but some, like the nuns of Swine, evidently preferred weaving to their liturgical duties and were reprimanded for missing the Office.[23]

In addition to the daily chores carried out during times of communal work, some of the brethren had extra duties associated with their office or 'obedience'. The cellarer, who was in charge of supplies within the monastery, distributed provisions to the refectorer and also the infirmarer, for the use of the sick. During mealtimes he made a circuit of the refectory to make sure that everything was in order and that all the brethren were content; after the meal he passed the leftovers to the porter or almoner to distribute to the poor. The cellarer also prepared warm water for the Maundy and each week checked that all the kitchen utensils were in order and nothing was missing.[24] Another key official was the sacrist who, as noted in Chapter 1, was in charge of timekeeping. The sacrist also cared for the vestments and holy vessels and was to make sure they were clean and in a good state of repair. The purity and cleanliness of the sacred linens was essential and the sacrist of St Augustine's, Canterbury, was warned not to dry these items in the sun or by the fire, or even in the wind lest they were soiled; should any fall on the ground they had to be consecrated once more. Another important task was the annual preparation of the altar bread which was a lengthy and time-consuming process. The sacrist selected the corn grain by grain and then sent it to the abbey mill, where it was specially cleaned. When it was time to make the bread, the sacrist and his helpers had to prepare themselves and their workplace appropriately for this holy work. They washed their hands and faces, covered their hands with amices (furred hoods) and wore albs (long vestments). The workplace was covered with clean linens and the servant who held the irons wore gloves. The monks might sing psalms while they prepared the bread, but otherwise were silent and conducted this work with due reverence. Once the hosts had been prepared, the sacrist sorted the good from the bad and stored the former in an extremely clean container for use throughout the year.[25]

It was important that each monk played his part and carried out whatever duties were assigned to him on the weekly rota in addition to any jobs allocated to him on account of his office or status. Accordingly, anyone who had received priestly orders was expected to take his turn preaching in Chapter. In 1261 the monks of Hailes Abbey (Gloucestershire) were reprimanded for shirking this duty and the prior was warned to punish offenders appropriately. This seemingly involved withholding their customary treat, which was likely to have been a meaty delicacy since it was served either in the abbot's chamber or conventual hall rather than the refectory. A similar mandate was issued to the monks of Abbey Dore (Herefordshire) following the visitation of the house in 1318.[26] In some cases monks were excluded from what they considered was a group activity and one that had perhaps been eagerly anticipated. A notable example concerns the opening of St Edmund's shrine at Bury in 1198. The entire community had been looking forward to this event with great excitement and were heartbroken when they learned that it had been carried out secretly at night by a chosen few who had seen and in some cases actually touched the martyr's holy remains. Jocelin of Brakelond, who describes the proceedings in his chronicle, was not himself present but was informed of the momentous events by one of the twelve witnesses. He explains that Abbot Samson had considered it inappropriate and impracticable for all the brethren to attend but his decision cut the others to the core. Those who were excluded felt betrayed and deeply saddened that they had not been present at this momentous event, and tearfully sang the *Te Deum*.[27] The two translations of St William of Norwich's body were conducted with similar secrecy by a select group of the monks when the others were sleeping. On the second occasion the monks were warned not to reveal anything of their covert mission to the rest of the community and were careful to leave no evidence that the shrine had been disturbed.[28]

RELATIONSHIPS IN THE CLOISTER

Friendship is a twinning of minds and spirits where two become as one. Your friend is a second self from whom you withhold nothing, hide nothing, fear nothing. . . . Friendship should be stable, unfaltering in affection, holding a mirror to eternity.[29]

As a member of the monastic community the monk was almost always surrounded by others and spent most of his day engaged in group activities. Yet for much of this time the monks did not converse with each other but observed silence and communicated when necessary by signing. Moreover, the brethren might engage in meditation while sitting together in the cloister and were thus mentally withdrawn even when sharing the same space. The cloister was accordingly a communal rather than a social place. Still, there was opportunity for conversation and special friendships. The Cistercians, for example, were allowed to pair off with their friends in the afternoons of major feasts and share their thoughts and feelings.[30]

All the brethren were united through their common goal, the pursuit of salvation. Their friendship was regarded as a foretaste of the pleasure in heaven where souls were reunited. For Aelred of Rievaulx (d. 1167), human friendship led to that with God and was the basis for progression to Christ. Yet there was scope within the cloister to form personal ties and special friendships, whether this was between novices who embarked together on the monastic life or between the old and young, the former relying on the latter as mentors and providing in return physical help. However, there was the potential for hostilities, rivalries and tensions to arise between individuals and groups. Jocelin of Brakelond describes how he lost the friendship of a fellow monk of Bury, who took umbrage at a comment he had made in confidence to another member of the community. Jocelin sought to heal the rift by appealing to the monk and making him gifts but to no avail and the two remained estranged some twenty years later.[31] While hostility of this nature would be awkward in any situation it must have been particularly difficult within the confinement of the cloister.

SPECIAL FRIENDSHIPS

> *Friendship yields a harvest both in this life and the next. . . . In consequence there can be no true happiness for the man without a friend.*[32]

The communal life afforded opportunity for companionship. Novices often forged a strong bond with their master or with each other, sharing their doubts and fears and offering mutual support during times of hardship. This close relationship might last throughout their lives. A notable example concerns Anselm and Gundulf, who both entered the Norman monastery of Bec in the mid-eleventh century. A friendship developed as each supported the other's progression; whereas Anselm was knowledgeable, Gundulf was renowned for his compunction – 'one spoke the other wept; one planted the other watered'. Anselm's and Gundulf's friendship remained strong even when Gundulf was sent from Bec to join the new community at Caen, and later, when he was elevated to the see of Rochester. The two corresponded with each other, writing letters and exchanging prayers, and were reunited in England in 1093 when Anselm was made Archbishop of Canterbury. Fifteen years later Bishop Gundulf died and, fittingly, it was Anselm, his friend and archbishop, who conducted the funeral.[33]

The sick who shared the infirmary together and were permitted to talk a little to regale each other might similarly establish close ties and a strong sense of camaraderie. A monk of Westminster Abbey, who suffered various afflictions including a swollen foot, was assigned to the infirmary of the house, where he slept beside an elderly member of the community. The two regaled each other with conversation before retiring for the night and on one occasion discussed the merits of their resident saint, Edward the Confessor, for whom the injured monk had a special devotion. He described to his elderly companion how the saint had already cured him of several ailments and explained that he intended to seek help for his foot. The following morning the monk awoke to find that the swelling had miraculously disappeared and shared this joyful news with his companion.[34]

A close relationship might develop between the sick or elderly and their carers. Juliana, a Gilbertine nun of Sempringham (Lincolnshire) who had suffered from leprosy since childhood, was cared for in the infirmary by her novice-mistress, Clarice, who diligently bathed and tended Juliana until she was eventually cured by the powers of St Gilbert.[35] While newcomers and juniors generally required encouragement and advice to strengthen them in their early years, the frail and elderly often needed physical assistance and might be assigned the help of a younger monk. The young and the old might therefore establish a symbiotic relationship, the one offering wisdom and spiritual guidance, the other providing practical assistance. When William of Duns, the former sacrist of Melrose Abbey (Scotland), was afflicted by blindness in his old age, he was allocated a monk helper to guide him around the monastery and help prise open his eyes, which were tightly sealed with blindness.[36]

Newcomers might feel lonely and isolated in their new surroundings, especially if they had come from another country and were faced with a foreign language and culture as well as a sea of unfamiliar faces. A special effort might therefore be made to welcome these new arrivals and make them feel that they were among friends. Abbot Anselm of Bec (Normandy) was concerned for the welfare of one of his favourite monks, Maurice, who was sent to study at Canterbury. Anselm wrote to several monks of Christ Church asking that they make Maurice feel welcome while living amid strangers and received regular updates on Maurice's progress with assurance that the monk was settling in well to his new community.[37] Newcomers might, however, be susceptible to bullying. A monk of the London Charterhouse who was sent to Mount Grace Priory in the sixteenth century complained that the monks of the Yorkshire house were jealous of him and mounting a conspiracy; he interpreted every laugh or cough as an attempt to ridicule him.[38] When Peter Abelard (d. 1142) was appointed abbot of St Gildas (Lower Brittany), he claimed that the 'dissolute' monks of the abbey were seeking to murder him. Peter alleged that he lived in fear for his life since the monks had first contrived to poison his food and drink, then the chalice and finally held a dagger to his throat; Peter maintained that each day he imagined a sword hanging over his head and could scarcely breathe at meals.[39] While both of these cases were likely fuelled by paranoia, bullying in the cloister was not unknown. The monks of Hailes (Gloucestershire) were on several occasions reprimanded for tormenting their companions. Their spitefulness caused one monk of the house, Thomas Ashby, to flee to Waverley Abbey (Surrey), where he was advised to remain on account of 'the malice of his rivals'.[40]

RIFTS AND RUCTIONS

No corner of the monastery was free from the sound of poisonous whisperings.[41]

While personal animosities might be injurious and disruptive, the emergence of rival factions within the monastery could cause deep rifts and tear the community apart. Following the Norman Conquest of England in 1066 there were tensions between the native English monks and newcomers from the Norman abbeys of Bec and Caen; the latter had been brought to England by Archbishop Lanfranc (d. 1089) to help implement his programme of reform. In some houses two rival camps were formed that were divided by language, customs and also by preference, as the Norman newcomers were generally appointed to positions of authority within the monastery. The native community at Christ Church, Canterbury, was deeply resentful of these foreign usurpers who occupied the senior offices, including that of prior. Their neighbours at St Augustine's actively resisted the imposition of a Norman abbot, Wido, in 1087. The community refused to attend Wido's installation ceremony and left the monastery *en masse*. Later, they plotted to murder the new abbot and encouraged the laity to join them and drive Wido out. Their behaviour was punished severely – the rebel monks were scourged while the laity were blinded. The community was dispersed and twenty-three monks from Christ Church were later sent to re-form the community.[42]

It was not uncommon for antagonisms to develop between the junior and senior members of the community. At the visitation of Norwich in the sixteenth century the senior monks were accused of exploiting their position and taking liberties. The juniors claimed that their superiors had stopped wearing the habit and now donned top hats and fancy headgear; moreover, they sought and indulged in female company. This hostility was mutual and it was alleged that the juniors were disorderly and that they played backgammon and cards rather than memorizing the Psalms.[43] Complaints of preferential treatment led to strife within the Gilbertine Order in the thirteenth century. The nuns complained that the canons enjoyed better food than they and further, were served ale while the nuns made do with water.[44] It was to avoid such discord that Benedict had ruled that all the brethren should receive the same allowances and share the chores equally.

Appointments to office were often the cause of division within the community. The election of a new prior at Bury St Edmunds in 1201 sparked off a bitter feud and exposed a deep rift between those who promoted learning in the cloister and those who undermined it. The community was torn over who would be the best successor to Prior Robert. Whereas Abbot Samson favoured the relatively young and junior monk, Herbert, the traditionalists supported their sub-prior, the experienced and learned Master Hermer. Jocelin of Brakelond reports the proceedings at length in his chronicle. He was a staunch advocate of learning and was deeply distressed at the turn of events and, not least, at Abbot Samson's attitude throughout. The election should have been a democratic process with Samson presenting four candidates, pointing out their relative strengths and weaknesses and leaving the community to make their decision. However, Samson effectively stitched up the election to ensure that his own candidate was appointed. He presented a dummy panel of four men who were young (under forty) and inexperienced. But crucially, he omitted Hermer from the shortlist. Jocelin was aghast that these junior monks should have been promoted over a senior member of the community with both learning and experience and argued that Bury needed an eloquent prior who would be an ambassador for the abbey; it would be scandalous if a 'speechless figurehead was set up and a block of wood put in its place'. Yet this is effectively what happened. Herbert was duly elected and when he expressed a concern that his lack of learning might prevent him from accepting office, Samson immediately dispelled his doubts and even suggested that Herbert should simply memorize old sermons that others had preached and deliver these to the Chapter in English or French rather than Latin. For Jocelin this undermined the entire system of learning and education in the cloister and made a mockery of the ethos at Bury. What was more shocking and even distressing was the fact that Jocelin had regarded Samson, his former novice-master, as a man of learning. Jocelin describes how the unlettered members of the community considered this a victory over the clerics and gloated over their triumph,

Our good clerks have done so much declining in the cloister they have all been declined. There has been so much sermonizing in chapter that they are all rebuffed.... They have declined musa, muse so often that their minds are reckoned to be muzzy![45]

Elections were a common cause of strife but occasionally ripped the entire brotherhood apart and might even assume national or international significance. A particularly vicious struggle for the abbacy erupted at the Yorkshire abbey of Fountains, following the death of Abbot Robert Burley (1383–1410). The community was split over the appointment of Robert's successor and the abbots of Rievaulx and Jervaulx were sent to resolve the matter. They chose Roger Frank, a monk of Fountains who had allegedly received the greatest number of votes. Their decision provoked a vehement response from Frank's chief opponent, John Ripon, who had previously officiated as cellarer of Fountains and was at this time abbot of the neighbouring house of Meaux. He claimed that Frank's appointment was unorthodox and took his complaint to Rome, where he engaged an English clerk as his proctor. This instigated a lengthy and complex case that was injurious to the house and Order and defamatory to both candidates, who each sought to besmirch the other's character. Frank undermined Ripon's suitability to preside over Fountains, claiming that as abbot of Meaux he had wasted the abbey's resources and behaved inappropriately by wandering around in public armed. His allegations were in vain, for the Pope decided in Ripon's favour. Ripon still had to convince Parliament of his legitimacy but nevertheless set about forcibly removing Frank from the abbacy. In response Frank's supporters launched a violent attack on Ripon and allegedly plotted his murder. There was turmoil and chaos as the tenants of each contender hit out at the opposing side by looting and destroying the abbey's granges and literally ripping Fountains apart. The situation was so serious that it was raised at the Council of Constance (1414–18) and brought to the attention of Parliament, which subsequently intervened. The matter was ultimately resolved in Ripon's favour and he remained in office until his death in 1434.[46]

The magnitude of the strife at Fountains was exceptional but feuds of this nature were not uncommon and were frequently sparked off when an outsider was imposed on the community. The situation at Newbattle Abbey (Midlothian) in the fourteenth century was not untypical. Prior Donald and the monks of Newbattle refused to admit John of Hailis, a monk of Melrose Abbey, to preside over the abbey, for they wanted one of their own brothers and not an outsider.

They strongly resisted John, even though he had papal and royal backing, and a lengthy legal battle ensued. This was eventually resolved in John's favour and on 5 January 1394 the pope sent a mandate to the abbots of Glasgow and Dunkeld instructing them to enforce the nomination of Abbot John to the monastery of Newbattle. John did not, however, remain long at Newbattle and in the fifteenth century transferred to the abbacy of Balmerino in Fife, where he established himself as a prominent figure in national and international affairs.[47]

ABSENCE AND LOSS

My soul is sorrowful and I will not be comforted until I return to you.[48]

While the monks took a vow of stability and were in theory to remain rooted to the monastery in which they made their profession, it was not uncommon for brethren to be moved to another house to take up office or settle a new community. This was particularly common amongst the Cistercians in the twelfth century, which was the highpoint of the Order's expansion. Established communities might send out colonies of monks and lay brothers to found daughter-houses. Each new foundation required an abbot and twelve monks as well as lay brothers to help with the building work and the cultivation of land. The departure of so many men from the mother-house – and in one fell swoop – would have had a considerable impact on morale and relationships, with the loss of friends, colleagues but also some of the most experienced members of the community. The exchange between Abbot Bernard of Clairvaux and Gerard, a monk of Clairvaux who was sent in 1143 to colonize the new foundation at Alvastra in Sweden, underlines just what a wrench this could be both for those who were leaving and those left behind. Gerard and the others chosen to go to Alvastra pleaded with Bernard to stay at Clairvaux, but to little avail, for while Bernard admitted that he was aggrieved at their departure, he insisted it was essential they go and teach the 'uncultivated and wild men' of Sweden the ways of the Cistercian Order. But Bernard promised that this would only be a temporary move and that Gerard and his companions would one day return to their home community. Gerard remained in Sweden for over fifty years and for most of this time presided as abbot of the house. He eventually returned to Clairvaux, where he died in the infirmary. Another striking example of the strong attachments monks might feel for their own community and their grief should they be promoted to office elsewhere concerns Ralph, a monk of Fountains Abbey in Yorkshire. He was sent to Norway in 1146 to preside as the first abbot of Lyse-Kloster, south of Bergen. Ralph evidently missed his home community terribly and also the Yorkshire landscape, for it was said that every time he saw the sun setting on the fjords he was reminded of his valley at Fountains. Like many of his contemporaries Ralph considered his transfer temporary and ultimately returned home to Fountains to die in familiar surroundings.[49]

The loss of members to another house would inevitably have affected the dynamics within the community and at times significantly so. But the arrival of temporary members could be equally unsettling and lead to rivalries, tensions and perhaps even a feeling of overcrowdedness. These transient recruits included monks from other houses who, as previously noted, had committed a serious offence and were sent to another community in the hope that they would reform their ways. They might also include members of other Orders whose arrival could cause disharmony and resentment. This was the case in the north of England in the early fourteenth century, following the trial of the Templars. It was decided that the twenty-four offenders should be absolved and sent as guests to religious houses in the area. While Rievaulx Abbey bluntly refused to receive a Templar, the monks of Fountains agreed to admit one of these guests but then complained that he was rude and unruly. The monks of Kirkstall seemingly allowed their visitor to escape and were probably glad to be rid of this guest.[50]

DEATH AND THE DYING

He was summoned by the Blessed Mother of God and passed from darkness into light, from faith to sight, from toil to rest, from deserving to reward, from the world to heavenly country.[51]

Monastic friendship persisted beyond the grave. Even after the monk died he remained a member of the community. A pittance was served in the refectory on the anniversary of his death and he was remembered by the brethren in their prayers. Death was not therefore an end but the loss of one's companions could nonetheless cause considerable grief, particularly in a small community where so much time was spent in the company of one's companions. It is interesting

Matthew Paris, monk of St Albans, on his deathbed, 13th c, British Library, Royal 14. C. VII, f. 218v.

to consider how death was regarded in the monastery and its impact on the community.

Death was a time for consolation and solace. The dying monk was shown compassion by his fellow brethren, who would offer comfort and allay any fears about what lay ahead. Support might come from outside the community and when the brethren at Pershore (Worcestershire) were struck down by the plague in c. 1111, a monk of Worcester visited to comfort one of the dying monks and dispel his fears.[52] Even those who had spent their life anticipating death and the joys of heaven might have their concerns when faced with its imminence. The process of dying was a communal affair and the brethren rallied around their companion in his final hours. They took turns to keep Vigil around the dying monk, to console and strengthen him and, importantly, to help in the final struggle between good and evil. According to Lanfranc's *Constitutions* of the late eleventh century there should always be two brothers by the monk's bedside to read to him continuously until he died. Narratives of the Passion and the Gospels were read when the monk still had his senses and thereafter passages from the Psalter.[53] At the point of death the monk was set on a sackcloth on top of ashes in the form of a cross. The door of the cloister was then beaten with sharp, rapid blows to notify the rest of the community that the end was in sight and they should gather immediately to be with their brother when he departed from this life and began his journey to the next. In Cistercian houses the entire community witnessed the last rites (unction, confession, absolution) and said the *Credo* three times but then withdrew, allowing the monk to die alone, for the actual moment of death was a private affair.[54]

The monk's death triggered off another set of rituals. Bells were sounded and while the corpse was stripped, washed and clad in a new or newly washed shift the community recited the Office of the Dead and the Psalter. The head, hands and feet of the deceased were covered in preparation for burial and once the body was ready the brethren were summoned to accompany the corpse into the church, where it remained until the funeral. Once again the monks kept constant Vigil and recited the psalmody continuously to ward off evil spirits. It was common to organize a shift so that the body was never left alone and the psalmody was not broken. Complete silence was observed within the cloister until the body had been buried, and nobody was permitted to leave the precinct until after the funeral; this applied also to any guests who happened to be staying at the house.[55]

The attendance of the dead and dying could be demanding, particularly if the monks were roused from their slumbers to tend their brother or were on the night shift. Monks of Worcester Cathedral Priory who were performing the psalmody at the body of Bishop Wulfstan (d. 1095) were 'wearied out with long watching' and slinked off into corners of the church to have a snooze. The dead bishop was clearly not impressed with their half-heartedness and reputedly roused them, demanding that they sing the Psalter for his soul.[56] Bernard of Clairvaux (d. 1153) worried that his monks of Clairvaux would be exhausted for Vigils and deliver a sloppy performance if they had to rise during the night to tend the deceased. Hence he would ask any dying member of the community to defer his death to an appropriate time so that the brethren would be fresh for the Office.[57]

WHAT IMPACT DID DEATH HAVE ON THE REST OF THE COMMUNITY?

> *After his glorious departure the blessed man came in an apparition to a*
> *certain Handmaid of Christ. He took the form of a child dressed in a robe,*
> *partly snow-white, partly purple.*[58]

The Carthusians generally ate alone in their cells but 'for the grace of consolation' came together in the refectory when one of their brethren was buried.[59] The community might feel great loss and sorrow at the death of one of their companions, particularly those who had been close to the deceased or if a notable member of the community had died. This might prompt unprecedented displays of emotion. Goscelin of St Bertin (d. c. 1099) describes the deep sorrow of Aelflaed, a senior nun of Wilton (Wiltshire), upon the death of her young abbess, Wulfthryth (c. 940–1010?), who was 'pained by an especially sharp wound'. At the funeral Aelflaed professed her love for Wulfthryth and thereafter showed her devotion to the abbess by remaining behind each day after the Office and reciting the whole Psalter for her soul. Aelflaed was rewarded for her 'faithful perseverance' and at Easter had a vision of the Paschal lamb emerging from Wulfthryth's tomb and making three circuits of the shrine to protect the sleeper, a sign that Christ resided in the late abbess's breast.[60] The death of Gilbert of Sempringham in 1189 caused considerable sorrow among the brethren of the Order he had founded. Such was the outpouring of grief that it was decided to leave the coffin open so that anyone who wished could kiss the corpse. This was not evidently commonplace or at least was not considered desirable, for Gilbert's biographer emphasizes that everyone who gathered for the funeral kissed the corpse yet felt 'no horror at kissing the lifeless body', since faith had given them the courage to touch the body and piety prompted them to show their love.[61] A poignant account of Aelred of Rievaulx's death in 1166 and the impact this had on his community is recorded by Walter Daniel, a monk of the Yorkshire abbey, who himself tended Aelred and cradled his head in his final hours. Walter recounts how the day before his death Aelred was unable to speak but nonetheless listened intently to the brother who read to him the story of the Lord's Passion. On occasion Aelred would show his great joy at a passage by raising his hands and even moving his lips 'in the likeness of a truly spiritual smile'. The brethren were clearly moved and experienced mixed emotions, shedding tears of grief at the imminent loss of their beloved abbot yet jubilant that he would soon be free from the toils of this world in Paradise.

Walter explains that shortly before his death Aelred, who had not spoken for two days, turned to look up at the wooden cross and recited the words of Luke 23.46: 'You are my God and Lord, my refuge and Saviour. Into Your hands I commend my spirit.' These were effectively the last words the holy man uttered. Walter vividly conveys his own personal reaction to Aelred's death and describes how he was unable to restrain himself from kissing the abbot's feet when preparing the body for burial, choosing the feet 'lest feeling rather than pure affection' should admonish him. The memory of this occasion, of one who had died in light and not darkness, continued to overwhelm Walter and fill him with joy.[62]

INTERCESSION AND INTERACTION

Death was also a time for jubilation since the deceased had gone to the place where all the brethren aspired to go. His passing would likely prompt the community to reflect on their own mortality and perhaps raise concerns for the welfare of their former companion. A number of stories circulated about the dead reappearing to members of their community to offer reassurance and comfort about their own well-being and tell of the joys awaiting all who persevered in the monastic life. A monk of Villers (Belgium) who died during the night reappeared to one of the monks, who saw his former friend ecstatic in the joys of heaven and free of the bodily afflictions and ailments he had suffered on earth.[63] From the twelfth century questions about the soul's passage through Purgatory were of considerable concern, in particular, how long the soul would remain in Purgatory before passing to Paradise and what, if anything, the living could do to hasten this journey. The dead might therefore return to shed light on these and other matters, acting as a personal link between the two worlds. A monk of Stratford Langthorne (London) received a vision of a former brother of the house in Purgatory, who reassured him that no Cistercian monk would spend more than thirty days in this temporary place. Another monk of Stratford twitched so violently when he died it seemed to his fellow brethren that he rose four feet above his bed. The next night he appeared to them as a ghost, peacefully surrounded by light. When asked what had made him twitch so severely he explained that in the instant of death his soul passed through Purgatory for a period that seemed a thousand years, even though it had only been a minute on earth.[64]

Ties of friendship and bonds with former members of the community could therefore provide the living with a direct link to the afterlife and an opportunity to access pertinent information that was otherwise beyond their reach. The living might make a pact that whoever died first would return and reveal to the other what awaited them. A formal agreement of this kind was drawn up between Alexander, a monk of the Cistercian abbey of Stratford Langthorne, and Roger, a lay brother of the house. The terms were set out formally in a cyrograph. Alexander was the first to die and in accordance with their agreement duly appeared to his friend after thirty days, when his soul was exiting Purgatory. Roger quizzed his former companion, wishing to know where he had gone and where he himself would eventually go when he died. Alexander reappeared a year later as a brilliant light and 'ravishing smell', for he was now in Paradise. Roger again questioned his friend and was particularly concerned to know who else was with him; he asked about specific saints and also members of the community who had recently died. Alexander explained that the ascent to Paradise was a slow one but reassured Roger that he too would eventually join him there.[65]

The dead did not simply provide information about the life hereafter. Their assistance was sometimes sought to bring relief from physical ailments. One elderly monk of Durham who was afflicted with blindness in his later years prayed for help at the shrine of his former friend, the illustrious Adam of Melrose. Adam had been a devout member of the community who was highly regarded for his spirituality and was thus an ideal intercessor. William implored Adam for assistance and was immediately cured when a marvellous clear light passed through the middle of 'the locked closets' of his eyes, bringing complete and immediate relief; indeed the old monk was able to return to the cloister unaided.[66]

THE PRESSURES OF COMMUNAL LIVING

Wishing to avoid upsetting her neighbours Ida made such brave efforts to summon back her bodily strength that her labouring face showed black all around from the distressing struggle.[67]

To live in a community where one was constantly surrounded by others fostered self-consciousness and a concern with how one was perceived. The brethren might worry that any unsavoury afflictions would repulse their companions or that idiosyncratic behaviour would invite ridicule. This is vividly conveyed in the story of Eadwacer, a monk of Ramsey. Eadwacer suffered from a cancerous growth in his jaw which caused him considerable pain and also embarrassment, for he feared that the hideousness of his deformity would disgust the other members of the community. Indeed, the flesh around Eadwacer's jaw was so badly worn away that it left his teeth and gums exposed. Hoping to conceal this grotesqueness, Eadwacer draped a cloth over his jawbone. The other monks were not, however, repulsed but felt great compassion for their friend, whose affliction struck them 'like a whip'. Nevertheless, Eadwacer was ashamed of his appearance and chose to withdraw to a little island near the monastery where he could live alone in dignity while serving God. On St Oswald's day (28 February), however, he returned to the abbey to celebrate the founder's feast and the brethren persuaded Eadwacer to join them. They sat together in the hospice and then dined in the refectory, but tactfully seated Eadwacer in a quiet corner of the room where he would feel less conspicuous. It was customary on Oswald's feast day to pass around the saint's cup after dinner so that each member of the community might drink from this in turn. Eadwacer was the last to receive the cup and upon holding it to his jaw was miraculously healed.[68]

The story of Eadwacer's affliction and cure was recounted to demonstrate the power of Ramsey's saint, who cared for the monks of his foundation, but it provides a striking insight into the sensitivities of those living in the cloister and is a testimony to the particular problems presented by communal living. It was clearly difficult for the brethren to be indifferent to their appearance and conduct when there were always others around. Hence Ida, the nun of La Ramée who was prone to fall into a state of ecstasy when receiving the Eucharist, struggled to retain control of her emotions lest she would shock or upset her fellow sisters. Ida ultimately sought to be alone, where she could succumb to her frenzy without the worry of the impact she was having on the others:

> She wished to be enclosed in solitude, in a place where she could be louder and more ardent in the groans and sobs her lamenting mind would offer to her Spouse and in the sighs of her vehement soul, a place where she could flex her limbs without shocking anyone, where she could conduct herself as her heart's desire might suggest.[69]

The monks might also fear that their behaviour would be mocked or ridiculed by the others. A novice of Dunfermline (Fife) who was struck by paralysis was reluctant to visit St Margaret's shrine in the abbey church for fear he would be scorned by his master.[70] The infirmarer of Villers (Brabant) was 'covered with embarrassment' when Arnulf, a lay brother of the house, threw his arms around him in delight on learning that he would soon die and be united with his Maker. The infirmarer was concerned that the other inmates who had witnessed this display might suspect it had other implications.[71]

For many in the monastery the pressures of communal living fostered self-consciousness, and the anxiety this caused might compel them to seek solitude and privacy. The next chapter considers the time the monk spent alone, whether in a secluded space away from the others or mentally withdrawn while in their company.

I'll have a cell all to myself alone
No comrade and no servant shall I own
Alone I'll sing, alone I'll take my meal
Alone at night my way to bed I'll feel.[1]

9

The Work of God (2): The Monk Alone

Carthusian monasticism combined eremitic and coenobitic living, with each monk leading a solitary life within the community. The cell was the focus of Carthusian life and the monks spent most of their time alone in their private cell where they ate, slept and meditated, joining the others only occasionally for communal meals and worship. For some the solitude of the Carthusian monastery could be overwhelming. Alexander, a twelfth-century monk of Witham Priory (Somerset), complained of the boredom and torpor of Carthusian life since they lacked the support of companionship and could look only at the walls of their cell. Alexander subsequently left Witham to become a Cluniac but later regretted his decision. Others were similarly struck by the seclusion of Carthusiasn life and one sixteenth-century monk of the London Charterhouse found this so unbearable he contemplated committing suicide; the prior responded by securing his release from the Order.[2] The isolation of Carthusian life was not typical and most who entered the cloister were surrounded by companions and spent much of their day engaged in communal activities. Nevertheless the monk could seek time and space alone or withdraw mentally to the inner recess of his mind while in the company of others. This chapter explores how monks spent their time alone and their desire for privacy in what must at times have been a rather claustrophobic environment; it considers the various worries and concerns that preoccupied the brethren and the opportunity for individualism within the communal life – that is, the chance each monk had to pursue personal interests and talents.

READING AND MEDITATION: INTROSPECTION

The purpose of the prayers and meditations that follow is to stir up the mind of the reader to the love of God or the fear of God or to self-examination.[3]

Every day the community gathered in the cloister to read and meditate on the Word of God (*Lectio Divina*) and thereby progress on the path to Truth and Understanding. Although this was a group activity it was a journey of introspection. Each monk embarked on a solo voyage of self-discovery, looking inwards to reach upwards. However, all the brethren shared the same destination and were united in their common purpose. The process of *Lectio Divina* was fourfold – the monks first read the text slowly, carefully studying the holy words, and thereafter meditated on the work, seeking a deeper understanding of its meaning; prayer followed whereby the heart yearned to find what was good and avoid what was bad, and finally the readers engaged in contemplation and lifted their hearts to God to be filled with knowledge of the sweetness of Heaven. Reading was not primarily a way to acquire information but was intended to stir the heart, provoking self-awareness and a true understanding of God. The monks were above all to seek God in the text and be transformed by what they learned. Reading therefore was the stimulus that ignited meditation and guided the monk on his journey heavenwards. As William of St Thierry explained, there was the same difference between attentive study and mere reading as between 'acquaintance with a passing guest, boon companionship and chance meeting'.[4]

St Anselm (d. 1109) recommended reading alone and in silence. This did not require that the monk was physically removed from the rest of the community, but rather that he was mentally withdrawn in the secret chamber of his soul.[5] Indeed meditation generally took place in communal areas and most often in the cloister, where the monks gathered at least once a day for the *Lectio Divina*. The importance of the cloister as a place of reading and contemplation is encapsulated in Abbot Richard of Melrose's (1136–48) declaration that a cloister without literature is 'a grave for living men'.[6] The monks might also read in the dormitory during the afternoon siesta, when the community retired to rest after dinner. Those who chose to do so were warned to be quiet and show consideration for others wishing to sleep. The monks of Durham meditated each day in their cemetery, where they remembered former members of the community, and it has recently been suggested that gardens within the precinct may have been used as places of solitary contemplation where the monk could focus on a flower or a tree as a stimulus to meditation.[7]

It was crucial that the monk remained focused while reading if he was to successfully withdraw into the recesses of his mind. For this reason silence was observed in the cloister and access to outsiders was restricted. The Cistercians were concerned that ornate carvings and decorations would distract the brethren. Accordingly their cloisters, like their churches, were almost minimalist in design, with little to divert the monks' attention. The great English Cistercian, Aelred of Rievaulx (d. 1166), launched a harsh attack on monasteries having 'ridiculous monstrosities' carved in their cloisters:

> Here we find filthy monkeys and fierce lions, fearful centaurs, harpies and striped tigers, soldiers at war and hunters blowing their horns. Here is one head with many bodies, there is one body with many heads. . . . All around there is such an amazing variety of shapes that one could easily prefer to take one's reading from the walls instead of a book. One could spend the whole day gazing fascinated at these things, one by one, instead of meditating on the law of God. Good Lord, even if the foolishness of it all occasion no shame at least one may balk at the expense.[8]

Various steps were taken to encourage the brethren to concentrate and cut themselves off from all distractions. They generally sat facing their neighbour's back to prevent them from communicating and were warned to keep their hoods down lest they were tempted to snooze under the cover of their cowls. Moreover, it was common for several of the senior monks to patrol the cloister, checking that everyone was focused on the task and nobody was idling; anyone who was not concentrating would likely be given some manual work to do so that his or her time was not wasted.[9] Reading was essential to the monk's journey to salvation and it was therefore imperative that the entire community attended the daily session in the cloister. Shirkers were likely to be punished. In 1394 the monks of Hailes (Gloucestershire) were warned that anyone who left the cloister through the door when they ought to be reading would be beaten in Chapter, while those who sneaked off by another route would be punished as for a carnal sin.[10] Although it was expected that all the brethren should be literate, that is able to read and write in Latin, this was not always the case. Gosbert, Count of Aspremont, who took the Cistercian habit at Villers-en-Brabant in c. 1238, could not read Latin but learnt the words for the Office so that he could join the others in the choir. As Gosbert did not actually understand the words he tended to get bored and would chew on a peppercorn to keep alert.[11] Peter Abelard (d. 1142) was insistent that all monks should be able to read Latin so that they could understand the words rather than simply repeating them; otherwise, he wrote, they were like an ass sitting before a lyre.[12]

WHAT MONKS READ

*Chew the honeycomb of his words, suck their flavour which is sweeter
than sap, swallow their wholesome sweetness. Chew by thinking, suck by
understanding, swallow by loving and rejoicing.*[13]

At the beginning of Lent each year the community gathered in the chapter house
for the annual distribution of books. The monks took their places in order of
seniority. When their name was called out they stepped forward, returned the
book they had borrowed the previous year and received a new text to meditate
upon in the year ahead.[14] Although the book remained in the monk's keeping
for the year, he returned it each night to the book cupboard for safe keeping. The
Ordinal of Barking Abbey (Essex), which dates from the early fifteenth century,
reveals that at this nunnery the librarian took charge of proceedings. She emptied
out all of the books from the cupboard onto a carpet on the chapter house floor
and then called each nun in turn, reading out the name of the book she had
borrowed. If the nun had finished with the text she placed it on the carpet, but
otherwise retained it for another year.[15] A unique record of the distribution
of books at Thorney Abbey (Cambridgeshire) over a four-year period in the
fourteenth century has been discussed by Professor Richard Sharpe. It survives
in an old mortuary roll that was reused to document this information and was
later refashioned to bind a translation of Bede's *History*; the medieval monks
clearly appreciated the benefits of recycling. The list is not a complete record of
the members of the community and the books they read, for there were a number
of absentees on distribution day. Nevertheless, it offers a fascinating insight into
the nature of reading material in the monastery and, not least, of how the Lenten
distribution of books was carried out at this particular house. The precentor of
Thorney compiled a list of all the monks, recording the title of each book he
had received and when. The process of distributing these books was conducted
with formality. The monks sat according to seniority and were called forward in
order of precedence, starting with the abbot. The monk stepped forward when
his name was read out and returned the book he had borrowed the previous year
unless he specifically asked to retain it; he then received a new text. The monks
were not limited to one book and might borrow others during the year but this
was uncommon and it was more usual to hold onto the same work for two or
more years. Indeed, the abbot of Thorney kept Gratian's *Decretum* for four years,
perhaps as his abbatial duties left him with little time for reading or because he

used it as a reference book.[16] It might seem excessive to retain the same book for a year or longer but it is important to realize that these texts were not simply read for information but were used as aids to meditation; the brethren were to chew over the words, reflect on their meaning and thereby receive enlightenment and understanding. The Carthusian monks each received two books from the library to read in the solitude of their cells and were expected to look after these works carefully, regarding them as the eternal food of their souls. They were warned explicitly that no book should be stained or soiled by dust or smoke.[17]

The choice of reading matter was given due consideration so that each monk received a text that was appropriate to his position and abilities. It was particularly important that novices were given suitable reading material, and guides were compiled advising them on which texts they should begin with and how they should progress thereafter. According to William of St Thierry (d. c. 1148), novices should start with works on Christ's deeds, since these provided an example of humility and a stimulant to charity and piety. They might also read the lives of saints and martyrs; not, however, for the historical detail but to stir them to the love of God.[18] The Cistercian abbot, Stephen of Sawley (d. 1252), provided a detailed guide on reading for novices in his spiritual directory, *Speculorum Novi* ('The Mirror of Novices'). He recommended the novice to begin with the four core texts, namely the customs of the Cistercian Order (the *Usages*), the Cistercian antiphonary (a choir book with chants for the Divine Office), the *Lives of the Fathers* and Gregory the Great's *Dialogues*. He could then advance to 'more solid food', studying the Old and New Testaments. Stephen was equally emphatic that these should not be read simply to acquire knowledge but should be used as a mirror, that the soul might see a reflection of its own image. Once the novice had mastered these texts he could proceed to more complex works such as the *Rule of St Benedict*, the *Confessions* of St Augustine and his commentaries on the Psalter; more contemporary texts such as the twelfth-century sermons of Gilbert of Hoyland on the 'Song of Songs' were also recommended. The novice was to read and cherish these works before moving onto others that included Cassian's *Conferences*, Jerome's *Letters* and contemporary works by Aelred of Rievaulx and William of St Thierry. The novice was advised to choose and read these works 'with discretion and not a little caution', that they might instruct him in modesty, perseverance and knowledge of the virtues.[19]

Those who had successfully progressed through the novitiate and were fully fledged members of the community could enjoy a greater choice of reading material. Office-holders might borrow books relating to their duties. In 1252 the infirmarer of Cluny was reading a work on prognostications about future life, while the wine-keeper of the community had a book on herbs.[20] Each monastery would have had a book cupboard (*armarium*) or a library for its collection of books. Some of these were large and wide-ranging and also included a number of reference works which were not distributed for personal reading. The great Cistercian abbey of Clairvaux, in north-east France, had about 350 books in its library while the English Benedictine libraries at Rochester and Christ Church, Canterbury, held almost 300 and 600 books respectively. The kinds of books stocked in these libraries varied and comparison of Cistercian, Benedictine and Augustinian houses suggests that the former were less diverse and more centred on theology. Some of these books have survived as a testimony to the nature of the medieval monastic library, but library catalogues are more revealing about the size and scope of the collections.[21] The late twelfth or early thirteenth-century catalogue for the Cistercian abbey of Rievaulx (Yorkshire), which is now in Jesus College, Cambridge (MS, 34), lists over 200 books that were in its library and thus available to the monks, although not necessarily read by them. The list is divided into sixteen sections labelled A to Q, with basic legal texts recorded under section A and the works of St Augustine under B and C. The books are wide-ranging and cover an array of subjects that encompasses history, grammar, philosophy and medicine. Nevertheless, the vast majority – around 85 per cent – is concerned with theology and includes Bibles and Psalters, authoritative writings by St Augustine and Bede, and works by renowned Cistercians, chiefly St Bernard of Clairvaux and Aelred of Rievaulx.[22] This seems fairly typical of a Cistercian monastic library and is comparable to the collection at Meaux Abbey, also in Yorkshire.[23] The libraries did not always include the most edificatory of works. The Cistercian abbey of Roche (Yorkshire) had a copy of the Anglo-Norman romance, *Li Romanz des Romanz*, while the Benedictines of Thorney seem to have had a rather bawdy book in their collection in the mid-fourteenth century which was described by the canon conducting a visitation of the house as 'shameful and not at all fit to be committed to writing'. He left orders for its destruction.[24]

'BOOKS HAVE WINGS'

Reading was intended as a stimulus for meditation and contemplation, to help advance each monk on his personal voyage to Truth. Hugh of Lincoln, prior of the Carthusian house of Witham and bishop of Lincoln (d. 1200), regarded books as the monk's lifeline. They were to be enjoyed as pleasures and riches in times of peace, as arms during war, and as food when hungry.[25] Importantly, books provided a way for monks to communicate with each other and with the world. At the request of his friends, St Anselm (d. 1109) committed to writing his prayers and meditations, hoping that these personal outpourings might inspire and guide others on their pilgrimage to salvation. Anselm's writings were read and appreciated by royalty, laity and religious alike. Durandus, abbot of Casa-Dei, wrote an enthusiastic letter of thanks, assuring Anselm that his writings had stirred his community to love God and him; Durandus requested that Anselm send any additional prayers.[26] The Carthusians spent much of their time copying and binding books in the solitude of their cells, both for their own use and for dissemination to others. In this way they 'preached with the pen' and communicated the Word while remaining secluded from the world and immersed in silence. Books were thus a way for monks to advance their own development and inspire others to hunger for God.

PRAYER AND PRIVATE DEVOTION

Prayer was closely related to meditation and both were part of the monk's progression to Truth and Understanding on his journey of self-discovery. As with reading, the monk might pray while in the midst of his companions, withdrawing mentally into the inner recesses of his mind. He might, however, seek a private space to pray, choosing to stay in the church after Vigils when the others returned to the dormitory to rest before Lauds. A monk of Westminster Abbey who was 'remarkably devoted' to St Edward the Confessor would remain behind after Vigils to recite five Psalms at a private altar 'for the repose of his soul'. When the same monk was struck with various afflictions he turned to Edward for relief. After Vigils, when his companions returned to the dormitory, the monk prayed to the saint, thanking him for his help in the past and asking for relief from his present suffering. He shed tears of compunction and was duly relieved when his chest was 'perfused with a dew from heaven', enabling him to breathe freely once more.[27] John, a monk of Dunfermline Abbey (Fife) who had three fingernails missing on his left hand, similarly sought help through private devotion. One evening after Compline had been celebrated and the rest of the community had retired to the dormitory, John stole away to the church, to the shrine of St Margaret, who was the resident saint. He spent the night there in vigil and was rewarded with 'a little healing sleep' and a vision of the saint, and woke to find he had been healed. John was later afflicted with a large swelling on his right hand and was unable to eat or use the hand in any way. He prudently ignored his brethren's advice to cut off the offending limb and once more sought relief through private devotion at the shrine of St Margaret. Six months later the swelling disappeared. John attributed this to the saint's miraculous intervention, believing that his prayers had been duly answered.[28] The medieval monk did not consider immediate relief essential to a miracle.

THE EUPHORIA OF DEVOTION

> *Thinking that he was quite alone and that no-one could see him, going down on his knees he then waved his hand in expressions of ecstasy and beat the ground intensely at the exquisite gaiety of being in the presence of the One he adored.*[29]

The brethren might experience great joy and euphoria when engaged in private devotion and deliberately seek a solitary spot, where they could express themselves freely without worrying about how their behaviour was perceived by their companions. It was previously noted that Ida the Gentle preferred to be alone when meditating on the body of Christ as she wanted privacy but also, and importantly, since she was prone to fits of ecstasy that could startle the others; hence she wished to find a private space to sob and 'flex her limbs' without shocking her sisters.[30] Others were similarly concerned that their rapturous frenzies should not be witnessed. Adam, a pious monk of Melrose Abbey, was rewarded for his devotion to the Virgin with a vision of the saint, which he received one day while praying at the altar of St Stephen in the abbey church. Thinking he was alone, Adam yielded to his emotions; he fell to his knees, waved his hands and beat the ground intensely out of sheer ecstasy. Unbeknown to Adam he had been observed by another member of the community but, significantly, the onlooker chose to remain silent lest Adam was embarrassed or

even angry that his behaviour might be deemed 'fatuous and inordinate'. The
monk, however, was puzzled and curious at what he had witnessed and later
approached Adam to ask why he had acted in this way and shown such elation.
Adam explained that the Virgin had appeared to him as the all-embracing
Church, and asked his companion not to tell anyone of this during his lifetime;
it was to remain their secret.[31]

THE INDIVIDUAL WITHIN THE COMMUNITY

*As often as the singing gives me more pleasure than the subject of this song, so
often do I confess I sin grievously.*[32]

Although the monastic life demanded self-abnegation, there was scope for
individuality. The monks might pursue their own interests and talents, whether
through personal devotion to a favourite saint, writing or painting. But, importantly, they used their gifts for the benefit of the community and to the glory of
God. Adam of Lexington, a devout monk of Melrose Abbey in Scotland, spent
the winter nights before the altar of the Blessed Virgin in the abbey church
playing the lute and singing songs in her honour. Prior Lawrence of Durham
(c. 1149–54) used his leisure time to compile a lengthy summary of passages on
the Redemption of Man in the Old and New Testaments; he called his work the
Hypognosticon.[33] There was opportunity for those who wished to develop their
musical abilities to do so. Monks of Durham who were keen to improve their
singing and participate in the Lady Mass and learn polyphony might take extra
lessons with the cantor. At Buckland Abbey (Devon) the monks could learn
organ-playing from Robert Derkeham, who was brought in around 1522 to teach
music to any of the brethren who were interested.[34] There was scope also for
monks to advance a cause that was dear to their heart, such as the promotion of a
favourite saint. Thomas of Monmouth, a twelfth-century monk of Norwich, was
a fervent devotee of the boy martyr, St William of Norwich, and self-proclaimed
keeper of the shrine. Thomas compiled a life of the saint and his miracles and
spearheaded support for his cult.[35]

   While the monk was to use his talents for the glory of God and not the self,
he might nonetheless derive considerable joy and contentment from pursuing
a personal interest, and appreciate the opportunity for time alone and away

from the demands of claustral life. A notable example is gardening, which was regarded as manual work and was in some cases essential to the self-sufficiency of the house, yet could be enjoyed as a tranquil and almost therapeutic activity. William Culross (d. 1504), the twenty-first abbot of Kinloss (Moray), was allegedly an avid gardener who worked until he was exhausted planting and grafting trees. Abbot Longdon of Abbey Dore (1500–16) evidently also found respite in nature and would gather the flowers of the saffron growing in one of the abbey's properties in Hereford.[36] For Walafrid Strabo ('Walafrid the Squinter'), a ninth-century monk of Reichenau in S. Germany, there was no joy greater than gardening or studying herbs for those living the secluded life.[37] Excavation of the Carthusian cells at Mount Grace Priory in Yorkshire indicates that gardening might offer an opportunity for self-expression. By the later Middle Ages it was common for each Carthusian to have a private garden attached to his cell, where he might meditate and work either cultivating the land or creating a pleasure garden. Recent research at Mount Grace suggests that what precisely was grown in these gardens and how they were cared for might vary depending on the monk's personal interests and abilities. Accordingly, whereas some of the brethren grew vegetables to supplement their diet, others specialized in flowers; those who had little interest in gardening probably allowed nature to take her course and more or less abandoned their gardens.[38]

The monks might employ their skills outside the community, although this too frequently benefitted the monastery, bringing in revenues and perhaps raising the profile of the house. Baldwin, a monk of St Denis (Paris) who officiated as physician to Edward the Confessor (1042–66), was rewarded with the abbacy of Bury St Edmunds, which he held from 1065 to 1097. During this time Baldwin continued to treat renowned patients and was regarded as the leading physician in the kingdom. Walter, who was the almoner of Bury in the late twelfth century, financed the building of the almonry at the house from the income he received from treating patients.[39] Thomas of Bamburgh, a monk of Durham, was employed to make large warlike engines for the defence of Berwick, while Brother Peter Lightfoot of Glastonbury made astronomical clocks in the fourteenth century; until recently one of these was in Wells Cathedral and it is now in the Victoria and Albert Museum, London.[40]

Thus, within the monastic life there was opportunity for each monk to follow and develop his personal interests and talents, but always for the fulfilment of the self in God. The brethren were not to take pride in these activities but must show humility for, as St Augustine warned, less pleasure should be taken in the singing of the song than in its subject. The monk might retain a sense of self within the community by withholding information from the others, thereby keeping part of himself private. It was not uncommon for monks to conceal a stash of candles or a treasured object. A striking example relates to Thomas of Monmouth, a twelfth-century monk of Norwich and fervent devotee of St William. Thomas was present when the body of the saint was exhumed in preparation for its translation from the chapter house to the church and spied two of the saint's teeth lying a little way from the corpse. He swiftly secreted these precious relics, wishing to retain them for himself, and carefully hid them away in a private place. Thomas did consider the ethicality of his actions but concluded that this was a 'pious theft' and said nothing of it to the others. But Thomas's secret was later exposed by the saint, who appeared in a vision to two of the brethren and recommended that they use his teeth, currently in Thomas's possession, to cure their sick companion. Thomas at first denied knowledge of the relics but eventually yielded to pressure and handed over the treasured objects.[41]

It was perhaps easier for abbots and office-holders to keep their affairs private, given that they often had a private chamber or suite of rooms and might use the excuse of their duties to absent themselves from claustral affairs. Samson, abbot of Bury St Edmunds (1182–1211), secretly stitched a white linen cross in advance of Henry II's visit to the abbey, for he planned to show this to the king when asking for permission to go on Crusade. Upon Henry's arrival Samson duly appeared with the cross in one hand and a needle and thread in the other. Alas, his efforts were in vain for the bishop of Norwich, who had already decided to go on Crusade, vetoed Samson's departure. The bishop was concerned for the safety of the counties of Suffolk and Norfolk if the two figures of authority were away at the same time.[42]

WORRIES

In the thirteenth century, a monk of Fountains Abbey (Yorkshire) was asked by his prior to illuminate leaves from the *Life of Godric*, which his community had borrowed from the monks of Durham. Having worked all day on these illuminations, the monk placed the pages to dry in the various nooks and crannies around the cloister. Just then the bell sounded for Compline and he joined his companions in the church to celebrate the Office. While the community was in the choir a fierce storm broke out and the monk grew anxious that his handiwork would be destroyed. However, there was little he could do to alleviate his fears, since all the brethren were obliged to remain in the church in silence and proceed to the dormitory immediately after the Office. Accordingly he had no opportunity to slip away to rescue the precious leaves. That night the monk lay awake, worrying what would become of the illuminations in the terrible storm, and sought comfort by praying to Godric to save these leaves from his *Life*. The saint duly appeared to the monk, commended him for his devotion and assured him that no wind or rain would touch the pages. The next morning the monk rushed to the cloister as soon as he was permitted and found, quite miraculously, that all the leaves were unharmed and just where he had left them.[43]

There were various worries that might trouble the monk in the cloister and a number of these have already been raised, such as concern over elections and problematic relationships. Other chief sources of angst included the stress of holding office and fears of inadequacy; these and other worries are now considered in greater detail.

THE BURDEN OF HOLDING OFFICE

> *You share in my wealth – in food and drink and travel and so on – but you scarcely give a thought to the things that worry me – the administration of the abbey and my household, and the many difficult matters that I encounter in my pastoral role. These are the things that cause me misery and heartache.*[44]

Matthew of Rievaulx, who officiated as precentor of the Cistercian abbey in the late twelfth and early thirteenth century, attributed his failing health to the stresses and strains of his office and begged to be released from his duties. Matthew vividly described his suffering and, strikingly, compared the intensity of his anguish to labour pains since he felt that his stomach was contracting and bursting out of his skin and that a razor was tearing out the skin from the crown of his head. He also complained of insomnia from rising early to lead the Night Office of Vigils and regretted having ever accepted the job, which he believed was too much for one man. Matthew reckoned that he would soon be carried from the singing in the choir to a grave in the cemetery.[45] But Matthew was not the only monk to seek relief from the stress of his office, and abbots in particular might suffer considerable strain. Jocelin of Brakelond conveys just what an impact this

St Cuthbert and monks, 12th c copy of Bede's *Life of St Cuthbert*, British Library,
Yates Thompson 26, f. 35v.

might have when he describes the physical change in Samson during his years as abbot of Bury. Jocelin notes that when Samson succeeded to the abbacy in 1182 at the age of forty-seven he had only a few grey hairs in his red beard, but fourteen years later it was snowy white. Indeed, Samson himself freely admitted that, had he foreseen the nature and scope of his abbatial duties, he would never have accepted office but served as master of the aumbry and librarian. On one occasion Samson asserted that, had it been possible for him to have returned to the way of life he had enjoyed before entering the monastery, he would gladly have done so and resumed his studies at the schools.[46]

The running of a monastery was an onerous task, particularly if there were financial problems to address. Samson's predecessor, Abbot Hugh (1157–80), left Bury in severe debt and the monastery's fiscal state was a source of grave concern and anxiety to the new superior. Upon succeeding to the abbacy Samson was approached by the abbey's creditors and became pale and thin with worry. Jocelin describes how one night he heard Samson 'unusually wakeful and sighing deeply'. He approached the abbot to find out the cause of his anxiety but met with an acrid reply, for Samson reeled off a list of matters that concerned him as superior of the house yet were rarely considered by the others. Jocelin raised his hands heavenwards, grateful that he was spared such anxieties.[47] Financial and legal wrangling was a common source of anxiety for superiors. In 1440 the prior of the Hull Charterhouse was greatly distressed about the monastery's legal problems and their impact on the community's resources. He was urged by the visiting priors of Beauvale and Mount Grace to set aside his worries and think of loftier matters and his own salvation. They stressed that he should not be submerged in temporal matters but ought to be a model for his monks – a 'light in a lantern' who would inflame eternal love (Matthew 5.14).[48] This, however, was often easier said than done and the burdens of abbatial office might cause some to resign from office and return to the relative solitude of claustral life. In 1229 Abbot Jens I of Øm stepped down as superior of the Danish abbey after seven years in office and returned to the position of prior, for he sought to be free from the travel, business and litigation that was required of him as abbot. A succeeding abbot, Magnus of Øm (1233–5), found the post to be so demanding that he asked God for relief. Magnus was soon released from his burdens, for that very day he was struck down with illness and died soon thereafter.[49] Hugh of Chepstow, who was abbot of the Cistercian monastery of Grace Dieu (Monmouthshire) in the fourteenth century, found the wrangling with the monastery's ruthless neighbours overwhelming. At the visitation of the house in 1351, Hugh explained that he felt the burden of administering the monastery was too much and wished to resign. Hugh's request was accepted and arrangements were made for his subsequent provision at Grace Dieu as a former abbot, since he was entitled to retain some of the dignity attached to the office. It was agreed that Hugh should have his own private chambers at the abbey, that he might eat with the abbot and, like him, be permitted to speak anywhere within the precinct. Hugh was also allowed to have at least one servant and an annual pension of £20.[50]

FEARS OF INADEQUACY

> When I examine myself carefully it seems to me that my whole life is either sinful or sterile. . . . O man, luke-warm and worthy to be spewed out.[51]

The monk might be plagued with self-doubt, fearing he was unworthy of salvation and unable to persist in the monastic life. Indeed, given that much of the monk's time was spent looking inwards in the hope that self-examination would bring realization of and horror at his sins, it is hardly surprising that this might lead to fears of inadequacy. Concerns of this kind might drive the monk to leave the monastery or even to take his own life; one lay brother apparently threw himself into a fish pond, having lost all hope of salvation.[52] A guilty conscience or crisis of faith might similarly prompt the monk or nun to contemplate suicide. A thirteenth-century nun who was tortured with feelings of guilt and shame threw herself down a well. It was alleged that a lay brother of the house had employed the black arts to entice her, but rather than confessing her feelings and sharing this burden the nun kept her shameful thoughts to herself. Finding the guilt intolerable, she sought to leave the convent, but when permission was withheld she took the only other route out – death.[53]

Occasionally, brethren suffered a crisis of faith which might similarly drive them to contemplate suicide. Caesarius of Heisterbach (d. c. 1240) recounts how one nun had recently attempted to drown herself after falling into a state of despondency and despair. The nun, who had been a model of virtue, was suddenly afflicted with doubts and disbelief, but when questioned by her companions simply retorted that she was a reprobate and there was no hope for her salvation. The prior of the house sought to help the nun return to her former ways and reminded her that if she died in this state he would be obliged to bury her in unconsecrated ground. This, however, had adverse effects for the nun considered it preferable to be drowned in a river than buried in an open field like a beast. She subsequently threw herself into the Moselle River but was rescued by a bystander who brought her back to the convent. Interestingly, her companions considered they were culpable for her lapse and vowed to look after her more carefully.[54] This story was recounted as a warning of how melancholia and doubt could strike even the most devout but offers an insight into the worries and concerns that might plague the brethren and drive them to extreme measures.

SOLITUDE AND ISOLATION: THE MONASTIC RETREAT

It was common for monasteries to have a retreat, to which the brethren could withdraw occasionally to escape the rigours of claustral life and perhaps recuperate from illness. Or they might seek time alone to meditate and get closer to God, experiencing a hermit-like existence. Peter the Venerable, abbot of Cluny (d. 1156), periodically withdrew into the forest near Cluny seeking peace and a solitary place where he could contemplate and meditate, free from the pressures of abbatial office. The senior monks of Cluny were similarly allowed to withdraw into the surrounding woods on occasion to meditate in private, but junior monks were unlikely to be granted this concession for it was feared that the isolation of these places exposed the less experienced to the devil. There was safety in numbers, and while the monks could as a community ward off evil, alone they were vulnerable to temptation. As Bernard of Clairvaux (d. 1153) warned, 'the desert, the shade of the forest and the solitude of silence offer plentiful opportunities for evil. . . . The Tempter approaches in perfect security'.[55] Hence only proven and mature monks were permitted to go on these retreats.

The retreat might instead function as a form of recreation or respite from the routine of claustral life and an opportunity for the monk to be physically and mentally refreshed. This was particularly important for anyone suffering from depression (*accidie*), for whom fresh air, exercise and a break from claustral life were considered restorative. The recreational retreat was not necessarily a solitary experience and the monks might be sent in relays to a manor or cell of the house to enjoy a more relaxed regime, a less austere diet and fresh air; not least they could benefit from the beauty of Nature. While the way of life was less restricted on retreat the brethren were nevertheless required to observe certain regulations and perform various liturgical duties. The monks of Durham were sent in groups of four to Finchale, a cell of their house, where they stayed for three weeks at a time enjoying a less rigorous programme.[56] A similar arrangement functioned between St Albans and its cell at Redbourne (Hertfordshire). From the late twelfth century Redbourne was used by St Albans as a rest house and a retreat, and the monks were sent in relays – three monks stayed with a prior for several weeks at a time. By the fifteenth century these breaks were occasionally more riotous than restful and some of the monks were reprimanded for late-night gatherings at Redbourne.[57] Others were guilty of hunting, hawking and drinking.

Some monasteries, particularly those situated in the towns and cities, sent their monks to their manors in the country or by the sea, believing that the healthier air would be beneficial to their physical and mental well-being. Monks of St Peter's, Westminster, went to the monastery's manors at Hendon, Hampstead and Wandsworth, as well as Combe in Kent, to recover from ill health. The prior had a house at Belsize (now Belsize Park), where he had blood let in 1512.[58] The convalescent and elderly monks of Norwich were sent to the abbey's cells at Lynn and Yarmouth, to benefit from the sea air. Brethren who were too ill to travel might go instead to the priory of St Leonard's overlooking Norwich. In some cases monks went there specifically to receive treatment – in the fourteenth century the precentor of Norwich had blood let at St Leonard's and received medication.[59]

Time away from the rigours and oppressiveness of the cloister helped restore the body and soul, enabling the monk to return reinvigorated to claustral life. But the monks did not necessarily have to leave the confines of the precinct to enjoy the benefits of fresh air and exercise. The community was often advised to take a walk through the gardens or vineyards or perhaps to stroll by the river to lift their spirits and refresh both body and soul. The Augustinian Canons of Barnwell, who were 'greatly disturbed in spirit', walking around half-dead and unable to participate fully in communal life, were sent to wander in the priory gardens or by the river but might be permitted to leave the precinct to walk through woods, fields or meadows.[60]

A GROWING DESIRE FOR PRIVACY

The monastic life combined solitude with communal living. Each monk progressed on a solo voyage to salvation through meditation and contemplation. But he undertook his journey alongside and in the presence of his companions, since the community as a group could resist temptations that were difficult to withstand alone. Communal living – that is eating and sleeping together and sharing the various chores – was also intended to foster unity and, importantly, to suppress jealousies and hostilities. However, as previously noted in Chapter 5, developments within the organization of the monastery contributed to its breakdown. From the twelfth century a number of abbots had their own quarters and soon after it was not uncommon for senior officials to have private chambers. The regularization of meat-eating in the monastery meant that mealtimes were no longer the communal affairs they had once been; whereas those who observed the routine diet ate in the refectory, meat-eaters dined in a separate room. The nature of communal living was affected also by developments outside the monastery, notably a growing desire for privacy, which in some houses led to the partitioning of the dormitory and infirmary to provide private cubicles. By the later Middle Ages various aspects of communal living that had been tolerated by earlier generations were more difficult to accept, and in some cases were rejected. Expectations were changing and had changed in accordance with the times. Yet the support of the community remained the essence of monastic life. Through fellowship and communion the monk could achieve his ultimate goal of salvation.

See to it, dearest friends, that the fear of God which you experience does not cool down under any pretext; but let it grow daily more fervent, as if fanned by your untiring zeal until, transformed, it shines brightly for you into eternal safety.[1]

Epilogue

When Abbot Gisilbert of Himmerod (Germany) was asked how his monks, who had been brought up with the fine things in life, managed to tolerate the frugal claustral diet, he revealed the three secret ingredients that ensured the brethren ate everything without complaint – long night watches, manual labour and the knowledge that nothing better was on offer.[2]

The monastic life was undoubtedly difficult if rewarding. The decision to take the habit and dedicate oneself to God was not to be taken lightly, for once the monk entered the cloister he was subject to the rules of the Order and the authority of his abbot. The rigorous and demanding daily regime and the pressures of communal living could be gruelling for even the most zealous of conscripts and not everyone managed to stay the course. Yet the monastery offered camaraderie and friendship, as well as security in this life and the promise of salvation in the next. Indeed, to die wearing the monastic habit, to be buried in holy ground and to secure the community's prayers for one's soul was the ultimate consolation. But above all the monastic life brought true fulfilment and joy. St Anselm (d. 1109) was happiest when he, like the owl, was safely with his chicks in the cloister rather than among the rooks and the crows in the secular world. Anselm spoke of the delights of monastic life and he and his contemporaries urged others to take the habit and experience for themselves the 'blissful abundance' they enjoyed within the cloister.[3] The monastery did not simply provide a path to Heavenly Salvation but was itself a kind of paradise. This is vividly evoked in Eadmer's account of a vision Anselm had when recovering from illness. He describes how the holy man was led into a large and spacious cloister where the walls were covered with bright, shining silver. The silvery grass was 'soft and delightful beyond belief' and like real grass yielded to those who lay upon it and sprang up once more when they rose. This scene, which was enchanting and truly beautiful, was an image of the 'true monastic life' and Anselm, we are told, rejoiced to have the cloister as his home.[4]

Glossary

(Terms in **bold** feature somewhere in the Glossary.)

abbot
: the superior of the monastic community who presides over the abbey and is to be obeyed in all matters. The head of a priory is a **prior**.

acolyte
: a minor church officer whose main duties are to light the candles on the altar and carry them in processions, to prepare water and wine for mass and attend the **priests** and **deacons**.

alb
: a white tunic worn as a liturgical vestment.

almoner
: this was an important monastic official (**obedientiary**) in benedictine houses who exercised charity on behalf of the community and distributed alms to the deserving poor. In *Cistercian* houses these duties were carried out by the monk **porter**.

amice
: this liturgical vestment is an oblong piece of white linen worn on the shoulders over the **alb**.

Augustinian Canon
: a regular canon who follows the ***Rule of St Augustine*** and like the monk lives in a community but does not withdraw from the world and carries out pastoral duties, after the example of the Apostles. The Augustinian Canons preached, taught, cared for the sick and administered the sacraments.

Benedictine
: monk who follows the ***Rule of St Benedict*** compiled by ***St Benedict of Nursia*** and promises to live a life of poverty, chastity and obedience, and pledges stability to the monastery and the way of life. Their customary clothing is a black habit, symbolic of humility. The Benedictines dominated religious observance from the

sixth to the late eleventh century when the emergence of the new religious orders challenged their monopoly.

St Benedict of Nursia — regarded as the founder of Western monasticism, he wrote a rule for his monks of Monte Cassino c. 480–550 which became and remains the bedrock of Western monasticism (see **Rule of St Benedict**).

Calefactory — the warming house, often located on the south claustral range. This was one of the few places in the monastery that was heated and the monks gathered here in silence to warm themselves, to grease boots or prepare ink.

Camaldolese Order — hermit group founded c. 1024 in the mountains near Arezzo by Saint Romuald, a monk of Ravenna, which was the first eremitical order in the West. The first Camaldolese lived in individual cells within the enclosure – their 'prison'. These monk-hermits led an austere and impoverished life and engaged in self-flagellation.

Camaldoli — seat of the **Camaldolese Order**, near Arezzo.

Canonical Hours/ Divine Office — the seven daytime Offices (**Lauds, Prime, Terce, Sext, None, Vespers, Compline**) and the night Office of *Vigils* that structured the monastic day. Lauds, the first Office, began at daybreak while Compline took place at sunset, marking the end of the monk's day.

Carthusian Order — a contemplative Order founded by St Bruno in 1084 at **La Grande Chartreuse**, near Grenoble. Carthusian monasticism combined **coenobitic** living (life in a community) with **eremitic** (the hermit's way of life). Each monk lived alone in a private cell where he ate, slept and prayed but joined the others to celebrate the **Office**. Every Sunday the monks dined together in the refectory and also ate together whenever one of their members died. The Carthusian life was and is regarded as one of the most testing forms of monasticism.

cellarer

he was one of the most important monastic officials (**obedientiaries**) and was chiefly responsible for the provisions within the monastery.

chapter house

the room where the community gathered for their daily meeting which began with a reading from the *Rule of St Benedict*. Thereafter business was discussed and disciplinary matters tended. The chapter house was usually on the east claustral range and was one of the most important buildings in the precinct. Hence this was often an impressive building and a desirable burial spot for abbots and leading members of the community.

Charter of Charity (*Carta Caritatis*)

this pioneering **Cistercian** document established the constitutional framework of the order and was first compiled c. 1114 but was revised and updated. It set out the familial organization of the abbeys which were united through bonds of unity and subject to annual visitation. Every Cistercian abbey was to have a copy of this document.

chartulary

a manuscript containing a collection of charters pertaining to land, rights and legal transactions.

chasuble

this sleeveless mantle covering the body and shoulders is worn over the **alb** by the celebrant at Mass.

choir

the area occupied by the monks' stalls in the east end of the church. Here they gathered to celebrate each of the **Canonical Hours** and the daily **Mass**.

Cistercian Order

one of the most important of the new religious Orders to emerge from the eleventh-century reform movement, the Cistercians had their origins in the swampy forests of **Cîteaux**, south of Dijon, where the **Benedictine** abbot, Robert of Molesme, sought to lead a life of greater simplicity and poverty. While Robert was compelled to return to his former abbey of Molseme, his small group of followers remained and were joined by other devotees. The arrival of

Bernard of Clairvaux c. 1112 transformed the Order
which quickly expanded throughout Europe. By
the mid-twelfth century the Cistercians had gained
international prominence and had houses the length
and breadth of Western Christendom. The Cistercians
were characterized by their desire to return to the
basic tenets of the *Rule of St Benedict* and to lead
a life of simplicity and poverty. They wore habits
of undyed wool and were sometimes known as the
'White Monks'; they embraced manual labour and
made **lay brothers** an integral part of the community
to achieve self-sufficiency. To implement unity and
uniformity of practice all the abbeys were organized
in a familial structure and each house was visited once
a year to ensure that standards were maintained. The
abbots attended an annual assembly at Cîteaux called
the **General Chapter**.

Cîteaux   the mother-house of the Cistercian Order in
                           Burgundy that was founded in 1098 and hosted the
                           annual assembly of abbots.

Cluniac Order   a reformed branch of the **Benedictine Order** that
                           emerged in the tenth century when the Burgundian
                           abbey of **Cluny** established a congregation of affiliated
                           houses throughout Europe. Cluniac monasticism was
                           characterized by its elaborate liturgy and magnificent
                           buildings. The Cluniacs dominated monastic
                           reform in the tenth and eleventh centuries but their
                           reputation faded in the eleventh century when their
                           excesses were criticized. The **Cistercians** emerged as a
                           chief opponent of Cluniac monasticism and a war of
                           polemic developed between the two orders.

Cluny   the Burgundian mother-house of the **Cluniac**
                           congregation founded by William of Aquitaine in 909.
                           Cluny spearheaded **Benedictine** reform in the tenth
                           century establishing a large network of houses and

reforming existing monasteries. Cluny alone was an abbey and all other houses within the congregation were priories. Cluny became synonymous with the restored Benedictine life but faced criticism for its opulence in the eleventh century.

coenobitic
communal living; refers to monks living as a community rather than as solitaries.

Collations
the daily reading from John Cassian's *Collationes Patrum* (*Conferences*) and other edifying texts. This took place before **Compline**, usually in the north cloister walk.

Compline
the seventh and last of the daytime **Canonical Hours** which brought the monk's day to a close. The name comes from the Latin *plenus* meaning complete.

corporal
the square pieces of linen on which the consecrated elements were placed during the Mass and which covered the remnants of the consecrated Host.

Corrody
a stipend awarded to an individual (corrodian) in return for gifts given to the community or as recompense for past services. The terms of the corrody varied but might include food, drink, fuel, lighting and accommodation within the precinct.

cowl
a full cloak with wide sleeves and a hood worn by monks over the tunic when they were in the church, at the chapter meeting and at meals.

Customary
a directory of customs relating to daily life, the administration of the house and liturgical arrangements.

daughter-house
a monastery founded by another was known as its daughter-house; the founding monastery was the **mother-house**.

deacon
an ordained member of the clergy below the rank of **priest**.

eremitic	living as a hermit; a life characterized by solitude and austerity.
Fontevrault	a double foundation for men and women founded by the preacher, Robert of Arbrissel, c. 1101. The abbey was situated near Anjou and was intended to provide for women from all walks of life but was soon popular among the nobility who made it their own. High status residents include Eleanor of Aquitaine who was buried here; her tomb, as well as that of her husband, Henry II (d. 1188), can still be seen.
General Chapter	annual general meeting attended by the heads of houses. The Cistercians were the first to make this an integral part of the administration of their order and held this general assembly at **Cîteaux** each September. Every abbot of the Order was expected to attend to discuss business and legislation.
Gilbertines/Order of Sempringham	an Order for women founded in 1131 by a Lincolnshire man, St Gilbert of Sempringham (d. 1189). The nuns followed the ***Rule of St Benedict*** and were assisted by **lay sisters** who carried out domestic duties and cared for guests; heavy labour was undertaken by **lay brothers**. Canons were incorporated to minister to the women; they followed the ***Rule of St Augustine***. The organization of the Gilbertines was greatly influenced by the **Cistercians**. Gilbert had hoped that the **General Chapter** of **Cîteaux** would incorporate his women within their congregation but his request was turned down. Nevertheless, the Cistercians offered Gilbert their support and guidance. The Gilbertines were the only English Order established in the Middle Ages and did not spread outside the country; most foundations were in Lincolnshire and Yorkshire.
La Grande Chartreuse	the **mother-house** of the **Carthusian** Order situated in the mountains near Grenoble. Here, St Bruno

	and his followers settled in 1084 to observe a life of contemplation and poverty.
Grandmontines/Order of Grandmontine	founded by St Stephen of Muret (d. 1124) in the late eleventh century near Limoges. The Grandmontines were noted for their austerity and were also known as the 'Bonshommes'. Like the **Carthusians** the Grandmontines were hermit monks but had greater contact with their fellow brethren and were more receptive to outsiders. The Grandmontines did not follow the ***Rule of St Benedict*** or the ***Rule of St Augustine*** but considered the Gospel their rule.
guestmaster	the monastic official (**obedientiary**) responsible for the reception and care of guests and the management of the monastery's guesthouse (hospice).
Habit	the customary clothing worn by the monk.
Hagiography	writings on saints and venerated persons.
Horarium	the daily timetable in the monastery that was structured around the **Canonical Hours**.
Infirmarer	the monastic official (**obedientiary**) who cared for the sick and managed the monastery's infirmary.
Kiss of peace/pax	the kiss was exchanged as a greeting of the faithful in Eucharistic liturgy and is a symbol of love and unity in Christ.
Kitchener	the monastic official (**obedientiary**) who was responsible for the management of the kitchen.
Knights Hospitaller (Knights of St John)	the origins of the Hospitallers are obscure but seemingly lie in the late eleventh century when a hospital for pilgrims was founded near the Holy Sepulchre, Jerusalem. In the twelfth century the Hospitallers were transformed into a Military Order and like the **Knights Templar** took vows of chastity and obedience and lived according to a rule; the Hospitaller rule was based largely on the ***Rule of St Augustine*** and not the ***Rule of St Benedict***. The

Hospitallers were chiefly concerned with caring for
pilgrims and crusaders to the Holy Land, where they
administered hospitality and charity. However they
had lands and houses in the West.

Knights Templar
they, like the **Knights Hospitaller**, developed into
a **Military Order** in the twelfth century and were
essentially intended to serve in the Holy Land,
protecting the crusader states and guarding pilgrim
routes to Jerusalem. However, they had outposts in the
West including houses and estates in Britain. These
fighting monks took vows of chastity and obedience
and lived according to a rule that was compiled by the
great Cistercian, St Bernard of Clairvaux (d. 1153),
who himself preached the Second Crusade. Victories
in the East and endowments in the West brought
prosperity to the Knights Templar but their reputation
was severely tarnished with the Fall of Acre in 1291
and also by allegations of greed and corruption
in their capacity as international financiers. The
Templar's centre in London was south of the Strand,
which is now Inner and Middle Temple. The church
survives and is in the characteristic circular design,
after the Church of the Holy Sepulchre.

Lauds
the first **Canonical Hour** of the day that was
celebrated at dawn.

Lay brother
(*Conversus*)
prior to the twelfth century this referred to one who
was an adult convert to the religious life. However,
with the emergence of the new monastic orders in the
twelfth century and particularly the **Cistercians**, the
lay brother (or sister) was one who was not a monk
yet had taken vows and was regarded as a member
of the community. The **Cistercians** were the first
to make the lay brothers an integral part of their
communities and compiled a rule for their use (*Usus
Conversorum*). These lay brothers were professed

members of the **Cistercian** family but whereas the monks' day revolved around their liturgical duties in the church, the lay brothers were chiefly responsible for agricultural and industrial work, ensuring the self-sufficiency of the house. The **Carthusians** similarly adopted **lay brothers** and **Gilbertine** communities included **lay brothers** and lay sisters.

Lectio Divina   'divine reading'. This refers to the meditative reading through which one could achieve communion with God.

Matins   a **Canonical Hour** that was celebrated before **Prime**. The term is rather ambiguous for what was in the Middle Ages called Matins is now referred to as **Lauds** and what was then called **Nocturns** or **Vigils** is now known as Matins. In the later Middle Ages Matins and Lauds were together referred to as Vigils.

Military Orders   see **Knights Hospitaller** and **Knights Templar**.

misericord   a separate room where the monks could eat meat when permitted since meat was forbidden in the refectory.

mother-house   the abbey which founded another was known as the mother-house; the new monastery was the **daughter-house**.

Nocturns   see **Vigils**.

None(s)   the fifth daytime **Canonical Hour** sung at the ninth hour of the day (mid-afternoon).

novice   a probationary member of the monastic community who was instructed and guided by the **novice-master** until he made his profession as a monk.

novice-master   the monastic official (**obedientiary**) in charge of the **novices** who offered guidance and support and instructed these newcomers on the monastic way of life.

novitiate	the probationary period that a newcomer had to complete before he was received within the community as a monk. Traditionally this lasted one year and was both a testing time and an instructive process.
obedientiary	a monastic office-holder responsible for the daily administration of the monastery. Important obedientiaries included the **cellarer** and **sacrist**.
Office (Divine)	see **Canonical Hours**.
Opus Dei	literally 'the work of God', this refers to the daily round of liturgical **Offices** in the church.
Porter	in some orders this was a monastic official (**obedientiary**) who manned the gate and welcomed visitors; in Benedictine houses a lay man held this post.
Pottage	a kind of pease pudding.
Precentor	the monastic official (**obedientiary**) who directed the church services. He encouraged singing and ensured the monks were vigilant during the service. The precentor was also responsible for the liturgical books.
Premonstratensian Order	founded by St Norbert in 1120 at Prémontré, the Order was influenced by the **Cistercians** but followed the *Rule of St Augustine* and not the *Rule of St Benedict*; accordingly these men were canons rather than monks. The Premonstratensians were sometimes referred to as the Norbertines after their founder, Norbert of Xanten, or the White Canons, after the colour of their habit.
Priest	an ordained member of the clergy above the rank of **deacon** who has the right to celebrate and administer the holy rites.
Prior	in an abbey he was the second in command who assisted and deputized for the abbot but in priories he officiated as the head of the community.
Prime	the first monastic **Office** of the day.

Refectorer	the monastic official (**obedientiary**) responsible for the organization and maintenance of the **refectory**.
Refectory	this was where the community gathered for their meals and listened to an edifying reading while they ate. In winter the monks ate here once a day but in summer they had a light supper to supplement their dinner. No meat was permitted in the refectory and was eaten instead in a separate chamber known as the **misericord**.
Regularis Concordia	a legislative document promulgated at Winchester in 970 that was intended to unify religious practice in England. The *Regularis Concordia* was based on the **Rule of St Benedict** and Benedict of Aniane's ninth-century revisions of the *Rule*.
Reredorter	the toilet block often accessed from the monks' dormitory.
Retrochoir	the area immediately behind the monks' **choir** occupied by the sick and infirm who followed a less rigid routine than the rest of the community, and often also by **novices**.
Rule of St Augustine	effectively a letter of guidance compiled by St Augustine of Hippo (d. c. 430), this underlines the importance of charity, obedience and individual poverty, and sets down a daily schedule for communal devotion. Its followers observe a regular life but unlike monks are not required to withdraw from the world.
Rule of St Benedict	'a little rule for beginners' compiled by **Benedict of Nursia**, c. 480–550, to regulate the life of his monks at Monte Cassino in Italy. Benedict underlined the abbot's powers of supremacy and made stability, chastity and obedience defining features of this way of life. The daily regime was structured around the liturgical offices in the church (**Opus Dei**), spiritual reading (**Lectio Divina**) and manual labour. From the

ninth century Benedict's *Rule* became and remains the blueprint for monasticism in the West.

Sacrist

the monastic official (**obedientiary**) responsible for the maintenance and upkeep of the church and liturgical vestments. His duties included opening and closing the church doors and making sure there was sufficient candles and oil. He prepared the hosts for the celebration of Mass and when **novices** made their profession and received the **tonsure** it was the sacrist's job to burn the hair clippings.

Savigniac Order/
Order of Savigny

this had its origins in the forest of Savigny, where Vitalis of Mortain established a hermitage in 1105. The community that evolved followed the ***Rule of St Benedict*** and the monks wore grey habits. A Savigniac Congregation was established with the foundation of **daughter-houses** but by the mid-twelfth century administrative and financial problems compelled the head of Savigny, Abbot Serlo, to request that the **Cistercians** incorporate his own congregation within their family. The Cistercian **General Chapter** of 1147 agreed and subsequently all Savigniac houses were visited and reformed according to Cistercian ideals.

Sempringham

the mother-house of the Order of Sempringham/ **Gilbertines**, founded by St Gilbert of Sempringham.

Sext

the third of the lesser **Canonical Hours** that was originally celebrated at the sixth hour of the day (midday).

Seyney

the process of bloodletting that was common in the Middle Ages both to prevent ill health and as a curative. The monks were routinely bled in groups to prevent sickness and followed a more relaxed regime when recuperating from the process; this included permission to eat a little meat.

Skilla	a small bell that hung in the refectory and was rung to summon the brethren to eat and to announce courses.
Statutes	regulations issued to the monastic community, usually following the visitation of the house, to correct and reform.
Tabula	a wooden board that usually hung outside the chapter house and was struck with a mallet. The prior or his deputy sounded the *tabula* to summon the monks to the **refectory** or to their duties. Whenever a monk was dying the board was struck repeatedly to call the community to attend their brother; the *tabula* was used during Easter in lieu of bells as bell-ringing was forbidden at this time. The community's notice-board was also called a *tabula*.
Terce	the third **Canonical Hour** that was celebrated mid-morning.
Tiron	the mother-house of the **Tironensian Order**, near Chartres, where Bernard of Tiron and his followers settled in the early twelfth century.
Tironensian Order	a new monastic Order that emerged from the eleventh-century reform movement and was the initiative of the **Benedictine**, Bernard of Tiron (d. 1117), who sought to live a hermit-like existence of great austerity in the forest of Craon. Here, he and his fellow solitaries, Robert of Arbrissel (founder of **Fontevrault**) and Vitalis of Mortain (founder of **Savigny**), were joined by followers; from this the order of Tiron was established near Chartres, in the early twelfth century. The Order was the first of the new religious orders to spread internationally and established abbeys and priories houses throughout France and the British Isles. King David of Scotland (d. 1153) brought the Tironensians to Scotland following his visit to Tiron in 1116 and settled the

monks at Selkirk in the Scottish Borders. They later
relocated to Kelso.

tonsure   the rite of shaving the crown of the head, this was
                   symbolic of both clerical and monastic status.

Vespers   the sixth **Canonical Hour** that was celebrated at the
                   approach of dusk. This was named after Hesperus, the
                   evening star.

Victorines/Order   Regular Canons founded in 1106 by William of
of St Victor   Champeaux. The abbey was in Paris and had a
                   theological school which was highly renowned,
                   particularly in the twelfth century, and drew a number
                   of important scholars. The Victorines observed a
                   modified version of the ***Rule of St Augustine***.

Vigils   the Night Office traditionally celebrated at midnight
                   in accordance with Psalm 119. 162 ('At midnight I rose
                   to give thanks to Thee').

visitation   a formal inspection of the monastery by the bishop
                   or his deputy or a member of the Order. This was
                   intended to ensure standards were maintained, to
                   punish and correct misdemeanours and to offer
                   advice and support.

Notes

Notes to the Preface

1 Bernard of Clairvaux, cited in A. A. King, *Cîteaux and her Elder Daughters* (London, 1954), p. 215.

2 See for example J. Kerr, *Monastic Hospitality: the Benedictines in England c. 1070–c. 1250* (Woodbridge, 2007), pp. 7, 16–17.

Notes to the Introduction

1 From St Anthony's *Vita Patrum* cited in *The Cistercian World: Monastic Writings of the Twelfth Century*, trans. and ed. with intro. P. Matarasso (Harmondsworth, 1993), p. 196.

2 For a general overview, see P. King, *Western Monasticism: A History of the Monastic Movement in the Latin Church* (Kalamazoo, 1999), chs 1–3; C. H. Lawrence, *Medieval Monasticism: Forms of Religious Life in Western Europe in the Middle Ages*, 3rd edn (Harlow, 2001), pp. 1–17; for an overview in the British Isles, see J. Burton, *The Monastic and Religious Orders in Britain 1000–1300* (Cambridge, 1994), pp. 1–20.

3 Canterbury, 'Instruction for Novices', in *The Monastic Constitutions of Lanfranc*, ed. and trans. D. Knowles, rev. ed. C. N. L. Brooke (Edinburgh, 2002), pp. 198–221 (199).

4 *The Rule of St Benedict*, ed. and tr. D. O. Hunter Blair, 5th edn (Fort Augustus, 1948), ch. 73 (p. 181).

5 G. Coppack and M. Aston, *Christ's Poor Men: the Carthusians in England* (Stroud, 2002), p. 44.

6 *The Ecclesiastical History of Orderic Vitalis*, ed. and trans. M. Chibnall, 6 vols (Oxford, 1969–80), 4, pp. 310–11.

7 Jacques de Vitry (d. c. 1240), cited by Lawrence, *Medieval Monasticism*, pp. 184–5.

8 For an overview see, King, *Western Monasticism*, pp. 195–228 and Burton, *Monastic and Religious Orders*, pp. 109–30; for pre-Conquest England see S. Foot, *Veiled Women: the Disappearance of Nuns from Anglo-Saxon England*, 2 vols (Aldershot, 2000).

9 William of St Thierry's advice to novices in *The Golden Epistle: A Letter to the Brethren at Mont Dieu*, trans. T. Berkeley (Kalamazoo, 1971), p. 54.

10 H. J. Richardson, 'Cistercian formularies', in *Formularies which bear on the History of Oxford, c. 1204–1420*, ed. H. E. Salter *et al.*, 2 (Oxford, 1942), pp. 279–327 (300–1); *The Early History of St John's College Oxford*, ed. W. H. Stevenson and H. E. Salter, Oxford Historical Society ns 1 (1939), pp. 6–7; *Concilia Scotia Ecclesiae Scotianae Statuta tam Provincialia quam Synodalia quae Supersunt 1225–1564*, 2 vols, ed. J. Robertson, Bannatyne Club (Edinburgh, 1866), 1, p. cclxxiv.

11 *St Peter Damian: Selected Writing on the Spiritual Life*, trans. and intro. P. McNulty (London, 1959), p. 42.

12 Matthew of Rievaulx, cited in M. Cassidy-Welch, *Monastic Spaces and their Meanings: Thirteenth-century English Cistercian Monasteries* (Turnhout, 2001), p. 65.

13 Caesarius of Heisterbach, *The Dialogue on Miracles*, trans. H. von E. Scott and C. C. S. Bland, 2 vols (London, 1929), 1, pp. 12, 244.

14 See A. H. Bredero, *Bernard of Clairvaux: Between Cult and History* (Grand Rapids, 1996), pp. 267–75.

15 *The Letters of Saint Anselm of Canterbury*, trans. and annotated W. Fröhlich, 3 vols (Kalamazoo, 1990–4), 1, no. 101 (pp. 253–4).

16 Professor Christopher Holdsworth, 'Bernard and his monastic family', paper given at the International Congress of Medieval Studies, Leeds 2007.

17 Adam of Eynsham, *Magna Vita Sancti Hugonis*, ed. and trans. D. Douie and D. H. Farmer, 2 vols (London, 1961–2; repr. Oxford, 1985), p. 78.

18 Walter Daniel, *The Life of Aelred of Rievaulx*, ed. and trans. F. M. Powicke (repr. Oxford, 1978), pp. 14–16; *Exordium*, cited in P. Matarasso, ed., trans. and intro., *The Cistercian World: Monastic Writings of the Twelfth Century* (Harmondsworth, 1993), p. 300.

19 Jocelin of Brakelond, *Chronicle of the Abbey of Bury St Edmunds*, trans. D. Greenway and J. Sayers (Oxford, 1989), p. 34.

20 Anselm, *Letters*, 1, no. 101 (p. 254).

21 Caesarius, *Dialogue on Miracles*, 1, p. 8.

Notes to Chapter 1: The Precinct, the People, the Daily Regime

1 Alexander of Neckam (d. 1217), *Alexandri Neckam, De Naturis Rerum Book 2*, ed. T. Wright (London, 1863), ch. 36 (pp. 149–50).

2 Bernard of Clairvaux, cited P. Meyvaert, 'The medieval monastic claustrum', *Gesta* 12: 1 (1973), 53–9 (57).

3 For an accessible analysis of the plan see L. Price, *The Plan of St Gall in Brief* (Berkeley, LA, London, 1982).

4 F. Woodman, 'The Waterworks drawing of the Eadwine Psalter', in *The Eadwine Psalter: Text, Image and Monastic Culture in Twelfth-Century Canterbury*, ed. M. Gibson/T. A. Heslop/R. W. Pfaff (London, 1992), pp. 168–77.

5 R. Gilchrist, *Norwich Cathedral Close: The Evolution of the English Cathedral Landscape* (Woodbridge, 2005), p. 64.

6   See Kerr, *Monastic Hospitality*, p. 92.

7   *The Observances in Use at the Augustinian Priory of St Giles and St Andrew at Barnwell, Cambridgeshire*, ed. and trans. J. W. Clark (Cambridge, 1897), pp. 193–5.

8   *De Obedientiariis Abbendoniae*, in *Chronicon Monasterii de Abingdon*, ed. J. Stevenson, 2 vols (London, 1858), 2, pp. 335–417 (404–5).

9   *Observances of Barnwell*, pp. 154–5.

10   C. Harper-Bill, 'Cistercian visitation in the late Middle Ages: the case of Hailes Abbey', *Bulletin of Historical Research* 53 (1980), 103–14 (109).

11   Jocelin, *Chronicle*, p. 65.

12   *Chronicon Abbatiae Ramseinsis*, ed. W. D. Macray (London, 1886), pp. lxviii, 397.

13   Cassidy-Welch, *Monastic Spaces*, pp. 161–2.

14   R. Sharpe, 'Monastic reading at Thorney Abbey 1323–47', *Traditio* 60 (2005), 243–78.

15   J. France, *The Cistercians in Scandinavia* (Kalamazoo, 1992), p. 88; 'The Chronicle of Melrose', in *Medieval Chronicles of Scotland: the Chronicles of Melrose and Holyrood*, trans. J. Stevenson (Llanerch facsimile, Felinfach, 1988), pp. 7–124 (61); E. M. Thompson, *The Carthusian Order in England* (London, 1930), p. 285.

16   Walter Daniel, *Life of Aelred*, p. 25.

17   B. Golding, *Gilbert of Sempringham and the Gilbertine Order c. 1130–c. 1300* (Oxford, 1995), pp. 147, 184.

18   Caesarius, *Dialogue on Miracles*, 1, pp. 247–8.

19   D. Sherlock and W. Zajac, 'A monastic sign list from Bury St Edmunds', *Proceedings of the Suffolk Institute of Archaeology* (1988), 251–73 (252).

20   Jocelin, *Chronicle*.

21   Walter Daniel, *Life of Aelred*, pp. 24–5.

22   Ulrich of Zell, 'Consuetudines Cluniacensis', *PL* 149, cols 643–779 (702).

23   B. Harvey, 'A novice's life at Westminster Abbey in the century before the Dissolution', in *The Religious Orders in Pre-Reformation England*, ed. J. G. Clark (Woodbridge, 2002), pp. 51–73 (61).

24   Caesarius, *Dialogue on Miracles*, 1, pp. 247–8.

25   S. G. Bruce, *Silence and Sign Language in Medieval Monasticism: the Cluniac Tradition c. 900–c. 1200* (Cambridge, 2007), p. 64; T. D. Fosbroke, *British Monachism or Manners and Customs of Monks and Nuns of England* (London, 1817), pp. 179–80.

26   Orderic, *Ecclesiastical History*, 6, p. 553.

27   Orderic, *Ecclesiastical History*, 6, pp. 553–7.

28   'The first Cistercians' from the *Exordium Parvum* in *Narrative and Legislative Texts from Early Cîteaux*, ed. and trans. C. Waddell (Cîteaux, 1999), p. 435

29   Thomas of Marlborough, *History of the Abbey of Evesham*, ed. and trans. J. Sayers/L. Watkiss (Oxford, 2003), appendix V, pp. 570–1; *Accounts of the Cellarers of Battle Abbey 1275–1513*, ed. E. Searle and B. Ross (Sydney, 1967), e.g. pp. 75, 82, 140, 145, 151, 159; Fosbroke, *British Monachism*, p. 195.

30   G. Oliver, *Historic Collections relating to the Monasteries in Devon* (Exeter, 1820), pp. 74–5.

31   R. Bowers, 'An early Tudor monastic enterprise: choral polyphony for the liturgical service', in *The Culture of Medieval English Monasticism*, ed. J. Clark (Woodbridge, 2007), pp. 21–54 (32).

32   *Victoria County History of Staffordshire*, 3, ed. M. W. Greenhill/R. B. Pugh (London, 1970), p. 232.

33   'The laye brethrens' statutes of Shene part 2', ed. C. P. Mathews, *Surrey Archaeological Collections* 39 (Frome, 1931), 112–43, clause 23 (140–3); Thompson, *Carthusian Order*, pp. 123–4.

34   D. H. Williams, *The Welsh Cistercians* (Leominster, 2001), p. 145.

35   See Williams, *Welsh Cistercians*, p. 145; K. Stöber, 'Social networks of late medieval Welsh monasteries', in *Monasteries and Society in the Later Middle Ages*, ed. J. Burton and K. Stöber (Woodbridge, 2008), pp. 12–24 (22–3).

36   R. Graham, *English Ecclesiastical Studies* (London, 1929), pp. 100–1.

37   Williams, *Welsh Cistercians*, p. 144.

38   'Chronicle of Melrose', p. 96.

39   Thomas of Marlborough, *History of Evesham*, pp. 168–9; *De Obedientiariis Abbendoniae*, p. 405; 'Customary of St Mary's' in *The Chronicle of St Mary's, York*, ed. H. H. E. Craster/ M. E. Thornton, SS 148 (London, 1934), pp. 80–108 (96–7).

40   Caesarius, *Dialogue on Miracles*, 1, pp. 265–6; J. Wardrop, *Fountains Abbey and its Benefactors 1132–1300* (Kalamazoo, 1987), p. 119, n. 247.

41   *Letters to the General Chapter from the English Abbots to the Chapter at Cîteaux 1442–1521*, ed. C. H. Talbot, CS series 4 (London, 1967), p. 191.

42   Idungus of Prüfening, 'A dialogue between a Cluniac and a Cistercian', trans. J. O'Sullivan, in *Idung of Prüfening, Cistercians and Cluniacs: the Case for Cîteaux* (Kalamazoo, 1977), p. 137.

43   *PL*, 189, col. 112 ff. (*Petrus Venerabilis, Epistolarum libri sex* (28)).

44   Walter Map, *De Nugis Curialium*, ed. and trans. M. R. James, rev. C. N. L. Brooke/ R. A. B. Mynors (Oxford, 1983), p. 77.

45   Idungus, 'Dialogue', p. 67.

46   *Statuta capitulorum generalium ordinis Cisterciensis ab anno 1116 ad annum 1786*, ed. Josephus-Mia Canivez, 8 vols (Louvain, 1933–41), 4, 1429: 69 (p. 337).

47   G. Constable, 'Horologium Stellare Monasticum', in *Consuetudines Benedictinae Variae*, Corpus Consuetudinum Monasticarum 6 (Siegburg, 1975), pp. 1–18.

48   For a detailed discussion of this manuscript from the Benedictine monastery of Santa Maria de Ripoll, see F. Maddison/B. Scott/A. Kent, 'An early medieval water-clock', *Antiquarian Horology* 3 (1962), 348–53. See also J. North, *God's Clockmaker: Richard of Wallingford and the Invention of Time* (London, 1995), pp. 148, 173.

49   Jocelin, *Chronicle*, pp. 94–5; *Les Ecclesiastica Officia Cisterciens du xiième Siècle*, ed. D. Choisselet and P. Vernet (Reiningue, 1989), ch. 114 (p. 318).

50   P. Wright, 'Time and Tithes', *History Today* 54 (2004), 22–7.

51 North, *God's Clockmaker*, p. 170.
52 J. North, 'Monasticism and the first mechanical clocks', in *Stars, Minds and Fate: Essays in Ancient and Medieval Cosmology*, ed. J. D. North (London, Ronceverte, 1989), pp. 171–86 (177).
53 North, *God's Clockmaker*, pp. 142, 662.

Notes to Chapter 2: The Severity of Monastic Life (1): Diet, Sleep, Clothing and Bathing

1 *Aelred of Rievaulx: The Mirror of Charity*, trans. E. Connor (Kalamazoo, 1990), p. 194.
2 C. M. Woolgar, *The Senses in Late Medieval England* (New Haven, Conn., 2006), p. 38; *Observances of Barnwell*, pp. 74–5.
3 *Calendar of Entries in the Papal Registers regarding Great Britain and Ireland: Papal Letters I 1198–1304*, ed. W. H. Bliss (London, 1893), pp. 355, 360; for Ely see also J. Greatrex, 'Benedictine observances at Ely: the intellectual, liturgical and spiritual evidence considered', in *A History of Ely Cathedral*, ed. P. Meadows/N. Ramsey (Woodbridge, 2003), pp. 77–93 (84).
4 See C. Harper-Bill, 'The labourer is worthy of his hire? Complaints about diet in late Medieval England Monasteries', in *The Church in Pre-Reformation Society*, ed. C. M. Barron and C. Harper-Bill (Woodbridge, 1985), pp. 95–107 (98). For the Gilbertines, see E. W. Iredale, *Sempringham and St Gilbert and the Gilbertines* (Pointon, 1992), p. 120; for the Carthusians see Thompson, *Carthusian Order*, p. 300.
5 G. J. McFadden, 'An edition and translation of the Life of Waldef, Abbot of Melrose, by Jocelin of Furness', PhD thesis, University of Columbia, 1952, pp. 240, 312.
6 *St Bernard's Apologia to Abbot William*, trans. M. Casey (Kalamazoo, 1970), pp. 57–8.
7 *The Letters of Bernard of Clairvaux*, ed. and trans. B. S. James, rev. edn with new introduction and bibliography by B. M. Kienzle (Stroud, 1998), ep. 1 (p. 8).
8 See B. Harvey, 'Monastic pittances in the Middle Ages', *Food in Medieval England: Diet and Nutrition*, ed. C. M. Woolgar, D. Serjeantson and T. Waldron (Oxford, 2006), pp. 215–27.
9 William of St Thierry, *Golden Epistle*, pp. 44–5.
10 *St Bernard's Apologia*, p. 57.
11 Harper-Bill, 'Cistercian visitation', 109.
12 Nigel Wireker, *A Mirror for Fools: The Book of Burnel the Ass*, trans. J. H. Mozley (Oxford, 1961), p. 62. Nigel was a monk of Christ Church, Canterbury, in the twelfth century and wrote this satirical poem on the religious Orders.
13 Harvey, 'Monastic pittances', pp. 220–1.
14 *The Chronicle of the Election of Hugh, Abbot of Bury St Edmunds and Later Bishop of Ely*, ed. and trans. R. M. Thomson (Oxford, 1974), pp. 62–4.
15 Harvey, 'Monastic pittances', p. 221; B. Harvey, *Living and Dying in England, 1100–1540: The Monastic Experience* (Oxford, 1993), p. 40.

16   B. Golding, 'Gerald of Wales and the monks', in *Thirteenth-Century England 5*, ed. P. R. Coss and S. D. Lloyd (Woodbridge, 1995), pp. 53–64 (57).

17   Walter Map, *De Curialium*, p. 77.

18   Harvey, 'Monastic pittances', p. 221.

19   J. Hogg, 'Carthusian abstinence', *Analecta Cartusiana, 35: 14: Spiritualität Heute und Gestern* 14, 5–15.

20   Adam of Eynsham, *Magna Vita*, 2, pp. 195–6.

21   *A Monk's Confession: The Memoirs of Guibert of Nogent*, trans. P. J. Archambault (Pennsylvania, 1996), pp. 31–2.

22   Walter Daniel, *Life of Aelred*, p. 30.

23   Cited in Woolgar, *Senses*, p. 301.

24   Golding, 'Gerald of Wales and the monks', p. 57.

25   Bruce, *Silence and Sign Language*, pp. 116, 123.

26   M. Cox, *The Story of Abingdon part 2: Medieval Abingdon 1186–1556* (Abingdon, 1989), p. 61; *Records of the Monastery of Kinloss*, ed. J. Stuart (Edinburgh, 1872), pp. xiv–xvi.

27   For example, see 'The Bursar's Book', in *The Memorials of the Abbey of St Mary of Fountains*, ed. J. S. Walbran, J. Raine and J. T. Fowler, 3 vols, SS 42, 67, 130 (Durham, 1863–1918), 3, pp. 1–91 (56); Gilchrist, *Norwich Cathedral Close*, p. 130.

28   H. W. Saunders, *An Introduction to the Obedientiary and Manorial Rolls of Norwich Cathedral Priory* (Norwich, 1930), p. 80; Gilchrist, *Norwich Cathedral Close*, p. 117.

29   *Accounts of Cellarers of Battle*, pp. 18–20.

30   *Accounts of Cellarers of Battle*, p. 20.

31   Harper-Bill, 'The labourer is worthy of his hire?', pp. 97–9, 101–2, 97–9; E. L. Taunton, *The English Black Monks of St Benedict*, 2 vols (London, 1897), 1, p. 288.

32   Thomas of Marlborough, *History of Evesham*, pp. 192–3; D. Robinson, *The Cistercians in Wales: Architecture and Archaeology 1130–1540* (London, 2006), pp. 217, 275, 289.

33   Caesarius, *Dialogue on Miracles*, 1, p. 293.

34   *St Bernard of Clairvaux, The Story of his Life as Recorded in the Vita Prima Bernardi by Certain Contemporaries, William of St Thierry, Arnold of Bonnevaux, Geoffrey and Philip of Clairvaux, and Odo of Deuil*, trans. G. Webb and A. Walker (London: 1960), p. 57.

35   Jocelin, *Chronicle*, p. 37

36   The Carthusian way of life described in *The Metrical Life of St Hugh of Lincoln*, ed. and trans. C. Garton (Lincoln, 1986), lines 283–91 (pp. 23–5).

37   'Chronicle of Melrose', p. 96.

38   *St Bernard of Clairvaux, The Story of his Life*, p. 39.

39   William of St Thierry, *Golden Epistle*, p. 56.

40   B. Collett, 'Holy expectations: the female monastic vocation in the diocese of Winchester on the eve of Reformation', in *The Culture of Medieval English Monasticism*, ed. J. Clark (Woodbridge, 2007), pp. 147–68 (153).

41   For example, see 'Westminster customary', in *The Customary of St Augustine's, Canterbury and St Peter's, Westminster*, ed. E. M. Thompson, 2 vols, Henry Bradshaw

Soc. 23, 28 (1902–4), 2, p. 41 (lines 4–8), 1, p. 100 (lines 3–7); *Ecclesiastica Officia*, ch. 115 (pp. 316–19).

42 Caesarius, *Dialogue on Miracles,* 1, p. 231.

43 Cited in Jean-François Leroux-Dhuys, *Cistercian Abbeys: History and Architecture* (Paris, 1998), p. 51; Caesarius, *Dialogue on Miracles,* 1, p. 516.

44 Lanfranc, *Monastic Constitutions*, pp. 117–19.

45 Harper-Bill, 'Cistercian visitation', 109.

46 Cassidy-Welch, *Monastic Spaces*, pp. 161–2; B. P. McGuire, *Friendship and Community: the Monastic Experience 350–1250* (Kalamazoo, 1988), pp. 369–73.

47 From the Gilbertine Rule cited in R. Graham, *St Gilbert of Sempringham and the Gilbertines: a History of the Only English Monastic Order* (London, 1901), p. 70.

48 Idungus, 'Dialogue', p. 136.

49 Walter Daniel, *Life of Aelred*, p. 5.

50 Thompson, *Carthusian Order*, p. 34.

51 Bruce, *Silence and Sign Language*, p. 84.

52 Lanfranc, *Monastic Constitutions*, p. 115; *De Obedientiariis Abbendoniae*, p. 364.

53 Bruce, *Silence and Sign Language*, pp. 85–6.

54 Graham, *St Gilbert*, pp. 71–2.

55 W. St John Hope, *The History of the London Charterhouse* (London, 1925), p. 61; L. Hendriks, *London Charterhouse* (London, 1889), p. 304.

56 P. Meyvaert, 'The medieval monastic claustrum', *Gesta* 12: 1 (1973), 53–9 (56).

57 Bruce, *Silence and Sign Language*, pp. 84–5.

58 'Westminster customary', p. 82 (lines 30–3); Bede, '*Vita Sancti Cuthberti*' ('The Life of St Cuthbert'), ed. and trans. J. A. Giles in *Venerabilis Bedae, Opera Quae Supersunt Omnia 4: Opuscula Historica* (London, 1843), pp. 202–357 (269).

59 Bruce, *Silence and Sign Language*, pp. 84–5.

60 'The laye brethrens' statutes of Shene', clause 19 (120).

61 *Observances of Barnwell*, pp. 106–7.

62 Iredale, *Sempringham*, p.132; Cassidy-Welch, *Monastic Spaces*, p. 124, Canivez, *Statuta capitulorum*, 2, 1225: 22 (p. 39).

63 Walter Daniel, *Life of Aelred*, p. 34.

64 Iredale, *Sempringham*, p. 132.

65 C. Rawcliffe, 'On the threshold of eternity': Care for the Sick in East Anglian monasteries', *East Anglia's History: Studies in Honour of Norman Scarfe*, ed. C. Harper-Bill, C. Rawcliffe and R. G. Wilson (Woodbridge, 2002), pp. 41–72 (60).

66 Taunton, *English Black Monks*, 1, p. 296.

67 Hence Abbot Roger (1253–73) of St Augustine's, Canterbury, brought in laymen to shave his monks, William Thorne, *Chronicle of St Augustine's, Canterbury*, trans. A. H. Davis (Oxford, 1933), pp. 248–9.

Notes to Chapter 3: The Severity of Monastic Life (2): Family Ties, Health and Sickness

1 Eadmer of Canterbury, The Life of St Anselm, Archbishop of Canterbury, ed. and trans. R. W. Southern, 2nd edn (Oxford, 1972), p. 76.

2 Eadmer of Canterbury, Historia Nouorum in England: History of Recent Events in England, trans. G. Bosanquet (London, 1964), pp. 13–14.

3 Anselm, Letters, 1, ep. 8 (pp. 89–90).

4 The Account Book of Beaulieu Abbey, ed. S. F. Hockey, CS series 4 (London, 1975), p. 271; C. H. Talbot, 'The account book of Beaulieu Abbey', Cîteaux de Nederlanden 9 (Westmalle, 1958), 189–210 (195).

5 J. Hogg, 'The Carthusians and the temptations of Eve', Analecta Cartusiana 35: 15: Spiritualität Heute und Gestern 15 (1992), 138–86 (179).

6 R. Graham, 'A papal visitation of Bury St Edmunds and Westminster in 1234', English Historical Review 27 (1912), 728–39 (734).

7 English Historical Documents 4, 1327–1485, ed. A. R. Myers (London, 1969), p. 789.

8 Harper-Bill, 'Cistercian visitation', 110–11.

9 Thomas of Monmouth, Life and Miracles of St William of Norwich, trans., intro. and notes A. Jessopp and M. R. James (Cambridge, 1896), p. 133.

10 Thomas, Life and Miracles of William of Norwich, p. 134; Goscelin of St Bertin, Legend of St Edith, trans. M. Wright and K. Loncar, 'Goscelin's Legend of Edith', in Writing the Wilton Women: Goscelin's Legend of Edith and Liber Confortatorius, ed. S. Hollis with W. R. Barnes, R. Hayward, K. Loncar and M. Wright (Turnhout, 2004), pp. 17–93 (86–7).

11 Account Book of Beaulieu, pp. 271–6.

12 Harvey, Living and Dying, p. 80; Taunton, English Black Monks, 1, p. 288.

13 De Obedientiariis Abbendoniae, pp. 350, 351; Graham, 'A papal visitation', 736.

14 Anselm, Letters, 3, ep. 405 (pp. 170–2).

15 Anselm, Letters, 1, ep. 17 (pp. 105–7).

16 Goswin de Bossut, 'The Life of Abundus the choirmonk', Send Me God: Trilogy of Cistercian lives by Goswin de Bossut, Cantor of Villers in Brabant, 3 vols, trans. Father M. Cawley (Guadalupe, 2000), 3, pp. 22–5.

17 Fosbroke, British Monachism, p. 265.

18 English Historical Documents 4, p. 789 (clause 9).

19 Graham, St Gilbert, pp. 56–7; Golding, Gilbert of Sempringham, pp. 127, 163.

20 D. H. Williams, The Cistercians in the Early Middle Ages (Leominster, 1998), p. 404; E. Power, Medieval English Nunneries c. 1275–1535 (Cambridge, 1922), pp. 399–400; The Victoria History of the County of York, 3, ed. W. Page (London, 1912), pp. 170–1.

21 Golding, Gilbert of Sempringham, p. 111, n. 142.

22 The Register of William Greenfield, Lord Archbishop of York 1306–1315, ed. W. Brown and A. H. Thompson, 5 vols, SS 145, 149, 151–3 (Durham, 1931–48), 3, no. 1158 (pp. 12–13).

23   Matarasso, *Cistercian World*, p. 296.

24   Goswin de Bossut, *Life of Abundus*, pp. 22–5.

25   *The Life of the Venerable Man, Gundulf, Bishop of Rochester*, trans. the nuns of Malling, Kent (Malling Abbey, 1968), p. 10.

26   St John Hope, *The London Charterhouse*, p. 61; Thompson, *Carthusian Order*, p. 278.

27   *Chronica Monasterii de Melsa*, ed. E. A. Bond, 3 vols (London, 1866–8), 3, pp. 277–9.

28   Golding, *Gilbert of Sempringham*, p. 110

29   *St Bernard of Clairvaux, The Story of his Life*, pp. 72–3.

30   See *Visitations in the Diocese of Norwich A.D. 1492–1532*, ed. A. Jessopp, CS ns 43 (London, 1888), pp. xix–xxi, 201.

31   *Observances of Barnwell*, pp. 204–5.

32   Harper-Bill, 'Cistercian visitation', 112.

33   N. Siraisi, *Medieval and Early Renaissance Medicine: An Introduction to Knowledge and Practice* (Chicago, London, 1990), pp. 115–16.

34   Taunton, *English Black Monks*, 1, p. 285.

35   Caesarius, *Dialogue on Miracles*, 1, pp. 223–30.

36   *St Bernard of Clairvaux, The Story of his Life*, pp. 63–4.

37   Caesarius, *Dialogue on Miracles*, 1, p. 242.

38   *St Bernard's Apologia*, p. 56.

39   Thompson, *Carthusian Order*, pp. 38–9.

40   *Observances of Barnwell*, pp. 200–1.

41   Taunton, *English Black Monks*, 1, p. 309.

42   Rawcliffe, 'On the threshold', p. 68.

43   *Rule of St Benedict*, ch. 36 (pp. 100–1).

44   Rawcliffe, 'On the threshold', p. 69.

45   Taunton, *English Black Monks*, 1, p. 304.

46   B. Harvey and J. Oeppen, 'Patterns of morbidity in late medieval England: a sample from Westminster Abbey', *The Economic History Review*, ns 54 (2001), 215–39 (220).

47   Fosbroke, *British Monachism*, p. 233.

48   *De Obedientiariis Abbendoniae*, p. 346.

49   Taunton, *English Black Monks*, 1, p. 304.

50   Eadmer, *Life of St Anselm*, pp. 22–3.

51   'St Augustine's Customary', in *The Customary of St Augustine's, Canterbury and St Peter's, Westminster*, ed. Thompson, 1, p. 329 (lines 26–36).

52   *Gesta Sacristarum*, in *The Memorials of St Edmund's Abbey*, ed. T. Arnold, 3 vols (London, 1890–6), 2, pp. 289–98 (293).

53   *De Obedientiariis*, p. 407.

54   Rawcliffe, 'On the threshold', pp. 49–50; see too *The Chronicle of Bury St Edmunds, 1212–1301*, ed. and trans. A. Gransden (London, 1964), p. 15; *Observances of Barnwell*, pp. 212–15.

Notes to Chapter 4: The Sound of Silence (1): The Silence of the Cloister

1 Goswin de Bossut, *Life of Abundus*, p. 1.
2 Jocelin, *Chronicle*, pp. 94–8.
3 Lanfranc, *Monastic Constitutions*, p. 167.
4 Idungus, 'Dialogue', pp. 36–7.
5 Thompson, *Carthusian Order*, pp. 357–8.
6 Eadmer, *Life of St Anselm*, pp. 48–50.
7 Jocelin, *Chronicle*, pp. 13–14.
8 *The History of William of Newburgh*, trans. J. Stevenson (Llanerch facsimile, Felinfach, 1996), pp. 430–2.
9 Arnulph of Bohéries, *Speculum Monachorum* ('A Mirror for Monks'), *PL* 184, col. 1175.
10 Taunton, *English Black Monks*, 1, p. 297.
11 Gerald of Wales, '*De Rebus a se Gestis*', trans. H. E. Butler, *The Autobiography of Giraldus Cambrensis* [Gerald of Wales], intro. C. H. Williams, guide to reading J. Gillingham (Woodbridge, 2005), pp. 70–2.
12 *St Bernard's Apologia*, p. 55.
13 See Bruce, *Silence and Sign Language*, esp. pp. 77–124.
14 D. Sherlock and W. Zajac, 'A monastic sign list from Bury St Edmunds', *Proceedings of the Suffolk Institute of Archaeology* (1988), 251–73, nos 192, 172 (264, 263); D. Sherlock, *Signs for Silence: the Sign Language of the Monks of Ely in the Middle Ages* (Ely, 1992), nos 56, 108 (pp. 18, 28).
15 D. Sherlock, 'Anglo-Saxon monastic sign language at Christ Church, Canterbury', *Archaeologia Cantiana* 107 (1989), 1–27, no. 94 (11); Sherlock, 'A monastic sign list from Bury', no. 198 (264).
16 Bruce, *Silence and Sign Language*, p. 168.
17 Bruce, *Silence and Sign Language*, p. 72.
18 *St Bernard of Clairvaux, The Story of his Life*, p. 59.
19 Lanfranc, *Monastic Constitutions*, p. 171.
20 Bowers, 'An early Tudor monastic enterprise', p. 34, n. 69.
21 *Ecclesiastica Officia*, ch. 114 (pp. 318–20); Lanfranc, *Monastic Constitutions*, e.g. pp. 41, 65.
22 Jocelin, *Chronicle*, pp. 79–80.
23 G. Haigh, *The History of Winchcombe Abbey* (Watford, 1947), pp. 62–3.
24 V. Spear, *Leadership in Medieval English Nunneries* (Woodbridge, 2005), p. 145, n 40; Jessopp, *Visitations of Norwich*, p. 76.
25 See for example, Jessop, *Visitations of Norwich*, p. 264.
26 G. G. Coulton, *A Medieval Panorama: the English Scene from Conquest to Reformation* (New York, 1955), p. 276; Spear, *Leadership in Nunneries*, p. 143.
27 Spear, *Leadership in Nunneries*, p. 143; Jessopp, *Visitations of Norwich*, p. 191.
28 *Accounts of Cellarers of Battle*, p. 45.

29 *A Monk's Confession: Memoirs of Guibert of Nogent*, p. 209; *Life and Miracles of William of Norwich*, pp. 136–45.

30 For example see Harper-Bill, 'Cistercian visitation', 105.

31 *Visitations of Religious Houses in the Diocese of Lincoln 1420–49*, ed. A. H. Thompson, 3 vols, Lincoln Record Society/Canterbury and York Society (1915–27), 2, 'Visitations held by William Alnwick pt 1' (London, 1919), pp. 175–6, 185.

32 *History of William of Newburgh*, p. 578.

33 *The Letter Books of the Monastery of Christ Church, Canterbury*, ed. J. B Sheppard, 3 vols (London 1887–9), 1, nos 168, 170, 171 (pp. 164–71).

34 Jocelin of Furness, *Life of Waldef*, ch. 21: 76 (pp. 296–7).

35 Jocelin, *Chronicle*, p. 85.

36 S. G. Bruce, 'Uttering no human sound: silence and sign language in western medieval monasticism', PhD thesis, University of Princeton, 2000, p. 14.

37 *De Obedientiariis Abbendoniae*, p. 417.

38 *Observances of Barnwell*, pp. 192–3. For further discussion of the reception and care of guests in the monasteries see Kerr, *Monastic Hospitality*, esp. pp. 94–176.

39 Fosbroke, *British Monachism*, p. 234; *Records of Kinloss*, p. lii.

40 *Observances of Barnwell*, p. 170.

41 Graham, 'A papal visitation', 730–1.

42 'Customary of St Mary's', p. 96.

43 *De Obedientiariis Abbendoniae*, p. 411.

44 *Chronica de Melsa*, 3, pp. 35–6.

45 *De Administratione*, ch. XXV 'Of the first Addition to the Church' and *De Ordinatio* in *Abbot Suger: On the Abbey Church of St Denis and its Art Treasures*, ed. and annotated E. Panofsky, 2nd edn G. Panofsky-Soergel (Princeton, 1979), pp. 43, 134–5.

46 *Life and Miracles of William of Norwich*, pp. 185–8.

47 Jocelin, *Chronicle*, pp. 48–50.

48 B. McGuire, *Conflict and Continuity at Øm Abbey* (Copenhagen, 1976), p. 12.

49 *Cistercian World*, trans. Matarasso, pp. 271–3; Spear, *Leadership in Nunneries*, p. 107.

50 Harper-Bill, 'Cistercian visitation', 109–10.

51 Jocelin, *Chronicle*, p. 94.

52 Jocelin, *Chronicle*, pp. 94–8.

53 *Historia Ecclesie Abbendonensis, The History of the Church of Abingdon*, 2, ed. and trans. J. G. H. Hudson (Oxford, 2002), pp. 30–3; Wright, 'Time and Tithes', 24–5.

54 'St Augustine's Customary' (c. 1250), 2, p. 308.

55 Harper-Bill, 'Cistercian visitation', 110; E. H. Pearce, *The Monks of Westminster Abbey* (Cambridge, 1916), p. 141.

56 *Observances of Barnwell*, p. 194; Reginald of Durham, *Libellus de Admirandis Beati Cuthberti Virtutibus*, ed. J. Raine (Durham, 1835), pp. 91–2.

57 *Chronica de Melsa*, 2, pp. xxi; 3, p. 69; Thompson, *Carthusian Order*, p. 18.

58 *A Monk's Confession: Memoirs of Guibert of Nogent*, pp. 78–84.

59 Suger, *De Consecratione*, in *Abbot Suger: On the Abbey Church of St Denis and its Art Treasures*, ed. Panofsky, pp. 82–181 (109).

60 *Observances of Barnwell*, pp. xix–xx.

61 *Ecclesiastica Officia*, ch. 89 (pp. 252–5).

62 *Ecclesiastica Officia*, ch. 89 (pp. 252–5).

63 *The Book of St Gilbert*, ed. and trans. R. Foreville and G. Keir (Oxford, 1987), pp. 284–9

64 *Twelfth-Century Statutes from the Cistercian General Chapter*, ed. C. Waddell (Brecht, 2002), 1194: 8 (285).

65 Fosbroke, *British Monachism*, p. 276.

66 Caesarius, *Dialogue on Miracles*, 1, pp. 532–3.

67 *Vita Lanfranci*, ed. Gibson, pp. 709–11; Eadmer of Canterbury, 'Miracles of St Dunstan', in *Lives and Miracles of Saints Oda, Dunstan and Oswald*, ed. and trans. A. J. Turner and B. J. Muir (Oxford, 2006), pp. 182–9.

68 *Liber Eliensis: A History of the Isle of Ely from the Seventh Century to the Twelfth Century*, trans. with notes by J. Fairweather (Woodbridge, 2005), pp. 247–8.

Notes to Chapter 5: The Sound of Silence (2): The Silence of the Night

1   William of St Thierry, *Golden Epistle*, p. 55.

2   *Life and Miracles of William of Norwich*, pp. 187–8.

3   *Life and Miracles of William of Norwich*, pp. xi–xii, 116–21.

4   'Instruction for Novices', p. 211.

5   Meyvaert, 'The medieval claustrum', 58.

6   Bruce, *Silence and Sign Language*, pp. 85–6.

7   Caesarius, *Dialogue on Miracles*, 1, p. 360.

8   'Instruction for Novices', p. 211.

9   *Observances of Barnwell*, pp. 166–7.

10 Caesarius, *Dialogue on Miracles*, 1, pp. 471–2, 362–4.

11 Caesairus, *Dialogue on Miracles*, 1, p. 285.

12 Goswin de Bossut, 'The Life of Ida the Gentle', *Send me God*, trans. Cawley, 1, pp. 16–18.

13 Caesarius, *Dialogue on Miracles*, 1, pp. 377–9.

14 Walter Daniel, *Life of Aelred*, p. 51.

15 *The Miracles of Saint Aebbe of Coldingham and Saint Margaret of Scotland*, ed. and trans. R. Bartlett (Oxford, 2003), pp. 132–5, 96–9.

16 Cited Woolgar, *Senses*, p. 122; Reginald of Coldingham/Durham, *De Vita et Miraculis S. Godrici, Hermitae de Finchale Auctore Reginaldo Monacho Dunelmensis*, ed. J. Stevenson, SS 20 (Durham, 1847), pp. 356–8.

17 Caesarius, *Dialogue on Miracles*, 1, pp. 532–3.

18 *Life and Miracle of William of Norwich*, pp. 136–45.

19 *Alice the Leper: Life of Alice of Schaebeek by Arnold II of Villers (?)*, trans. Father M. Cawley (Guadalupe, 2000), pp. 9–10, 12–13.

20 *Observances of Barnwell*, pp. 166–7; 'Westminster Customary', p. 139 (lines 5–8); *The Chronicle of Battle Abbey*, ed. and trans. E. Searle (Oxford, 1980), pp. 306–7.

21 Cited in Bruce, *Silence and Sign Language*, p. 22; *Life and Miracles of William of Norwich*, pp. 211–13.

22 *Stephen of Sawley, Treatises*, trans. J. F. O'Sullivan, ed. B. F. Lackner (Kalamazoo, 1984), p. 112.

23 Stephen of Sawley, *Treatises*, p. 112.

24 John of Ford's *Life of Wulfric*, trans. Matarrasso, *Cistercian World*, pp. 246–7.

25 Harvey, *Living and Dying*, pp. 130–1.

26 Harper-Bill, 'Cistercian visitation', 109.

27 See for example, D. Bell, 'Chambers, cells and cubicles: the Cistercian General Chapter and the development of the private room', in *Perspectives for an Architecture of Solitude: Essays on Cistercians, Art and Architecture in Honour of Peter Fergusson*, ed. T. N. Kinder (Turnhout, 2004), pp. 187–98.

28 M. C. Erler, 'Private reading in the fifteenth and sixteenth-century English nunnery', in *Culture of Medieval Monasticism*, pp. 134–46 (141).

Notes to Chapter 6: A Life of Obedience

1 William of St Thierry, *Golden Epistle*, pp. 44–5.

2 Golding, *Gilbert of Sempringham*, p. 159.

3 Anselm, *Letters*, 1, ep. 6 (p. 86).

4 Jocelin, *Chronicle*, p. 65.

5 *The Letters of James V*, coll. and ed. R. K. Hannay, ed. D. Hay (Edinburgh, 1954), p. 169.

6 William of St Thierry, *Golden Epistle*, p. 46.

7 William of St Thierry, *Golden Epistle*, pp. 48–9.

8 Gerald of Wales, *The Journey through Wales/The Description of Wales*, trans. L. Thorpe (Harmondsworth, 1978), pp. 85–6.

9 *Book of St Gilbert*, p. 103.

10 William of St Thierry, *Golden Epistle*, p. 45.

11 *A Monk's Confession: Memoirs of Guibert of Nogent*, p. 105.

12 A. Gray, 'A Carthusian *carta visitationis* of the fifteenth century', *Bulletin of the Institute of Historical Research* vol. 40, no. 101 (1967), 91–100 (97).

13 Lanfranc, *Monastic Constitutions*, pp. 147–53, 167.

14 Anselm, *Letters*, 1, ep. 99 (pp. 248–9).

15 *Cistercian World*, trans. Matarasso, pp. 301–4.

16 *Narratio de fundatione Fontanis monasterii*, trans. A. W. Oxford, *The Ruins of Fountains Abbey* (London, 1910), appendix 1, pp. 127–230 (191–2).

17 Goswin de Bossut, *Life of Ida the Gentle*, pp. 28–9; Caesarius, *Dialogue on Miracles*,1, pp. 516–17.

18 Eadmer, *Life of Anselm*, p. 34.

19 For an important article on the monastic roundsman, see S. G. Bruce, '"Lurking with spiritual intent": a note on the origin and functions of the monastic roundsman (*circator*)', *Revue Bénédictine* 109 (1999), 75–9.

20 Lanfranc, *Monastic Constitutions*, pp. 117–19.

21 Bruce, 'Lurking with spiritual intent', esp. 81–4; Lanfranc, *Monastic Constitutions*, pp. 117–19; *De Obedientiariis Abbendoniae*, p. 368; Taunton, *English Black Monks*, 1, pp. 282–3.

22 Eadmer, *Life of Anselm*, pp. 38–9.

23 *Book of St Gilbert*, p. 67.

24 *Rule of St Benedict*, ch. 28 (p. 87).

25 Anselm, *Letters*, 1, ep. 96 (pp. 239–41).

26 Anselm, *Letters*, 3, ep. 313 (p. 17).

27 Idungus, 'Dialogue', pp. 134–5.

28 Stephen of Sawley, 'Mirror for Novices', in *Stephen of Sawley, Treatises*, pp. 102–3.

29 Taunton, *English Black Monks*, 1, p. 300.

30 Harper-Bill, 'Cistercian visitation', 107.

31 *Vita Lanfranci*, pp. 709–11; *Life of Gundulf*, p. 13.

32 *The Rites of Durham*, material selected, edited and rendered into modern English by R. W. J. Austin (Durham, 1985), p. 33.

33 H. E. Bell, 'Esholt Priory', *Yorkshire Archaeological Journal* 33 (1938), 5–33 (28–9); C. Cross and N. Vickers, *Monks, Friars and Nuns in Sixteenth-Century Yorkshire*, Yorkshire Archaeological Society Record Series 150 (Huddersfield, 1995), p. 565.

34 G. Coppack, *Fountains Abbey: the Cistercians in Northern England* (Stroud, 2003), pp. 99–100.

35 Fosbroke, *British Monachism*, p. 261.

36 Cassidy-Welch, *Monastic Spaces*, p. 123; Canivez, *Statuta capitulorum* 2, 1226: 25 (p. 53).

37 Lanfranc, *Monastic Constituions*, pp. 147–53; Taunton, *English Black Monks*, 1, p. 301.

38 Cassidy-Welch, *Monastic Spaces*, p. 123; Canivez, *Statuta capitulorum*, 1, 1218: 47 (p. 494).

39 *The White Book of Worcester: Glimpses of Life in a Great Benedictine Monastery in the Fourteenth Century*, trans. J. M. Wilson (Llanerch facsimile, Felinfach, 1999), pp. 66–7.

40 Thompson, *Carthusian Order*, p. 283.

41 Thompson, *Carthusian Order*, pp. 289–90, 294–5.

42 Anselm, *Letters*, 1, ep. 67 (p. 189).

43 *Stephen of Lexington, Letters from Ireland 1228–9*, trans. and intro. B. W. O'Dwyer (Kalamazoo, 1982), pp. 26, 27, 32, 55–61, 129.

44 *Register of William Greenfield*, 3, no. 1224 (p. 45); see also no. 1180 (pp. 45, 23–5).

45 *Register of William Greenfield*, 3, nos 1630, 1634 (pp. 235–8, 238–40).

46 Cited by Peter Abelard in his 'Letters of Direction', trans. B. Radice, *The Letters of Abelard and Heloise* (Harmondsworth, 1974), p. 223.

47 J. Fletcher, *The Cistercians in Yorkshire* (London, 1919), p. 92.

48 Harper-Bill, 'Cistercian visitation', 104.

49 *Visitations of Religious Houses in Diocese of Lincoln, 2*, pp. 47, 50.

50 See Jessopp, *Visitations of Norwich*, pp. xiv–xv; Rawcliffe, 'On the threshold', p. 71; France, *Cistercians in Scandinavia*, pp. 453–4.

51 Harper-Bill, 'Cistercian visitation', 112.

52 Jessopp, *Visitation of Norwich*, pp. xxii, 267.

53 Jocelin, *Chronicle*, p. 65.

54 *Visitations of Religious Houses in Diocese of Lincoln, 2*, pp. 47–9.

Notes to Chapter 7: Crimes and Misdemeanours

1 Caesarius, *Dialogue on Miracles*, 1, p. 313.

2 J. Gøering and F. A. C. Martello, 'The *Perambulavit Iudas* (*Speculum Confessionis*) attributed to Robert Grosseteste', *Revue Bénédictine* 96 (1986), 125–68.

3 Lanfranc, *Monastic Constitutions*, p. 209.

4 *English Historical Documents 4*, pp. 796–8.

5 Graham, 'A papal visitation', 730; Jessopp, *Visitations of Norwich*, pp. 200–1.

6 Gerald of Wales, *Speculum Ecclesiae*, in *Giraldi Cambrensis Opera*, ed. J. S. Brewer, J. F. Dimock and G. F. Warner, 8 vols (London, 1861–91), 4, pp. 1–354 (213–5).

7 *Visitations of Religious Houses in Diocese of Lincoln, 2*, pp. 133–4; Jessopp, *Norwich Visitations*, pp. xvii; 75.

8 Harper-Bill, 'Cistercian visitation', 111.

9 Harper-Bill, 'The labourer is worthy of his hire?', pp. 101–2.

10 *Visitations of Religious Houses in Diocese of Lincoln, 2*, pp. 47, 50.

11 Jocelin, *Chronicle*, pp. 103–6.

12 For documents relating to Downom's expulsion from Fountains in 1449 see *Letters from the English Abbots to the Chapter at Cîteaux*, pp. 22–40.

13 *Book of St Gilbert*, pp. 310–15.

14 'Letter to Maurice', in Walter Daniel, *Life of Aelred*, pp. 65–81 (80).

15 King, *Cîteaux and her Elder Daughters*, p. 58.

16 *Records of the Monastery of Kinloss*, ed. Stuart, p. xlii; France, *Cistercians in Scandinavia*, p. 153.

17 Henry V's reforms for the Benedictines in England, 1421, *English Historical Documents 4*, p. 789.

18 Caesarius, *Dialogue on Miracles*, 1, pp. 302–3.

19 Woolgar, *Senses*, p. 176; '*Perambulavit Iudas*', 136–7, 149–50.

20 Hope, *London Charterhouse*, p. 61.

21 Adam of Eynsham, *Magna Vita*, 1, pp. 28–30; 2, pp. 48–52.

22 Chapter 21 of Guiges' Customs of 1128, trans. in Thompson, *Carthusian Order*, p. 26.

23 Goswin de Bossut, *Life of Abundus*, pp. 8–9.

24 Graham, 'A papal visitation', 731, 734.

25 Jessopp, *Visitations of Norwich*, pp. xx, 3–4, 75, 200.

26 Jessopp, *Visitations of Norwich*, pp. 199, 268.

27 Thomas of Monmouth, *History of Evesham*, pp. 192–3; *Calendar of Papal Supplications relating to Scotland 1418–1422*, ed. E. R. Lindsay and A. I. Cameron (Edinburgh, 1934), pp. 246–8.

28 Gerald of Wales, *Journey Through Wales*, pp. 118–19; 'Gemma Ecclesiastica' in *Giraldi Cambrensis Opera*, 2, p. 248.

29 *English Historical Documents 4*, pp. 796–9.

30 Bruce, 'Lurking with spiritual intent', p. 86.

31 Golding, *Gilbert of Sempringham*, p. 169; 'Gemma Ecclesiastica', 2, pp. 247–8.

32 Wireker, *Mirror for Fools*, p. 69.

33 Golding, *Gilbert of Sempringham*, pp. 69, 109, 127.

34 G. Constable, 'Aelred of Rievaulx and the nun of Watton: an episode in the early history of the Gilbertine Order', in D. Baker (ed.), *Medieval Women* (Oxford, 1978), pp. 205–26; Golding, *Gilbert of Sempringham*, pp. 33–8.

35 *Visitations of Religious Houses in Diocese of Lincoln*, 2, pp. 47, 50; *Register of William Greenfield*, 3, pp. 188, 190, 55, 56.

36 Bell, 'Esholt Priory', 29; Cross and Vickers, *Monks, Friars and Nuns*, p. 563.

37 Caesarius, *Dialogue on Miracles*,1, pp. 501–2.

38 Cited in Cassidy-Welch, *Monastic Spaces*, p. 195; *The Register of John Le Romeyn, Lord Archbishop of York, 1286–1296*, ed. W. Brown, 2 vols, SS 123, 128 (1913–17), 1, p. 437.

39 Adam of Eynsham, *Magna Vita*, 1, pp. 81–3; Thompson, *Carthusian Order*, p. 128.

40 Anselm, *Letters*, 1, ep. 97 (pp. 242–6).

41 Golding, *Gilbert of Sempringham*, pp. 164–5; Cassidy-Welch, *Monastic Spaces*, pp. 126, 209.

42 Caesarius, *Dialogue on Miracles*, 1, pp. 21–2.

43 *Vita Lanfranci*, pp. 672–3.

44 Caesarius, *Dialogue on Miracles*, 1, pp. 22–3.

45 Caesarius, *Dialogue on Miracles*, 1, pp. 22–3.

46 Bell, 'Esholt Priory', 29; Cross and Vickers, *Monks, Friars and Nuns*, p. 563; Cassidy-Welch, *Monastic Spaces*, p. 196.

Notes to Chapter 8: The Work of God (1): The Communal Life

1 Matthew of Rievaulx, fl. early thirteenth century, cited in Cassidy-Welch, *Monastic Spaces*, p. 65.

2 Peter Damian (d. 1072), cited in Graham, *English Ecclesiastical Studies*, p. 42.

3 *Aelred of Rievaulx: The Mirror of Charity*, trans. E. Connor (Kalamazoo, 1990), pp. 209–12.

4 Harper-Bill, 'Cistercian visitation', 108.

5 Hendriks, *London Charterhouse*, pp. 89–90.

6 Spear, *Leadership in Nunneries*, p. 122.

7 E. M. Thompson, *A History of the Somerset Carthusians* (London, 1885), pp. 35–6; *Observances of Barnwell*, pp. 81, 87.

8 Goswin de Bossut, *Life of Ida the Gentle*, pp. 27, 37–8, 51, 57.

9 Goswin de Bossut, 'The Life of Arnulf the Wagoneer', *Send me God*, trans. Cawley, 2, pp. 43–5.

10 *St Bernard of Clairvaux, The Story of his Life*, pp. 63–4.

11 Aelred of Rievaulx, *The Life of Edward the Confessor*, trans. J. Bertram (Southampton, 1997), pp. 120–1.

12 Hugh of St Victor (d. 1142), cited in Coulton, *Medieval Panorama*, p. 280.

13 Taunton, *English Black Monks*, 1, p. 288.

14 C. S. Jaeger, *The Envy of the Angels: Cathedral Schools and Social Ideals in Mediaeval Europe* (Philadelphia, 1994), p. 272.

15 *Ecclesiastica Officia*, ch. 76 (p. 226); Taunton, *English Black Monks*,1, p. 218.

16 Coulton, *Medieval Panorama*, pp. 278–80.

17 *Ecclesiastica Officia*, ch. 76 (p. 226); Abelard, 'Letters of Direction', trans. Radice, *Letters of Abelard and Heloise*, p. 248; *Observances of Barnwell*, pp. 162–3.

18 William of St Thierry, *Golden Epistle*, p. 40.

19 W. Williams, 'Saint Robert of Newminster', *Downside Review* 58 (1939), 137–49 (148).

20 Idungus, 'Dialogue', p. 94; Ulrich of Zell, 'Consuetudines Cluniacensis', col. 677.

21 *Gesta Abbatum Monasterii Sancti Albani*, ed. H. T. Riley, 3 vols (London, 1867–9), 1, p. 314.

22 Goscelin of St Bertin, *Vita et translatio S. Ethelburgae*, ed. M. L. Colker, Jocelyn of St Bertin, 'Life and miracles of St Ethelburga', *Studia Monastica* 7 (1965), 398–417 (414).

23 *Register of William Greenfield*, 3, no. 1629 (p. 233).

24 See for example *Rule of St Benedict*, ch. 35 (p. 99); *Ecclesiastica Officia*, ch.117 (p. 330).

25 Taunton, *English Black Monks*, 1, pp. 286–7; *Ecclesiastica Officia*, ch. 114 (p. 320).

26 Harper-Bill, 'Cistercian visitation', 108.

27 Jocelin, *Chronicle*, pp. 98–102.

28 *Life and Miracles of William of Norwich*, pp. 122–5, 185–7.

29 Aelred, *On Spiritual Friendship*, trans. Matarasso, *Cistercian World*, p. 179.

30 Cawley, intro. to Goswin de Bossut, *Life of Abundus*, p. xvi.

31 Jocelin, *Chronicle*, pp. 14–15.

32 Aelred, *On Spiritual Friendship*, trans. Matarasso, *Cistercian World*, pp. 173–4.

33 *Life of Gundulf*, pp. 8 ff., 15, 17, 21, 71–2.

34 Aelred, *Life of St Edward*, pp. 121–2.

35 *Book of St Gilbert*, pp. 282–5.

36 'Chronicle of Melrose', p. 95.

37 Anselm, *Letters*, 1, ep. 34, 35 (pp. 129–31).

38 Thompson, *Carthusian Order*, pp. 289–90, 294–5.

39 Peter Abelard, *Historia calamitatum*, trans. Radice, *Letters of Abelard and Heloise*, pp. 57–106 (104).

40 Harper-Bill, 'Cistercian visitation', 106–7.

41 Jocelin, *Chronicle*, p. 71.

42 R. W. Southern, *Saint Anselm: A Portrait in a Landscape* (Cambridge, 1990), pp. 313–14; D. Knowles, *The Monastic Order in England: A History of its Development from the Times of St Dunstan to the Fourth Lateran Council, 940–1216*, 2nd edn (Cambridge, 1963), p. 116.

43 Jessopp, *Visitations of Norwich*, pp. xix–xxi, 198–201.

44 Golding, *Gilbert of Sempringham*, p. 162.

45 Jocelin, *Chronicle*, pp. 111–15.

46 E. F. Jacob, 'The disputed election at Fountains 1410–1416', in *Medieval Studies Presented to Rose Graham* (Oxford, 1950), pp. 78–97.

47 *Calendar of Papal Letters to Scotland of Clement VII of Avignon, 1378–1394*, ed. and trans. C. Burns and A. I. Dunlop (Edinburgh, 1976), p. 197.

48 Bernard of Clairvaux, *Letters*, ep. 146 (p. 214).

49 France, *Cistercians in Scandinavia*, p. 112.

50 G. Barnes, *Kirkstall Abbey 1147–1539: an Historical Study*, Publications of the Thoresby Society 58 (Leeds, 1984), p. 75; *The Register of William Greenfield, Lord Archbishop of York, 1306–1315*, V, SS 153 (Durham, L. 1938), pp. 1–5; 8, fn. 1; xxxix.

51 On Walter Birbach, monk of Himmerod, *see* Caesarius of Heisterbach, *Dialogue on Miracles*, 1, p. 518.

52 'Miracles of St Oswald', in *Eadmer: Lives and Miracles*, pp. 318–21.

53 Lanfranc, *Monastic Constitutions*, pp. 122 ff.

54 *Ecclesiastica Officia*, ch. 93 (pp. 266–8).

55 Lanfranc, *Monastic Constitutions*, pp. 124–5.

56 William of Malmesbury, *Life of Wulfstan*, p. 96.

57 Matarasso, *Cistercian World*, pp. 296–7.

58 Goswin de Bossut, *Life of Arnulf*, p. 77.

59 Thompson, *Carthusian Order*, p. 40.

60 Goscelin of St Bertin, *Legend of St Edith*, pp. 75–6.

61 *Book of St Gilbert*, pp. 130–1.

62 Walter Daniel, *Life of Aelred*, pp. 60–3.

63 Goswin de Bossut, *Life of Abundus*, pp. 29–31.

64 C. Holdsworth, 'Eleven visions connected with the Cistercian monastery of Stratford Langthorne', *Cîteaux* 13 (1962), 185–204 (196); *The Laicorum Speculum*, cited in P. Binski, *Medieval Death* (London, 1996), p. 187.

65 Holdsworth, 'Eleven visions', 197–201.

66 'Chronicle of Melrose', p. 95.

67 Goswin de Bossut, *Life of Ida the Gentle*, p. 26.

68 Eadmer, *Miracles of Oswald*, pp. 308–13.

69 Goswin de Bossut, *Life of Ida the Gentle*, pp. 26, 50.

70 'Miracles of St Margaret', in *Miracles of Aebbe of Coldingham and Margaret of Scotland*, ed. and trans. Bartlett, pp. 96–9.
71 Goswin de Bossut, *Life of Arnulf*, p. 76.

Notes to Chapter 9: The Work of God (2): The Monk Alone

1 Nigel Wireker, *Mirror of Fools*, p. 65.
2 Adam of Eynsham, *Magna Vita*, 1, p. 81; Thompson, *Carthusian Order*, p. 298.
3 Anselm's preface to his 'Prayers and Meditations', in *The Prayers and Meditations of Saint Anselm with the Proslogion*, trans. and intro. Sister B. Ward (Harmondsworth, 1973), p. 89.
4 William of St Thierry, *Golden Epistle*, p. 52.
5 Anselm, 'Proslogion', ch. 1, in *Prayers and Meditations*, p. 239.
6 Williams, *Cistercians in the Middle Ages*, p. 100.
7 C. Noble, 'Norwich Cathedral Priory Gardeners' Accounts 1329–1530', *Farming and Gardening in Late Medieval Norfolk*, Norfolk Record Society, 61 (1997), p. 12; C. Noble, 'Spiritual practice and the designed landscape: monastic precinct gardens', *Studies in the History of Gardens and Designed Landscape* 20 (2000), 197–205.
8 *St Bernard's Apologia*, p. 66.
9 Golding, *Gilbert of Sempringham*, p. 69; see for example, *Rule of St Benedict*, ch. 48 (p. 127); *Ecclesiastica Officia*, ch. 71 (p. 212); Iredale, *Sempringham*, p. 128.
10 Harper-Bill, 'Cistercian visitation', 109.
11 Leroux-Dhuys, *Cistercian Abbeys*, p. 51.
12 *The Letters of Abelard and Heloise*, p. 263.
13 Anselm, 'Meditation 2', in *Prayers and Meditations*, p. 230.
14 *Rule of St Benedict*, ch. 48 (p. 127).
15 M. C. Erler, *Women, Reading and Piety in Late Medieval England* (Cambridge, 2002), p. 31.
16 Sharpe, 'Monastic reading at Thorney'.
17 Carthusian Customs, ch. 28, compiled c. 1127 by Guigues, fifth prior of La Grande Chartreuse, and printed in 1510. A facsimile of this was published in 1998 by the Archives générales du Royaume, Brussels. The customs are also printed in *PL* 153, cols 635ff.
18 William of St Thierry, *Golden Epistle*, pp. 67–8.
19 Stephen of Sawley, 'Mirror for Novices', pp. 106–8.
20 Meyvaert, 'The medieval claustrum', 54–5.
21 For details of these and other library holdings see *Corpus of British Medieval Library Catalogues 3: Libraries of the Cistercians, Gilbertines and Premonstratensians*, ed. D. N. Bell (London, 1992); *Corpus of Medieval Library Catalogues 4: English Benedictine Libraries: The Shorter Catalogues*, ed. R. Sharpe, J. P. Carley, R. M. Thomson and A. G. Watson (London, 1996); D. Bell, *An Index of Authors and Works in Cistercian Libraries in Great Britain* (Kalamazoo, 1992); D. Bell, *What Nuns Read: Books and Libraries in Medieval*

English Nunneries (Kalamazoo, 1995); A. J. Piper, 'The monks of Durham and the study of scripture', in *The Culture of Medieval Monasticism*, ed. Clark, pp. 86–103; D. Bell, 'What nuns read: the state of the question', in *The Culture of Medieval Monasticism*, ed. Clark, pp. 113–33.

22   This thirteenth-century manuscript includes two library catalogues, bound together. For a recent edition of the two copies see *Corpus of Library Catalogues 3*, pp. 87–120.

23   D. Bell, 'The books of Meaux Abbey', *Analecta Cisterciensa* 40 (1984), 25–83 (29).

24   For Roche see Bell, *Index of Authors and Works*, pp. 252–3; for Thorney see Sharpe, 'Monastic reading at Thorney' and J. Arberth, *Criminal Churchmen in the Age of Edward II: the case of Bishop Thomas de Lisle* (Penn State University, 1996), pp. 28–30.

25   Adam of Eynsham, *Magna Vita*, 1, p. 85.

26   Anselm, *Prayers and Meditations*, p. 220; Eadmer, *Life of Anselm*, p. 14.

27   Aelred, *Life of St Edward*, p. 121.

28   'Miracles of St Margaret', nos. 15, 14 (pp. 106–7).

29   'Chronicle of Melrose', pp. 94–5.

30   Goswin de Bossut, *Life of Ida the Gentle*, e.g. pp. 23, 25, 45–6, 50, 58.

31   'Chronicle of Melrose', pp. 94–5.

32   St Augustine (d. 430), cited by Caesarius of Heisterbach in his *Dialogue on Miracles*, 1, p. 204.

33   'Chronicle of Melrose', p. 96; Piper, 'Monks of Durham', pp. 86–7.

34   See Bowers, 'An early Tudor monastic enterprise', esp. p. 37.

35   This work is published as *Life and Miracles of William of Norwich*.

36   D. H. Williams, 'The abbey of Dore', in *A Definitive History of Dore Abbey*, ed. R. Shoesmith and R. Richardson (Woonton, 1997, repr. 2000), pp. 15–36 (31); *Records of Kinloss*, p. xliii.

37   Walafrid Strabo, *Hortulus or the Little Garden: A Ninth-Century Poem by Walafrid Strabo*, trans. R. S. Lambert (Wembley Hill, 1923), lines 1–4.

38   Coppack and Aston, *Christ's Poor Men*, pp. 91–2.

39   Knowles, *Monastic Order*, pp. 517–18.

40   Fosbroke, *British Monachism*, p. 184. For an authoritative account of Peter Lightfoot, see W. W. Starmer, 'The clock jacks of England', *Journal of Royal Music Association* 44 (1917), 1–17.

41   *Life and Miracles of William of Norwich*, pp. 116–25, 174–6.

42   Jocelin, *Chronicle*, p. 48.

43   Meyvaert, 'Medieval claustrum', 56–7.

44   Jocelin, *Chronicle*, p. 33.

45   Cassidy-Welch, *Monastic Spaces*, pp. 161–3; McGuire, *Friendship and Community*, pp. 369–73.

46   Jocelin, *Chronicle*, pp. 36, 33.

47   Jocelin, *Chronicle*, p. 36.

48   Gray, 'A Carthusian *carta visitationis*', 95–7.

49   McGuire, *Øm*, pp. 56–7.

50   Harper-Bill, 'Cistercian visitation', 106.

51   Anselm, *Prayers and Meditations*, pp. 221–2.

52   Caesarius, *Dialogue on Miracles*, 1, pp. 239–40.

53   Caesarius, *Dialogue on Miracles*, 1, pp. 240–1.

54   Caesarius, *Dialogue on Miracles*, 1, pp. 237–9.

55   Cited in *A History of Private Life II: Revelations of the Medieval World*, ed. G. Duby, trans. A. Goldhammer (Cambridge, Mass. and London, 1988), p. 516.

56   Taunton, *English Black Monks*, 1, pp. 87–8.

57   M. Heale, *The Dependent Priories of Medieval English Houses* (Woodbridge, 2004), pp. 145–6, 149.

58   Harvey, *Living and Dying*, pp. 80, 99.

59   Rawcliffe, 'On the threshold', pp. 71–2.

60   *Observances of Barnwell*, pp. 206–7.

Notes to the Epilogue

1   Anselm, *Letters*, 1, ep. 51 (p. 159).

2   Caesarius of Heisterbach, *Dialogue on Miracles*, 1, p. 280.

3   See for example, Eadmer, *Life of St Anselm*, p. 70; Anselm, *Letters*, 3, no. 418 (p. 189); 1, nos 36 (pp. 131–2), 117 (p. 281).

4   Eadmer, *Life of St Anselm*, pp. 35–6.

Bibliography

SOURCES

The Account Book of Beaulieu Abbey, ed. S. F. Hockey, CS series 4 (London, 1975).

Accounts of the Cellarers of Battle Abbey 1275–1513, ed. E. Searle and B. Ross (Sydney, 1967).

Adam of Eynsham, *Magna Vita Sancti Hugonis*, ed. and trans. D. Douie and D. H. Farmer, 2 vols (London, 1961–2; repr. Oxford, 1985).

Aelred of Rievaulx, *On Spiritual Friendship*, trans. M. E. Laker (Kalamazoo, 1977).

——*Mirror of Charity*, trans. E. Connor (Kalamazoo, 1990).

——*The Life of St Edward the Confessor*, trans. J. Bertram (Southampton, 1997).

Alexander of Neckam, *Alexandri Neckam, De Naturis Rerum Book 2*, ed. T. Wright, RS (London, 1863).

Alice the Leper: Life of Alice of Schaebeek by Arnold II of Villers (?), trans. Father M. Cawley (Guadalupe, 2000).

Anselm of Bec/Canterbury, *The Prayers and Meditations of Saint Anselm with the Proslogion*, trans. and intro. Sister B. Ward (Harmondsworth, 1973).

——*The Letters of Saint Anselm of Canterbury*, trans. and annotated W. Fröhlich, 3 vols (Kalamazoo, 1990–4).

Arnulph of Bohéries, *Speculum Monachorum* ('A Mirror for Monks'), PL 184.

Bede, '*Vita Sancti Cuthberti*' ('The Life of St Cuthbert'), ed. and trans. J. A. Giles, in *Venerabilis Bedae, Opera Quae Supersunt Omnia 4: Opuscula Historica* (London, 1843), pp. 202–357.

Bernard of Clairvaux, *St Bernard's Apologia to Abbot William*, trans. M. Casey (Kalamazoo, 1970).

——*The Letters of Saint Bernard of Clairvaux*, trans. B. S. James, with new intro. and bibliography by B. M. Kienzle (Surrey, 1998).

St Bernard of Clairvaux, The Story of his Life as Recorded in the Vita Prima Bernardi by certain of his Contemporaries, William of St Thierry, Arnold of Bonnevaux, Geoffrey and Philip of Clairvaux, and Odo of Deuil, trans. G. Webb and A. Walker (London, 1960).

The Book of St Gilbert, ed. and trans. R. Foreville and G. Keir (Oxford, 1987).

Caesarius of Heisterbach, *The Dialogue on Miracles*, trans. H. von E. Scott and C. C. S. Bland, 2 vols (London, 1929).

Calendar of Entries in the Papal Registers regarding Great Britain and Ireland: Papal Letters I 1198–1304, ed. W. H. Bliss (London, 1893).

Calendar of Papal Letters to Scotland of Clement VII of Avignon, 1378–1394, ed. and trans. C. Burns and A. I. Dunlop (Edinburgh, 1976).

Calendar of Papal Supplications relating to Scotland 1418–1422, ed. E. R. Lindsay and A. I. Cameron (Edinburgh, 1934).

Chronica Monasterii de Melsa, ed. E. A. Bond, 3 vols, RS (London, 1866–8).

The Chronicle of Battle Abbey, ed. and trans. E. Searle (Oxford, 1980).

The Chronicle of Bury St Edmunds, 1212–1301, ed. and trans. A. Gransden (London, 1964).

The Chronicle of the Election of Hugh, Abbot of Bury St Edmunds and Later Bishop of Ely, ed. and trans. R. M. Thomson (Oxford, 1974).

'The Chronicle of Melrose', in *Medieval Chronicles of Scotland: the Chronicles of Melrose and Holyrood*, trans. J. Stevenson (Llanerch facsimile, Felinfach, 1988), pp. 7–124.

The Chronicle of St Mary's, York, ed. H. H. E. Craster and M. E. Thornton, SS 148 (London, 1934).

Chronicon Abbatiae Ramensiensis, ed. W. D. Macray, RS (London, 1886).

Concilia Scotia Ecclesiae Scotianae Statuta tam Provincialia quam Synodalia quae Supersunt 1225–1564, 2 vols, ed. J. Robertson, Bannatyne Club (Edinburgh, 1866).

The Customary of the Benedictine Abbey of Bury St Edmunds in Suffolk, ed. A. Gransden, Henry Bradshaw Society 99 (Chichester, 1973).

The Customary of the Benedictine Abbey of Eynsham in Oxford, ed. A. Gransden, *Corpus Consuetudinum Monasticarum* 2 (Siegburg, 1963).

The Customary of St Augustine's, Canterbury and St Peter's, Westminster, ed. E. M. Thompson, 2 vols, Henry Bradshaw Society 23, 28 (1902–4).

'*De Obedientiariis Abbendoniae*', in *Chronicon Monasterii de Abingdon*, ed. J. Stevenson, 2 vols, RS (London, 1858), 2, pp. 335–417.

Eadmer of Canterbury, *Historia Nouorum in England: History of Recent Events in England*, trans. G. Bosanquet (London, 1964).

——*The Life of St Anselm, Archbishop of Canterbury*, ed. and trans. R. W. Southern, 2nd edn (Oxford, 1972).

——*Lives and Miracles of Saints Oda, Dunstan and Oswald*, ed. and trans. A. J. Turner and B. J. Muir (Oxford, 2006).

Les Ecclesiastica Officia Cisterciens du xiième Siècle, ed. D. Choisselet and P. Vernet (Reiningue, 1989).

——(English translation) *The Ancient Usages of the Cistercian Order (Ecclesiastica Officia)*, Guadalupe Translations (Lafayette, 1998).

English Historical Documents 4, 1327–1485, ed. A. R. Myers (London, 1969).

Gerald of Wales, *Giraldi Cambresensis Opera*, ed. J. S. Brewer, J. F. Dimock and G. F. Warner, 8 vols, RS (London, 1861–91).

——*The Journey Through Wales/The Description of Wales*, trans. L. Thorpe (Harmondsworth, 1978).

——*The Autobiography of Giraldus Cambrensis*, ed. and trans. H. E. Butler, intro. C. H. Williams, guide to reading J. Gillingham (Woodbridge, 2005).

Goscelin of St Bertin, *Vita et translatio S. Ethelburgae*, ed. M. L. Colker, 'Jocelyn of St Bertin, Life and miracles of St Ethelburga', *Studia Monastica* 7 (1965), 398–417.

——*Vita et Translatio S. Edithae*, trans. M. Wright and K. Loncar, 'Goscelin's Legend of Edith', in *Writing the Wilton Women: Goscelin's Legend of Edith and Liber Confortatorius*, ed. S. Hollis with W. R. Barnes, R. Hayward, K. Loncar and M. Wright (Turnhout, 2004), pp. 17–93.

Goswin de Bossut, 'The Life of Abundus the choirmonk', *Send Me God: Trilogy of Cistercian Lives by Goswin de Bossut, Cantor of Villers in Brabant*, 3 vols, trans. Father M. Cawley (Guadalupe, 2000), 3.

——'The Life of Arnulf the Wagoneer', *Send Me God*, trans. Cawley, 2.

——'The Life of Ida the Gentle', *Send Me God*, trans. Cawley, 1.

Guibert of Nogent, *A Monk's Confession: The Memoirs of Guibert of Nogent*, trans. P. J. Archambault (Pennsylvania, 1996).

Guiges of la Grande Chartreuse, 'Customs', facsimile of Johann Amorbach's 1510 book (unpaginated) published by the Archives générales du Royaume, Brussels, in *Statuta ordinis cartusiensis a domino Guigone priore cartusie edita* (Brussels, 1998).

Hildegard of Bingen, *Explanation of the Rule of St Benedict*, trans. with intro., notes and commentary H. Feiss (Toronto, 1998).

Historia Ecclesie Abbendonensis, The History of the Church of Abingdon, 2, ed. and trans. J. G. H. Hudson (Oxford, 2002).

Idungus of Prüfening, 'A dialogue between a Cluniac and a Cistercian', trans. J. O'Sullivan in *Idung of Prüfening, Cistercians and Cluniacs: the Case for Cîteaux* (Kalamazoo, 1977).

'*Instructio Noviciorum*', in *The Monastic Constitutions of Lanfranc*, ed. and trans. D. Knowles, rev. edn. C. N. L. Brooke (Edinburgh, 2002), pp. 198–22.

Jocelin of Brakelond, *Chronicle of the Abbey of Bury St Edmunds*, trans. D. Greenway and J. Sayers (Oxford, 1989).

Jocelin of Furness, 'An edition and translation of the Life of Waldef, Abbot of Melrose, by Jocelin of Furness', G. J. McFadden, unpublished PhD thesis, University of Columbia, 1952.

Lanfranc of Bec/Canterbury, *The Monastic Constitutions of Lanfranc*, ed. and trans. D. Knowles, rev. edn. C. Brooke (Oxford, 2002).

'The laye brethrens' statutes of Shene part 2', ed. C. P. Mathews, *Surrey Archaeological Collections* 39 (Frome, 1931), 112–43.

The Letter Books of the Monastery of Christ Church, Canterbury, ed. J. B Sheppard, 3 vols RS (London 1887–9).

Letters to the General Chapter from the English Abbots to the Chapter at Cîteaux 1442–1521, ed. C. H. Talbot, CS series 4 (London, 1967).

The Letters of James V, coll. and ed. R. K. Hannay, ed. D. Hay (Edinburgh, 1954).

Liber Eliensis: A History of the Isle of Ely from the Seventh Century to the Twelfth Century, trans. with notes by J. Fairweather (Woodbridge, 2005).

The Life of the Venerable Man, Gundulf, Bishop of Rochester, trans. the nuns of Malling, Kent (Malling Abbey, 1968).

Matthew Paris, *Gesta Abbatum Monasterii Sancti Albani*, ed. H. T. Riley, 3 vols, RS (London, 1867–9).

The Memorials of St Edmund's Abbey, ed. T. Arnold, 3 vols, RS (London, 1890–6).

The Memorials of the Abbey of St Mary of Fountains, ed. J. S. Walbran, J. Raine and J. T. Fowler, 3 vols, SS 42, 67, 130 (Durham, 1863–1918).

The Metrical Life of St Hugh of Lincoln, ed. and trans. C. Garton (Lincoln, 1986).

The Miracles of Saint Aebbe of Coldingham and Saint Margaret of Scotland, ed. and trans. R. Bartlett (Oxford, 2003).

Narratio de fundatione Fontanis monasterii, trans. A. W. Oxford, *The Ruins of Fountains Abbey* (London, 1910), appendix 1, pp. 127–230.

Narrative and Legislative Texts from Early Cîteaux, ed. and trans. C. Waddell (Cîteaux, 1999).

Nigel Wireker/Longchamp, *A Mirror for Fools: The Book of Burnel the Ass, by Nigel Longchamp*, trans. J. H. Mozley (Oxford, 1961).

The Observances in Use at the Augustinian Priory of St Giles and St Andrew at Barnwell, Cambridgeshire, ed. and trans. J. W. Clark (Cambridge, 1897).

Orderic Vitalis, *The Ecclesiastical History of Orderic Vitalis*, ed. and trans. M. Chibnall, 6 vols (Oxford, 1969–80).

Patrologia Cursus Completus, Series Latina, ed. J. P. Migne *et al.*, 221 vols (Paris, 1844–64).

'The *Perambulavit Iudas* (*Speculum Confessionis*) attributed to Robert Grosseteste', J. Gøering and F. A. C. Martello, *Revue Bénédictine* 96 (1986), 125–68.

Peter Abelard, *The Letters of Abelard and Héloise*, ed. and trans. B. Radice (Harmondsworth, 1974).

Peter Damian, *St Peter Damian: Selected Writing on the Spiritual Life*, trans. and intro. P. McNulty (London, 1959).

Peter the Venerable, *The Letters of Peter the Venerable*, ed. G. Constable, 2 vols (Cambridge, Mass., 1967).

Ralph of Diceto, *Opera Historica*, ed. W. Stubbs, 2 vols, RS (London, 1876).

Records of the Monastery of Kinloss, ed. J. Stuart (Edinburgh, 1872).

Reginald of Coldingham/Durham, *Libellus de Admirandis Beati Cuthberti Virtutibus*, ed. J. Raine, SS 1 (Durham, 1835).

——*De Vita et Miraculis S. Godrici, Hermitae de Finchale Auctore Reginaldo Monacho Dunelmensis*, ed. J. Stevenson, SS 20 (Durham, 1847).

The Register of John Le Romeyn, Lord Archbishop of York, 1286–1296, ed. W. Brown, 2 vols, SS 123, 128 (1913–17).

The Register of William Greenfield, Lord Archbishop of York 1306–1315, ed. W. Brown and A. H. Thompson, 5 vols, SS 145, 149, 151–3 (Durham, 1931–48).

The Register of William Wickwane, Lord Archbishop of York, 1279–1285, ed. W. Brown, SS 114 (Durham, 1907).

The Rites of Durham, material selected, edited and rendered into modern English by R. W. J. Austin (Durham, 1985).

The Rule of St Benedict, ed. and trans. D. O. Hunter Blair, 5th edn (Fort Augustus, 1948).

Statuta Capitulorum Generalium Ordinis Cisterciensis ab Anno 1116 ad Annum 1786, ed. Josephus-Mia Canivez, 8 vols (Louvain, 1933–41).

Stephen of Lexington, *Letters From Ireland 1228–9*, trans. B. O'Dwyer (Kalamazoo, 1982).

Stephen of Sawley, Treatises, trans. J. F. O'Sullivan, ed. B. F. Lackner (Kalamazoo, 1984).

Suger, *Abbot Suger: On the Abbey Church of St Denis and its Art Treasures*, ed. and annotated E. Panofsky, 2nd edn G. Panofsky-Soergel (Princeton, 1979).

Thomas of Marlborough, *History of the Abbey of Evesham*, ed. and trans. J. Sayers and L. Watkiss (Oxford, 2003).

Thomas of Monmouth, *Life and Miracles of St William of Norwich*, trans., intro. and notes A. Jessopp and M. R. James (Cambridge, 1896).

Twelfth-Century Statutes from the Cistercian General Chapter, ed. C. Waddell (Brecht, 2002).

Ulrich of Zell, 'Consuetudines Cluniacensis', PL 149, cols 643–779.

Visitations of Religious Houses in the Diocese of Lincoln 1420–49, ed. A. H. Thompson, 3 vols, Lincoln Record Society/Canterbury and York Society (1915–27).

Visitations in the Diocese of Norwich A.D. 1492–1532, ed. A. Jessopp, CS ns 43 (London, 1888).

Vita Lanfranci, ed. M. Gibson, in *Lanfranco di Pavia e l'Europe del secolo xinel lx centenario della morte [1089–1989] (Pavia 21–24 September 1989)*, ed. G. D'Onofrio (Rome, 1993), pp. 659–715.

Walafrid Strabo, *Hortulus or the Little Garden: A Ninth-Century Poem by Walafrid Strabo*, trans. R. S. Lambert (Wembley Hill, 1923).

Walter Daniel, *The Life of Aelred of Rievaulx*, ed. and trans. F. M. Powicke (repr. Oxford, 1978).

Walter Map, *De Nugis Curialium*, ed. and trans. M. R. James, rev. C. N. L. Brooke and R. A. B. Mynors (Oxford, 1983).

The White Book of Worcester: Glimpses of Life in a Great Benedictine Monastery in the Fourteenth Century, trans. J. M. Wilson (Llanerch facsimile, Felinfach, 1999).

William of Malmesbury, *Life of Wulfstan of Worcester*, trans. J. H. F. Peile (Llanerch facsimile, Felinfach, 1996).

——*Gesta Regum Anglorum*, ed. and trans. R. A. B. Mynors, R. M. Thomson and M. Winterbottom, 2 vols (Oxford, 1998–9).

William of Newburgh, *The History of William of Newburgh*, trans. J. Stevenson (Llanerch facsimile, Felinfach, 1996).

William of St Thierry, *The Golden Epistle: A Letter to the Brethren at Mont Dieu*, trans. T. Berkeley (Kalamazoo, 1971).

William Thorne, *Chronicle of St Augustine's, Canterbury*, trans. A. H. Davis (Oxford, 1933).

SECONDARY READING

Arberth, J., *Criminal Churchmen in the Age of Edward II: the Case of Bishop Thomas de Lisle* (Penn State University, 1996).

Barnes, G., *Kirkstall Abbey 1147–1539: An Historical Study*, Thoresby Society 58 (Leeds, 1984).

Bell, D., 'The books of Meaux Abbey', *Analecta Cisterciensa* 40 (1984), 25–83.

——*An Index of Authors and Works in Cistercian Libraries in Great Britain* (Kalamazoo, 1992).

——*What Nuns Read: Books and Libraries in Medieval English Nunneries* (Kalamazoo, 1995).

——'Chambers, cells and cubicles: the Cistercian General Chapter and the development of the private room', in *Perspectives for an Architecture of Solitude:*

Essays on Cistercians, Art and Architecture in Honour of Peter Fergusson, ed.
T. N. Kinder (Turnhout, 2004), pp. 187–98.

——'What nuns read: the state of the question', in *The Culture of Medieval English Monasticism*, ed. J. Clark (Woodbridge, 2007), pp. 113–33.

Bell, H. E., 'Esholt Priory', *Yorkshire Archaeological Journal*, 33 (1938), 5–33.

Binski, P., *Medieval Death* (London, 1996).

Bowers, R., 'An early Tudor monastic enterprise: choral polyphony for the liturgical service', in *The Culture of Medieval Monasticism*, ed. J. Clark (Woodbridge, 2007), pp. 21–54.

Bruce, S. G., '"Lurking with spiritual intent": a note on the origin and functions of the monastic roundsman (*circator*)', *Revue Bénédictine* 109 (1999), 75–9.

——'Uttering no human sound: silence and sign language in western medieval monasticism', unpublished PhD thesis, University of Princeton, 2000.

——*Silence and Sign Language in Medieval Monasticism: the Cluniac Tradition c. 900–c. 1200* (Cambridge, 2007).

Burton, J. E., *The Yorkshire Nunneries in the Twelfth and Thirteenth Centuries* (York, 1979).

——*The Monastic and Religious Orders in Britain 1000–1300* (Cambridge, 1994).

——*The Monastic Order in Yorkshire 1069–1215* (Cambridge, 1999).

Bredero, A. H., *Bernard of Clairvaux: Between Cult and History* (Grand Rapids, 1996).

Cassidy-Welch, M., *Monastic Spaces and their Meanings: Thirteenth-century English Cistercian Monasteries* (Turnhout, 2001).

Clark, J., ed., *The Culture of Medieval English Monasticism* (Woodbridge, 2007).

Collett, B., 'Holy expectations: the female monastic vocation in the diocese of Winchester on the eve of Reformation', in *The Culture of Medieval English Monasticism*, ed. J. Clark (Woodbridge, 2007), pp. 147–68.

Constable, G., '*Horologium Stellare Monasticum*', in *Consuetudines Benedictinae Variae*, Corpus Consuetudinum Monasticarum 6 (Siegburg, 1975), pp. 1–18.

——'Aelred of Rievaulx and the nun of Watton: an episode in the early history of the Gilbertine Order', in *Medieval Women*, ed. D. Baker (Oxford, 1978), pp. 205–26.

Coppack, G., *The White Monks: the Cistercians in Britain 1128–1540* (Stroud, 1998).

——*Fountains Abbey: the Cistercians in Northern England* (Stroud, 2003).

Coppack, G. and Aston, M., *Christ's Poor Men: the Carthusians in England* (Stroud, 2002).

Corpus of Mediaeval Library Catalogues 3: The Libraries of the Cistercians, Gilbertines and Premonstratensians, ed. D. N. Bell (London, 1992).

Corpus of Mediaeval Library Catalogues 4: English Benedictine Libraries: The Shorter Catalogues, ed. R. Sharpe, J. P. Carley, R. M. Thomson and A. G. Watson (London, 1996).

Coulton, G. G., *Five Centuries of Religion*, 4 vols (Cambridge, 1923–50).

——*Life In the Middle Ages*, 4 vols, 2nd edn (Cambridge, 1928–30).

——*Scottish Abbeys and Social Life* (Cambridge, 1933).

——*A Medieval Panorama: the English Scene from Conquest to Reformation* (New York, 1955).

Cox, M., *The Story of Abingdon part 2: Medieval Abingdon 1186–1556* (Abingdon, 1989).

Cross, C. and Vickers, N., *Monks, Friars and Nuns in Sixteenth-Century Yorkshire*, Yorkshire Archaeological Society Record Series 150 (Huddersfield, 1995).

Dictionary of National Biography, ed. H. C. G. Matthew and B. Harrison (Oxford, 2004).

Dobson, B., 'The monks of Canterbury in the later Middle Ages, 1220–1540', *A History of Canterbury Cathedral*, ed. P. Collinson, N. Ramsey and M. Sparks (Oxford, 1995), pp. 69–157.

Dodwell, B., 'The monastic community', in *Norwich Cathedral: Church, City and Diocese 1096–1996*, ed. I. Atherton, E. Fernie, C. Harper-Bill and H. Smith (London, 1996), pp. 231–54.

Duby, G., ed., *A History of Private Life II: Revelations of the Medieval World*, trans. A. Goldhammer (Cambridge, Mass. and London, 1988).

Dugdale, W., *Monasticon Anglicanum*, ed. Sir William Dugdale, rev. J. Caley, H. Ellis and B. Bandinel, 6 vols in 8 (London, 1817–30).

Erler, M. C., *Women, Reading and Piety in Late Medieval England* (Cambridge, 2002).

——'Private reading in the fifteenth and sixteenth-century English nunnery', in *The Culture of Medieval English Monasticism*, ed. J. Clark (Woodbridge, 2007), pp. 134–46.

Evans, J., *Monastic Life at Cluny 910–1157* (London, 1931).

Fletcher. J., *The Cistercians in Yorkshire* (London, 1919).

Foot, S., *Veiled Women: the Disappearance of Nuns from Anglo-Saxon England*, 2 vols (Aldershot, 2000).

Fosbroke, T. D., *British Monachism or Manners and Customs of Monks and Nuns of England* (London, 1817).

France, J., *The Cistercians in Scandinavia* (Kalamazoo, 1992).

——*The Cistercians in Medieval Art* (Stroud, 1998).

Gilchrist, R., *Norwich Cathedral Close: the Evolution of the Cathedral Landscape* (Woodbridge, 2005).

Golding, B., *Gilbert of Sempringham and the Gilbertine Order, c. 1130–c. 1300* (Oxford, 1995).

——'Gerald of Wales and the monks', in *Thirteenth-Century England 5*, ed. P. R. Coss and S. D. Lloyd (Woodbridge, 1995), pp. 53–64.

Graham, R., *St Gilbert of Sempringham and the Gilbertines: a History of the Only English Monastic Order* (London, 1901).

——'A papal visitation of Bury St Edmunds and Westminster in 1234', *English Historical Review* 27 (1912), 728–39.

——*English Ecclesiastical Studies* (London, 1929).

Gransden, A., *Historical Writing in England c. 550–c. 1307* (London, 1974).

Gray, A., 'A Carthusian *carta visitationis* of the fifteenth century', *Bulletin of the Institute of Historical Research* 40 (1967), 91–100.

Greatrex, J., 'Benedictine observances at Ely: the intellectual, liturgical and spiritual evidence considered', in *A History of Ely Cathedral*, ed. P. Meadows and N. Ramsey (Woodbridge, 2003), pp. 77–93.

Haigh, G., *The History of Winchcombe Abbey* (Watford, 1947).

Harper-Bill, C., 'Cistercian visitation in the late Middle Ages: the case of Hailes Abbey', *Bulletin of the Institute of Historical Research* 53 (1980), 103–14.

——'The labourer is worthy of his hire? Complaints about diet in late Medieval England Monasteries', in *The Church in Pre-Reformation Society*, ed. C. M. Barron and C. Harper-Bill (Woodbridge, 1985), pp. 95–107.

Harvey, B., *Living and Dying in England c. 1100–1540: The Monastic Experience* (Oxford, 1993).

——'The aristocratic consumer in England in the long thirteenth century', in *Thirteenth-Century England 6*, ed. M. Prestwich, R. H. Britnell and R. Frame (Woodbridge, 1997), pp. 13–37.

——'A novice's life at Westminster Abbey in the century before the Dissolution', in *The Religious Orders in Pre-Reformation England*, ed. J. G. Clark (Woodbridge, 2002), pp. 51–73.

——'Monastic pittances in the Middle Ages', in *Food in Medieval England: Diet and Nutrition*, ed. C. M. Woolgar, D. Serjeantson and T. Waldron (Oxford, 2006), pp. 215–27.

Harvey, B. and Oeppen, J., 'Patterns of morbidity in late medieval England: a sample from Westminster Abbey', *The Economic History Review*, ns 54 (2001), 215–39.

Harvey, J., 'Westminster Abbey: the Infirmarer's garden', *Garden History* 20:2 (1992), 97–115.

Heale, M., *The Dependent Priories of Medieval English Houses* (Woodbridge, 2004).

Hendriks, L., *London Charterhouse* (London, 1889).

Hogg, J., 'Carthusian abstinence', *Analecta Cartusiana* 35: *Spiritualität Heute und Gestern* 14 (1991), 5–15.

——'The Carthusians and the temptations of Eve', *Analecta Cartusiana* 35: *Spiritualität Heute und Gestern* 15 (1992), 138–86.

Holdsworth, C., 'Eleven visions connected with the Cistercian monastery of Stratford Langthorne', *Cîteaux* 13 (1962), 185–204.

Hope, W. St John, *The History of the London Charterhouse* (London, 1925).

Iredale, E. W., *Sempringham and St Gilbert and the Gilbertines* (Pointon, 1992).

Jacob, E. F. 'The disputed election at Fountains 1410–1416', in *Medieval Studies Presented to Rose Graham* (Oxford, 1950), pp. 78–97.

Jaeger, C., *The Envy of the Angels: Cathedral Schools and Social Ideals in Mediaeval Europe* (Philadelphia, 1994).

Kerr, J., *Monastic Hospitality: the Benedictines in England c. 1070–c. 1250* (Woodbridge, 2007).

——'Health and safety in the medieval monasteries of Britain', *History* 93 (2008), 3–19.

——'Cistercian hospitality in the later Middle Ages', in *Monasteries and Society in the Later Middle Ages*, ed. J. Burton and K. Stöber (Woodbridge, 2008), pp. 25–39.

Kinder, T., ed., *Perspectives for an Architecture of Solitude: Essays on Cistercians, Art and Architecture in Honour of Peter Fergusson* (Turnhout, 2004).

King, A. A., *Cîteaux and her Elder Daughters* (London, 1954).

King, P., *Western Monasticism: a History of the Monastic Movement in the Latin Church* (Kalamazoo, 1999).

Knowles, D., *The Monastic Order in England: A History of its Development from the Times of St Dunstan to the Fourth Lateran Council, 940–1216*, 2nd edn (Cambridge, 1963).

Knowles, D., Brooke, C. N. L. and London, V. C. M., *The Heads of Religious Houses in England and Wales, 940–1216* (London, 1972).

Knowles, D. and Hadcock, R. N., *Mediaeval Religious Houses, England and Wales*, 2nd edn (Harlow, 1971).

Lawrence, C. H., *Medieval Monasticism: Forms of Religious Life in Western Europe in the Middle Ages*, 3rd edition (Harlow, 1989).

Lekai, L. J., *The Cistercians: Ideals and Reality* (Kent, Ohio, 1977).

Leroux-Dhuys, J. -F., *Cistercian Abbeys: History and Architecture* (Paris, 1998).

Maddison, F., Scott, B. T. and Kent, A., 'An early medieval water-clock', *Antiquarian Horology* 3 (1962), 348–53.

Mason, E., *St Wulfstan of Worcester, c. 1008–95* (Oxford, 1990).

Matarasso, P., ed., trans. and intr., *The Cistercian World: Monastic Writings of the Twelfth Century* (Harmondsworth, 1993).

Matthew, D., *The Norman Monasteries and their English Possessions* (Oxford, 1962).

McGuire, B., *Conflict and Continuity at Øm Abbey* (Copenhagen, 1976).

——'The collapse of a monastic friendship: the case of Jocelin of Brakelond and Samson of Bury', *Journal of Medieval History* 4 (1978), 369–97.

——*Friendship and Community: the Monastic Experience 350–1250* (Kalamazoo, 1988).

Meyvaert, P., 'The medieval monastic claustrum', *Gesta* 12: 1 (1973), 53–9.

Morton, V., *Guidance for Women in Twelfth-Century Convents* (Cambridge, 2003).

Mullin, F., *A History of the Cistercians in Yorkshire* (Washington, 1932).

Noble, C., 'Norwich Cathedral Priory Gardeners' Accounts 1329–1530', *Farming and Gardening in Late Medieval Norfolk*, Norfolk Record Society 61 (1997).

——'Spiritual practice and the designed landscape: monastic precinct gardens', *Studies in the History of Gardens and Designed Landscape* 20 (2000), 197–205.

North, J., 'Monasticism and the first mechanical clocks', in *Stars, Minds and Fate: Essays in Ancient and Medieval Cosmology*, ed. J. D. North (London and Ronceverte, 1989), pp. 171–86.

——*God's Clockmaker: Richard of Wallingford and the Invention of Time* (London, 1995).

Oliver, G., *Historic Collections relating to the Monasteries in Devon* (Exeter, 1820).

Pearce, E. H., *The Monks of Westminster Abbey* (Cambridge, 1916).

Piper, A. J., 'The monks of Durham and the study of Scripture', in *The Culture of Monasticism*, ed. Clark, pp. 86–103.

Power, E., *Medieval English Nunneries, c. 1275–1535* (Cambridge, 1922).

Price, L., *The Plan of St Gall in Brief* (Berkeley and London, 1982).

Rawcliffe, C., '"On the threshold of eternity": Care for the Sick in East Anglian monasteries', in *East Anglia's History: Studies in Honour of Norman Scarfe*, ed. C. Harper-Bill, C. Rawcliffe and R. G. Wilson (Woodbridge, 2002), pp. 41–72.

Richardson, H. J., 'Cistercian formularies', in *Formularies which bear on the History of Oxford, c. 1204–1420*, ed. H. E. Salter, W. A. Pantin and H. G. Richardson, 2 (Oxford, 1942), pp. 279–327.

Robinson, D., *The Cistercians in Wales: Architecture and Archaeology 1130–1540* (London, 2006).

Saunders, H. W., *An Introduction to the Obedientiary and Manorial Rolls of Norwich Cathedral Priory* (Norwich, 1930).

Savine, A., *The English Monasteries on the Eve of the Dissolution* (London, 1909).

Sharpe, R., 'Monastic reading at Thorney Abbey 1323–47', *Traditio* 60 (2005), 243–78.

Sherlock, D., 'Anglo-Saxon monastic sign language at Christ Church, Canterbury',
   Archaeologia Cantiana 107 (1989), 1–27.
——*Signs for Silence: the Sign Language of the Monks of Ely in the Middle Ages* (Ely,
   1992).
Sherlock, D. and Zajac, W., 'A monastic sign list from Bury St Edmunds', *Proceedings
   of the Suffolk Institute of Archaeology* (1988), 251–73.
Siraisi, N., *Medieval and Early Renaissance Medicine: An Introduction to Knowledge
   and Practice* (Chicago and London, 1990).
Smith, D. M. and London, V. C. M., *The Heads of Religious Houses in England and
   Wales 2, 1216–1377* (Cambridge, 2001).
Southern, R. W., *Saint Anselm and his Biographer: A Study of Monastic Life and
   Thought 1059–c. 1130* (Cambridge, 1963).
——*Saint Anselm: A Portrait in a Landscape* (Cambridge, 1990).
Spear, V., *Leadership in Medieval English Nunneries* (Woodbridge, 2005).
Starmer, W. W., 'The clock jacks of England', *Journal of Royal Music Association* 44
   (1917), 1–17.
Stevenson, W. H. and Salter, H. E., eds, *The Early History of St John's College Oxford*,
   Oxford Historical Society ns 1 (1939).
Stil, M., *The Abbot and the Rule: Religious Life at St Albans 1290–1349* (Aldershot,
   2002).
Stöber, K., 'Social networks of late medieval Welsh monasteries', in *Monasteries and
   Society in the Later Middle Ages*, ed. J. Burton and K. Stöber (Woodbridge, 2008),
   pp. 12–24.
Swift, E., 'The obedientiary rolls of Battle Abbey', *Sussex Archaeological Collection* 78
   (1937), 37–62.
Talbot, C. H., 'The account book of Beaulieu Abbey', *Cîteaux de Nederlanden* 9
   (Westmalle, 1958), 189–210.
Taunton, E. L., *The English Black Monks of St Benedict*, 2 vols (London, 1897).
Thompson, E. M., *A History of the Somerset Carthusians* (London, 1885).
——*The Carthusian Order in England* (London, 1930).
Vaughan, R., *Chronicles of Matthew Paris: Monastic Life in the Thirteenth Century*
   (Stroud, 1984).
Victoria History of the Counties of England (London, 1900–).
Ward, B., *Miracles and the Mediaeval Mind: Theory, Record and Event
   1000–1215* (London, 1982).
——*Signs and Wonders: Saints, Miracles and Prayers from the Fourth Century to the
   Fourteenth Century* (London, 1992).
Wardrop, J., *Fountains Abbey and its Benefactors 1132–1300* (Kalamazoo, 1987).

Williams, D. H., *The Cistercians in the Early Middle Ages* (Leominster, 1998).

——'The abbey of Dore', in *A Definitive History of Dore Abbey*, ed. R. Shoesmith and R. Richardson (Woonton, 1997, repr. 2000), pp. 15–36.

——*The Welsh Cistercians* (Leominster, 2001).

Williams, W., 'Saint Robert of Newminster', *Downside Review* 58 (1939), 137–49.

Woodman, F., 'The Waterworks drawing of the Eadwine Psalter', in *The Eadwine Psalter: Text, Image and Monastic Culture in Twelfth-Century Canterbury*, ed. M. Gibson, T. A. Heslop and R. W. Pfaff (London, 1992), pp. 168–77.

Woolgar, C. M., *The Senses in Late Medieval England* (New Haven, Conn., 2006).

Wright, P., 'Time and Tithes', *History Today* 54 (2004), 22–7.

Index

Page numbers in **bold** refer to illustrations, glossary entries and the main sections on the topic

violence (*continued*)
  of devils and saints 56, 106, 107, 144
  of superiors 128–30
Virgin Mary 24, 55, 70, 98, 105, 106, 107, 144,
  184–5
visions *see* dreams
visitors 25, **34–7**, 83, 89, 92, 95; *see also* family,
  hospitality, pilgrims, women
  entertainment of 22, 48, 52–3, 67–8,
    134–5, 155, 156
  guest accommodation 23–4, 60, 67, 157

restrictions imposed on 21, 22, 91, 93,
  168
women 22, 66–7, 91–2, 128, **139–42**
viticulture 20

women 22, 66–7
work/manual labour 4, 5, 8, 11, 22, 23, 28, 32,
  37–8, 46, 98, 151, 155, **156–9**, 179, 186, 197;
  see also gardening, lay brother
worries and fears 13, 27, 70, 72, 103, 119, 139,
  146–7, 167, 171–3, **187–93**; *see also* suicide